Richard of St.

On the Trinity

Richard of Saint Victor,

On the Trinity

English Translation and Commentary

⌇

RUBEN ANGELICI

CASCADE *Books* · Eugene, Oregon

RICHARD OF SAINT VICTOR, *ON THE TRINITY*
English Translation and Commentary

Cascade Books
A Division of Wipf and Stock Publishers
199 W. 8th Ave., Suite 3
Eugene, OR 97401

www.wipfandstock.com

ISBN 13: 978-1-61097-012-9

Cataloging-in-Publication data:

Angelici, Ruben.

    Richard of Saint Victor, on the Trinity : English translation and commentary / Ruben Angelici.

    xii + 246 p. ; 23 cm. Includes bibliographical references and index.

    ISBN 13: 978-1-61097-012-9

    1. Richard, of St. Victor, d. 1173. 2. Trinity—Early works to 1800. I. Title. II. Angelici, Ruben.

BT110.R514 A80 2011

Manufactured in the U.S.A.

To my wife
To my mother

Contents

Contents

Acknowledgements

The author would like to express his warm appreciation to the Revd. Dr. David L. Rainey for his guidance and encouragement in the preparation of this study; to the late Professor David F. Wright for his careful advice and critical appraisal in the preliminary stages of the present translation; and to Cascade Books, for the decision to publish this work on Medieval Theology in their imprint.

Ruben Angelici
September 2010

Abbreviations

Series

BH	Bibliothèque Historique, Paris.
FCTM	Fonti Cristiane per il Terzo Millennio, Rome.
PL	Patrologiae Cursus Completus Series Latina, Paris.
BPC	Bibliothèque de Philosophie Contemporaine, Paris.
DTC	Dictionnaire de Théologie Catholique, Paris.
BSM	Bibliothèque de Spiritualité Médiévale, Metz.
TPMA	Textes Philosophiques du Moyen Âge, Paris.
SC	Sources Chrétiennes, Paris.
WAA	Works of Aurelius Augustine, Edinburgh.
NPNF	The Nicene and Post-Nicene Fathers, Grand Rapids.
NBA	Nuova Biblioteca Agostiniana, Rome.
PG	Patrologiae Cursus Completus Series Graeca, Paris.
AARA	American Academy of Religion – Academy Series, Atlanta.
ANF	The Ante-Nicene Fathers, Peabody.
GDE	Grande Dizionario Enciclopedico, Turin.
CCL	Classics of Contemplative Life, London.
OST	Opere di San Tommaso, Milan.
CWS	Classics of Western Spirituality, New York.
LCL	Loeb Christian Library, London.
LCC	Library of Christian Classics, Philadelphia.
OCT	Oxford Classical Texts or Scriptorum Classicorum Bibliotheca Oxoniensis, Oxford.

Periodicals

HP	The Heythrop Journal, Oxford.

RMAL	Revue du Moyen Âge Latin, Lyons.
EHLDMA	Études d'Histoire Littéraire et Doctrinale du Moyen Âge, Paris.
MRANL	Memorie della Reale Accademia Nazionale dei Lincei: Classe di Scienze Morali, Storiche e Filologiche, Rome.

PART ONE

Introduction and Commentary

Introduction and Commentary

The Twelfth Century Milieu and the Victorine School

Without doubt, in the history of the Middle Ages, the twelfth century shines for its intellectual vitality and decisive originality. Gilson writes, "If considered in its entirety, the intellectual movement of the twelfth century presents itself as the preparation of a new age in the history of Christian thought."[1] It was a time of progress and cultural renaissance[2] of arts and letters, bringing to full maturity a number of positive tendencies that had originated in the previous century. In many ways, this period constitutes "the high peak of the Middle Age . . . therefore, a prolific and dynamic time, which does not oppose the Renaissance-Humanism,[3] but which rather leads up to it."[4] In society the economic

1. "Envisagé dans son ensemble, le mouvement intellectuel du xiie siècle se présente comme la préparation d'un âge nouveau dans l'histoire de la pensée chrétienne." Gilson, *Philosophie*, 337.

2. See Benson, et al., *Renaissance and Renewal*. See Paré, et al., *Renaissance du xiie Siècle*. From a historical perspective, it is important to mention that the first extensive analysis of the twelfth century, which recognised the importance of this century as a moment of Renaissance of arts and letters, was carried out by Haskins at the beginning of the twentieth century. See Haskins, *Renaissance*.

3. In spite of any inherent difficulty encountered in formulating an all-encompassing definition of Humanism as the cultural tendency of the Quattrocento, and in light of more recent studies (See: Celenza, *Lost Italian*; Nauert, *Humanism*; Trinkaus, *Scope*; Adorno, *Arte*), it might be helpful to clarify that for the sake of this present commentary, the term Renaissance-Humanism should be understood as indicating simply the particular activity of cultural, political, educational, and artistic reform carried out primarily during the course of the fifteenth century in Italian centers of culture such as Florence (and exported throughout the Italian peninsula and the rest of Europe to the end of the sixteenth century) and which originated from a renewed interest in classical literature, art, and philosophy.

4. "Il culmine del Medioevo . . . un'età, quindi, florida e dinamica che non si oppone, bensì prelude, all'Umanesimo-Rinascimento." Spinelli, *La Trinità*, 12.

3

rebirth produced new wealth and facilitated the spread of knowledge. New centres of learning were established in cathedral schools to counterbalance the *scholae abbatiarum*—the centres of learning associated with abbeys—creating a greater audience for new ideas and engaging a wider public in new debates. While Plato's, Augustine's, and Boethius' works continued to be studied with attention, John Scot Eriugena's translations of the writings of Greek fathers[5] attracted increasing appreciation. Latin translations of Aristotle's works also started making their first appearance. In summary, in Dumeige's words, the twelfth century "is . . . the dawn, which announces a great brightness."[6] Indeed, this is the century of Abelard and Bernard of Clairvaux, Innocent II and Alexander III, Roscelin of Compiègne and Gilbert Porreta.[7]

In such a time, William of Champeaux founded the Abbey of Saint Victor on the banks of the river Seine. The Victorines were to follow the rule of Saint Augustine, whose demands are considerably less restrictive than those of other monastic orders. They were to uphold the ideal of a contemplative life dedicated to studying the sacred books, the writings of the church fathers, and works of pagan authors. Immediately, the newly organised monastery became the see of one of the most prestigious schools of its time; a leading centre in academic discussions.[8] The theological influence of the Victorines is undeniable.[9] Hugh, a very prolific author, was known amongst his contemporaries as, "the most important theologian of our time"[10]—the second Augustine.[11] Adam was a very famous liturgical poet who perfected the *Sequentiae* meters and their use as liturgical hymns recited in Eucharistic celebrations.[12] Yet, as Spinelli argues, "the one who displays the most genius is certainly Richard of Saint Victor."[13]

5. For Eriugena's translations of the works of Maximus the Confessor, Gregory of Nyssa, and Pseudo-Dionysius the Areopagite, see Migne, *Joannis Scoti*, 1023D–1222A.

6. "Il [le xiie siècle] est . . . l'aube annonciatrice d'une grande clarté." Dumeige, *Richard de Saint-Victor*, 1.

7. For a more in depth analysis, see Gilson, *Philosophie*, 259–343.

8. See Spinelli, *La Trinità*, 15. Dumeige, *Richard de Saint-Victor*, 6ff.

9. See Dumeige, *Richard de Saint-Victor*, 16.

10. Richard of Saint Victor, "Benjamin Major," I.4.

11. Spinelli, *La Trinità*, 18.

12. Ibid., 17.

13. "Il più geniale è certamente Riccardo di San Vittore." Ibid., 17.

Richard was a Scottish monk who joined the monastery some time between 1120 and 1135[14] and became Prior in 1162.[15] He was a profound thinker and a passionate teacher, a devout believer whose worldview found "its profound inspiration in a theological life intensely lived out."[16] He was primarily a mystical author, a "Doctor of Contemplation,"[17] as Spinelli calls him, and a model of spiritual devotion to his contemporaries. About a century later, Dante would commend Richard's mysticism, pointing out the Prior of Saint Victor among the other *Spiriti Sapienti*—the souls of the wise of Paradise—who brought spiritual light to the world. According to him, "Richard . . . was in contemplation more than man."[18]

Studies on Richard's theology are today regrettably very few in number: the twelfth-century Prior of Saint Victor is almost exclusively renowned for his spiritual and allegorical treatises;[19] as a "theologian of the spiritual life."[20] Yet, he is also the author of one of the most significant mediaeval works on the dogma of the Trinity—the only purely dogmatic treatise that he produced.[21]

This masterpiece awakened profound admiration in Richard's contemporaries. Latin codices of the *De Trinitate* are found scattered throughout Europe, and the work held a key place of influence at least until the end of the sixteenth century,[22] becoming a *must-read classic* of dogmatic literature.[23] Quite surprisingly, its fortune slowly declined and today it is hardly ever included in average, theological curricula.

---

14. Ibid., 66. The chronology offered by Spinelli has been preferred to those presented by Ottaviano and Dumeige, as this seems to be the most accurate.

15. For further biographical information, see Fritz, "Richard de Saint-Victor," 13:2676–95.

16. "Trouve son inspiration profonde dans une vie théologale intensément vécue." Ethier, Le *"De Trinitate,"* 7.

17. "Doctor Contemplationis." Spinelli, *La Trinità*, 27.

18. "Riccardo/ . . . a considerar fu più che viro." Dante, *Paradiso*, X, 131–32.

19. In addition to the anthology edited by Zinn [see below], modern versions of some of Richard's mystical compositions can be found in Richard of Saint Victor, *Benjamin Minor*; and Richard of Saint Victor, *Sermons et Opuscules*.

20. "Un théologien de la vie spirituelle." Ethier, Le *"De Trinitate,"* 8.

21. Spinelli, *La Trinità*, 30.

22. Ibid., 59.

23. See Ribaillier, *Richard*, 71.

Nonetheless, in recent times, there have been clear signs of a renewed interest in Richard's dogmatics, especially within the English-
speaking academia. Scholars of the likes of Colin Gunton have seen the
Victorine's trinitarianism as a corrective source to certain Augustinian
tendencies.[24] More recently, Dennis Ngien has dedicated a significant
portion of his study on the *filoque* clause in mediaeval theology to
Richard of Saint Victor's use of *condilectio*,[25] while Matthew Knell has
used Richard's defence of the *filioque* to insert Victorine trinitarianism into a broader discussion of Western, mediaeval developments in
Pneumatology.[26] It is all the more disheartening, then, to see how such
genuine renewal of interest towards Richard's dogmatics shown by these
astute academics is at the same time tragically hampered by a limited—
and ultimately very superficial—knowledge of Richard's *De Trinitate*.
Due to the lack of a clear and available English translation, these recent
studies are mostly confined to the analysis of Book III, condemning serious enquiry to an understanding of Richard's argument which is only
partial. As a thoroughly scholastic masterpiece, the *De Trinitate* can be
truly understood only if it is analysed in its entirety. Never before has
the enthusiasm of the academia in its eagerness to develop a more enlightened understanding of Richard of Saint Victor's theology, together
with the serious lack of availability of primary sources in English, made
the present work more urgent and needed.

The Need for a Modern, English Translation
of Richard of Saint Victor's *De Trinitate*

The heavy prose of the Victorine's Latin and his sometimes excessively
analytical approach to the topic have probably discouraged more than
one attempt at translation. Richard's style is indeed prolix; his verbos-
ity and repetitions are at times difficult to follow, and his mysticism is
pervaded by a mannerism of a very mediaeval gusto. All these factors
can probably explain why translations of the *De Trinitate* into modern
languages have been very limited, often condemning Richard's dogmatics to oblivion.

24. Gunton, *Promise*, 42–55 and *passim*.

25. Ngien, *Apologetic for Filioque.*

26. Knell, *Holy Spirit.*

The first, full, modern version of the work has been completed in French by Salet, during the second half of the twentieth century.[27] The only other full translation existing today is that completed in Italian by Spinelli, and published in 1990.[28] The *De Trinitate* has never been translated into English or German.[29] Currently, only brief excerpts are available in:

- The English anthology, *The Twelve Patriarchs, The Mystical Ark, Book Three of the Trinity.* Edited by G. A. Zinn. New York: Paulist, 1979.

- The English anthology, *A Scholastic Miscellany: Anselm to Ockham,* LCC 10. Edited by Eugene R. Fairweather. Philadelphia: Westminster, 1961.

- The German anthology, *Die Viktoriner Mystische Schriften.* Edited by P. Wolff. Leipzig: Hegner, 1936.

The sharpness of Richard's achievement, however, is such to reproach the current lack of any type of full, English version of *De Trinitate.* And, as has already been noted, in spite of the recent renewal of interest in Richard's dogmatics, the absence of a translation is a key factor in explaining the regrettable lack of serious critical studies emerging from the English-speaking academy on the wealth and value of Victorine, trinitarian theology. The situation certainly demands that at least an attempt be made at filling the gap, so that the Victorine's accomplishments might be enjoyed by a wider theological public.

The translation offered here is based on the Latin text published by Salet, which represented an edition of Jean de Toulouse's codex (as transcribed by Migne), improved on the basis of the *Mazarienus Codex.* My goal has been to offer an English edition of Richard's work that is as literal a translation of the original Latin as possible, without appearing pedantic. Priority has obviously been given to faithfulness to the original intention and even formal style of the mediaeval author. Particular

27. Salet, *La Trinité.*

28. See above, Spinelli, *La Trinità.*

29. In truth, Ribaillier writes in 1958 that an English translation edited by J. Bligh was due to be published soon (Ribaillier, *Richard,* 8). However, this translation has never appeared, and Book Three is the only portion that has ever been available in English.

care has also been taken to maintain the most solid basis of faithfulness in rendering Richard's tight, technical, theological language. Yet, the needs of modern English also require a clear and flowing text and I have endeavoured to produce such.

The State of the Question: General Overview of the History of Trinitarian Thought

The dogma of the Trinity is certainly the central doctrine of the Christian faith. It developed from the Church's need to account for Christ's unity with the Father and it constitutes the basic tenet to present justification as a fully objective act of God's grace.[30] Yet, while the cause of a Trinitarian definition of faith, enshrined in the Creeds, is to be sought in deep christological concerns, its consequences also show radical, ontological effects. In Christian understanding, God—the supreme and only fountain of being—presents in himself both oneness and plurality.

The image we receive from the New Testament is that of God revealing himself in the economy of salvation in Christ (God as he is *in relation to creation*). Yet, the Trinity in its immanence (God as he *in himself*) remains by definition *totally other* to the human being, whose knowledge of divine essence cannot but ultimately result in being incomplete, as Augustine, quoting from Paul, notes.[31] Only an infinite intellect could ever entirely comprehend infinity, thus in order to fully understand God one must be God himself. Nonetheless, the needs of a sound soteriology are met only by a continual attempt to understand the being of God *in se* (God as he is *in himself*). The development of

---

30. See Athanasius, *Incarnation*, III.14–17 and *passim*. If the Son, who becomes incarnate, is not God himself—one with the Father—then he cannot carry a vicarious redemption for humanity. Indeed, if the Son does not share the very same substance of the Father, then he becomes simply another enlightened creature, who has happened to achieve goodness. Salvation, therefore, would be the product of human works of righteousness, obtained by an imitation of the work of Christ. Christ would become humanity's prophet without being humanity's representative redeemer, failing to carry humanity with himself. Such was the necessary consequence of Arian theology, for example, against which Athanasius fought his entire life, and which must be kept in mind in order to understand the reasons behind Athanasius' strong, trinitarian positions.

31. Augustine, *Trinity*, XV.8.14—10.18. See also Dante, *Paradiso*, XXXIII, 124–26.

models to "account for who ... these three [are],"[32] then, have remained through history the constant effort of Christian Trinitarian theology.

Athanasius

This present overview is not the appropriate place where one should attempt to provide a detailed analysis of pre-Nicene formulations made by theologians such as Origen, Irenaeus, and Tertullian. For the sake of this study, it will be sufficient to mention that one of the oldest properly trinitarian models developed in the Christian tradition was that presented by Athanasius in his theology. In recent decades, it has received renewed attention by a certain group of Reformed theologians, led by Thomas F. Torrance, who have tried to revive it.[33] According to Athanasius, the Trinity itself cannot be explained outside the *ousia* (being) of God, and that *ousia* is *one*. The perichoretic relationship—the mutual indwelling of the divine persons—then, is based on the divine *ousia*, which becomes also the source and origin of the procession of the Son and the Spirit.[34] In truth, Athanasius did not actually write a treatise on the Trinity to describe his model in a detailed way; rather, his views are to be extrapolated out of his anti-Arian writings and the Nicene Creed he endorsed. Maybe this factor is one reason why a trinitarian model based on the *ousia* as the source of the persons seems never to have been re-elaborated or re-used after Athanasius' attempt.[35] The main trinitarian models of West and East that have had a permanent impact on theological speculations are to be found in the accomplishments of Augustine and the Cappadocian fathers.

---

32. Augustine, *Trinity*, V.8.10.

33. Torrance, *Trinitarian Faith*.

34. While this model might overcome the whole dispute regarding the *Filioque* clause and the issue of double procession in the Trinity, as Torrance notes (Torrance, *Trinitarian Faith*, 231–47.), it also presents the great disadvantage of not being able to describe the specific office of the Father. In fact, while the Cappadocians could speak of monarchy as the unity of the Trinity, in which the Father is the origin of the Son and the Spirit (see Basil of Caesarea, "Holy Spirit," XVIII.44–47.), by the identification of the *ousia* with the fountain of divine procession, Athanasius does not seem able to describe any *specific* role of the Father in the divine relationship.

35. See Torrance, *Trinitarian Faith*, 241.

Augustine

Augustine started with a simple observation on dogmas that are re-vealed to us by faith. He noticed that divine truths can generally be based on fundamental principles of which we, as humans, have some notion.[36] For example, we can believe that Jesus was born of the Virgin Mary because we know what we mean by "virgin" and what we mean by "birth," although we have never seen a virgin giving birth.[37] Likewise, we have a generic understanding of "nature," "species," and "gender," so although we have never seen the apostle Paul, we believe about him that which we believe about the entire human race, i.e., that he was a human being like us and that his soul lived united to his body.[38] Indeed, it is only because we possess these analytical notions in ourselves that we can articulate in our minds a broad understanding of things that we do not know or that we have never encountered and these notions offer us a basis on which to formulate our faith convictions.

In the same manner, experience can also offer a helpful substrate on which to base our beliefs of faith concepts that in general terms are alien to us. Although the resurrection of our Lord is an unrepeatable act, which we have never seen, we can believe in it because we have experience of life and we have seen people dead and dying. Such experiences of death and life allow us to express our understanding of resurrection as the act of coming back to life from death.[39]

Lastly, according to Augustine, absolute concepts—which we cannot explain analytically, but which we know intuitively—can also offer a foundation to our beliefs. For example, we immediately know what the concept of Truth is, if someone asks, although it becomes almost impossible to define it in its most spiritual terms, without relapsing into corporeal images. Yet, our intuition of Truth provides us with a medium by which we can associate God with Truth.[40] Ultimately, every accent

---

36. Remember that according to Augustine, revealed truth only *invites* one to faith (Augustine, *Trinity*, IX.12.17.) so a firm foundation on which to base our faith is essential.

37. Ibid., VIII.5.

38. Ibid., VIII.5.8.

39. Ibid., VIII.5.8.

40. Ibid., VIII.2.3. Besides having an experiential knowledge of human nature, we also possess an innate understanding of the concept of human being (Ibid., VIII.4.7).

of our faith, which elicits belief, is communicated through and rests on a foundation of which we have some notion. However, Augustine's dilemma consisted of wondering how we as people can believe in the Trinity if we have no mediating concepts on which to base our faith.[41] Indeed, how can we believe if we do not have any idea of what it is that in which we should believe?

His is a reformulation in a Christian, trinitarian fashion of the question of knowledge, as raised by Plato. To the Greek philosopher, knowledge was recognition of the Ideas seen by the soul in the Hyperuranium—the Ideas' metaphysical dwelling place—which by being literally "beyond the heavens," transcended reality in its perfection of static immutability.[42] In order to understand Augustine's position, it might be helpful to examine Plato's theory of knowledge in a little more detail. As the philosopher expounds in great depth, in order to investigate something, one must first identify the object of his/her investigation. Yet, this means that the seeker must already know which object he/she is to identify and indeed he/she already must *know* such object in a certain way. In fact, if the seeker were to lack any kind of knowledge of the object sought, he/she would not be able to find it or even to identify it, even though the sought object might very well be in the seeker's plain sight. Indeed, as Plato has Meno wonder, "How will you enquire . . . into that which you do not know? What will you put forth as the subject of enquiry? And if you find what you want, how will you ever know that this is the thing which you did not know?"[43] This is often referred to as Meno's paradox: if enquiry of what is known is implausible—as the object to know is already known—enquiry of the unknown is utterly impossible—as the object sought can never be identified. Thus, Plato's answer to Meno is that knowledge is not *acquired* but rather *recollected*. As the immortal soul has been in contemplative contact with the Ideas in the company of the gods[44] and has passed through a series of embodied reincarnations,[45] it is now capable to bring

41. Ibid., VIII.5.8. "What then do we know, whether specially or generally, of that most excellent Trinity?"

42. Plato, *Phaedrus*, 247c; 249d. See also Reale and Antiseri, *Pensiero*, 1:100–101, 106–8.

43. Plato, *Meno*, 80d.

44. Plato, *Phedrus*, 249d.

45. Plato, *Meno*, 81d.

back the latent knowledge, which it already possesses in itself. [46] Indeed, his specific understanding of the acquisition of knowledge constituted the primary reason why Plato seems to endorse belief in reincarnation and metempsychosis.[47] Although Augustine was quick to reject Plato's conclusions on souls' re-embodiments and transmigrations,[48] he still accepted the philosopher's staring point as valid: knowing had to be equivalent to recognizing.[49] In summary, if the capacity of knowledge is inborn in humans, its presence testifies that *in some way* full knowledge of the unknown is already potentially existing in each human being.

The solution Augustine presented to the question is then remarkable: if knowing means recognizing, it is necessary to make an effort and find a *vestigium Trinitatis*, a trace of the Trinity, a clear image on which we can establish our faith so to believe. He found that which he

46. Ibid, 81d. Masterfully, Plato gives an empirical demonstration of his theory of knowledge as *anamnesis* by describing Socrates in an experiment of maieutics. Indeed, Socrates is able to lead an illiterate slave to the solution of a geometrical demonstration, which requires knowledge of the Pythagorean Theorem. Ibid, 82–86b. As Reale and Antiseri comment, "Since the slave had not previously learnt geometry, and since nobody had provided him with the solution . . . one cannot but conclude that he has drawn it from within himself . . . i.e., that he has remembered it . . . Every human . . . can . . . derive from him/herself truths, which he/she did not know before and which nobody has taught him/her." ("Poiché lo schiavo non aveva prima imparato geometria, e poiché non gli era stata fornita da nessuno la soluzione . . . non resta che concludere che egli l'ha tratta dal di dentro di se stesso . . . ossia che se ne è ricordato . . . Ogni uomo . . . può . . . ricavare da se medesimo verità che prima non conosceva e che nessuno gli ha insegnato.") Reale and Antiseri, *Pensiero*, 1:107.

47. Indeed, the mention of reincarnation and its association with knowledge as the product of the soul's recognition of the Ideas in the "world beyond" appears several times in Plato's works (Plato, *Phaedrus*, 246–54; Plato, *Republic*, 614–21; Plato, *Phaedo*, 106E–15). Although through history some commentators have disputed the fact that Plato himself held to a doctrine of reincarnation (Ficino, *Platonic Theology*, 17.4; for a discussion on how myth and allegory are used in Plato's thought see also Brisson, *How Philosophers*, *passim*), most of the Neoplatonists and virtually all of the Church Fathers read into Plato's myths a clear narrative of soul reincarnation and transmigration, also defined as metempsychosis (Plotinus, *Enneads*, 1.1.11; 3.4.2; 4.3.8–9; 4.3.12; 5.2.2; 6.7.6–7; Augustine, *City*, X.30; Irenaeus, *Against Heresies*, 2.33; Tertullian, *On the Soul*, 1.28ff).

48. Augustine, *Trinity*, XII.15.24.

49. Ibid., X.1.3. "And unless he knew what knowing means, no one could say confidently, either that he knew, or that he did not know."

considered to be the best image of this in the analysis of the human mind (memory, understanding, and will).[50]

The Trinitarian model Augustine preferred clearly emphasises God's unity. From that, one moves on to describe God's plurality. Augustine's understanding of the Trinity can ultimately be summarized by saying that God is three persons *ad intra,* and one essence *ad extra,*[51] utterly one in will and action.[52]

The Cappadocian Fathers

The Cappadocian fathers, instead, followed a pattern that seems opposite to the one that Augustine employed in his *De Trinitate.* Their major concern was not primarily that of responding to the question of knowledge, as it had been set out by Plato, but that of fighting the Sabellians, the Arians, and the Semi-Arian Pneumatomachi—the endemic problems of the Eastern Church.[53] By analyzing the *hypostaseis*—the "persons" in the Trinity—and by redefining the meaning of the terminology they employed, the Cappadocians began their speculations by developing a social model of the Trinity as persons-in-relationship. From this basis they moved on to describe divine unity.[54]

The emphasis of this kind of theological approach clearly lies on plurality. The Father is seen as the only source of the divine *monarchy,* the fountain of the other two persons' procession. In Cappadocian understanding, then, the Trinity is described as three persons in relationship, in the unity of will.

Comparing Augustine and the Cappadocians

Both the psychological (Augustinian) and the social (Cappadocian) trinitarian models present disadvantages. The first seems almost to

50. Ibid., X.11.17—12.19.

51. Ibid., V.8.10.

52. Ibid., II.10.18. "The Trinity works indivisibly."

53. See Basil of Caesarea, "Holy Spirit," *passim.*

54. Gregory Nazianzen, "Holy Spirit," XXXI.3, 7:318. See also Gregory Nazianzen, "On Holy Baptism," XL.41, 7:360. It is important to note that the Cappadocians were able to follow this scheme because they re-defined the significance of the word *person,* as will be argued later in this commentary.

encourage the *I* to turn towards itself[55] and to present three different manifestations of the same mind, which remains standing behind memory, understanding, and will.[56] Augustine, who preferred to use this model, as it has been said, was indeed conscious of its dangers and justified his choice by saying that the Trinity is not *in* one God, but it *is* one God. He specified that his was just an image, and as such it was imperfect.[57] On the other hand, the social model presents the opposite inconvenience: by highlighting plurality it seems almost to describe three gods. Gregory of Nyssa, in fact, felt compelled to write the oration "On Not Three Gods."[58]

This is perhaps the reason why ultimately both Augustine and the Cappadocians did not deliberately contrast the two models, but whilst demonstrating preferences for one over the other, they ended up making use of both of them. Augustine, in fact, offered one of the most vivid exegetical applications of the social trinitarian image, basing it on a paradigm situation of persons-in-relationship, united by the Spirit.[59] On the other hand, both Gregory of Nyssa and Gregory Nazianzen made brilliant uses of psychological imagery.[60]

The Development of Eastern and Western Trinitarian Thought

Unfortunately the Cappadocian relational *eikōn* and the Augustinian psychological *vestigium* became crystallized with time in a very rigid manner. Later developments in the traditions treated them as two almost incompatible frameworks of analysis. Increasingly Greek theology turned towards doctrinal positions that assumed God's triunal relationship *a priori,* and tried to study it in light of the Trinity's activity and involvement with creation. God's essence (*ousia*)—the "inef-

---

55. Augustine, *Trinity*, VIII.6.9. See also Augustine, *Religione*, XXXIX.72.

56. See Gunton, *Promise*, 42ff.

57. Augustine, *Trinity*, XV.22.42—23.43.

58. Gregory of Nyssa, "Quod non Sint," 115–36.

59. Augustine, *Lectures or Tractates*, XIV.9. In light of passages such as this, Gunton's judgment, which sees in Augustine an exclusive use of the psychological, trinitarian analogy, appears to be ultimately quite superficial (Gunton, *Promise*, 42–55).

60. Gregory Nazianzen, "To His Father," XII.1; Gregory of Nyssa. "Oratio Catechetica," II, 13.

fable being of God in Godself,"[61]—started to be contrasted with God's energy (*energeia* or *dynamis*)—"the characteristic activity of God in relation to creation."[62] While the Trinity had to remain ineffable, the doctrine of God also had to include, at the same time, the reality of human divinization understood as participation in the perichoretic life of Father, Son, and Holy Spirit.[63] This was the point of view that was to culminate in the thirteenth-century Byzantine theology defended by Gregory Palamas at the Synod of Constantinople in 1341. Yet, while Christology could clarify the Trinity's involvement with creation,[64] the constant challenge of this system, based as it was on the exclusive use of a relational understanding of the Trinity, remained that of avoiding charges of tritheism.

Latin, mediaeval theology, on the other hand, progressively tended to start from the consideration of the immense abyss between creation and God's being, emphasising God's simplicity and unity *ad extra*. "The radical difference between creator and creation was taken for granted, and the task was to clarify how God could be trinitarian."[65] In fact, rather than distinguishing between God's essence and his energy, like the Greeks, Latin theologians preferred to identify God with *pure actuality,* in whom there could be no difference between *substance* and *attributes,* since everything coincides with supreme fullness.[66] Under this perspective, the Trinity of persons appears to be almost an independent issue that concerns only God *within himself,* with hardly any practical application at all. This position, stemming from an overemphasis of God's unity, would also receive its most elaborate formulation in the

---

61. Reid, *Energies*, 26.

62. Ibid., 26.

63. As Maximus the Confessor had already argued, we will be transformed into everything that God is, except his being God (*ousia*). See Maximus the Confessor, "Ambiguorum," 1308B.

64. Reid, *Energies*, 21.

65. Ibid., 21.

66. This is also the reason why a doctrine of divinization has always remained foreign to Western theology. If there is no real difference between God's being and his energy, then we cannot be simply transformed into *anything that God is except for his being God* (See Maximus the Confessor, "Ambiguorum," 1308B.), as "anything that God is" also corresponds necessarily with his very substance.

thirteenth century in the works of Thomas Aquinas, during the debate over the relationship between *essence* and *existence*.[67]

It would be quite inaccurate, however, to say that Eastern and Western theology in the Middle Ages developed in parallel ways without influencing each other. Ethier is right in stressing that, particularly in the West, the attention of the Latin world towards the Greeks increased at a rapid pace following the events of 1204, often with contradictory effects.[68] Yet, embryonic signs of thirteenth-century theological tendencies were already detectable in earlier authors. In the ninth century, John Scot Eriugena had already made the writings of Gregory of Nyssa, Maximus the Confessor, and Pseudo-Dionysius the Areopagite available in Latin. With his translations he became, to later theologians, the archetype and inspiration[69] of that portion of academia which increasingly showed its preference for Greek patristic tradition, considering it to be much more meaningful in its expressions than Latin theology.[70]

However, in this work it is probably sufficient to limit ourselves to the acknowledgment that at the dawn of the twelfth century, the theological milieu presented quite a composite situation. It is true that the West was experiencing a growing interest in Greek perspectives, but Eastern authors continued to be generally interpreted through a markedly Western perception. Numerous Greek ideas imported by Eriugena had been misused and revealed to be potentially dangerous,[71] while the ostentatious, escalating use of Greek technical terms did not always communicate much in a Latin context.

67. Reale and Antiseri, *Pensiero*, 1:423–25, 427–28.

68. See Ethier, *Le "De Trinitate,"* 12–13.

69. A "Chef de file," as Ethier describes him. Ibid., 12.

70. "Graeci, autem, solito more res acutius considerantes expressiusque significantes." ("On the other hand, the Greeks, as usual, analyze the matter in a sharper manner and express it in a more meaningful way.") Eriugena, *Divisione*, V.35, 955. Other sectors of the Western theological world had indeed acquired familiarity with the Greek heritage but had preferred to take a non-critical stance before it. This is the case with Peter Lombard, who limited himself to juxtaposing the Greek Fathers to the Latin ones, without interpreting or critiquing them (See Ethier, *Le "De Trinitate,"* 13). Lastly, a third position is that represented by Peter Abelard, who read authors from both Latin and Greek traditions and elaborated them according to a very personal criterion (see ibid., 13).

71. See Spinelli, *La Trinità*, 9.

Richard's brusque words in response to this situation should not appear to be very surprising, then. To him, "We are not Greek."[72] The Victorine's trinitarian theology sets out to be wholly Latin and profoundly Augustinian,[73] without presenting the one-sidedness that too often taints other Western, mediaeval, trinitarian works. In agreement with Augustine,[74] Richard finds it necessary to use a language that is understandable by the average, Latin reader. Yet, from a thoroughly Latin background he finds a way to describe the Trinity in a perspective that both Latin *and* Greek authors could perhaps be able to appreciate.

Richard of Saint Victor: Faith, Reason, and the Analysis of the Problem of Knowledge in *De Trinitate*

It is now time to turn our attention to a direct analysis of the text of Richard's *De Trinitate*. Before starting his dogmatic analysis, Richard finds it necessary to begin by clarifying his stance on the methodology necessary to speculate on the Trinity. Understanding the correct relationship between revealed truths and human investigation, *Auctoritates*—the authorities[75]—and *Rationes Necessariae*—the logical, necessary reasons[76]—is indispensable for a healthy comprehension of the subject. Richard's personal answer to the question is precise: "Faith is . . . the origin and foundation of all good."[77] Yet, to him, "If faith is the origin of all good, knowledge is its consummation and perfection . . . Let us . . . mak[e] our best effort to understand what we believe."[78]

---

72. Richard of Saint Victor, *Trinity*, 4.IV.

73. Ethier also recognizes the importance of appreciating that, "Richard serait donc *latin* dans sa conception fondamentale de la Trinité." ("Thus, Richard will be *Latin* in his fundamental conception of the Trinity.") Ethier, *Le "De Trinitate,"* 23, my emphasis.

74. Augustine, *Christian Doctrine*, IV.10.24. "He . . . who teaches will avoid all words that do not teach."

75. Richard, *Trinity*, 1.I.

76. Ibid., 1.IV.

77. Ibid., Prologue.

78. Ibid., Prologue.

The tension noticeable in the apostles' writings[79] is the same that remains evident in subsequent patristic literature.[80] Yet, the Fathers' attitude progressively tended to be more conciliating, seeking to find a middle way that did not oppose the two concepts (authority and reason) against each other. The background concept, which seems to have been accepted in patristic thought from late antiquity, was the existence of objective, rational truths that could not be denied by the intellect without contradiction. Indeed, in Augustine's words, "Authority requires faith and prepares man to reason. Reason leads to understanding and knowledge."[81]

The Augustinian and Anselmian influence over the Victorine's position is evident. According to Augustine, revealed truth *invites* one to faith, which develops after one meditates on it and accepts it.[82] Grace, in fact, guides rational comprehension in such a way that the same truth gained from both faith and enquiry comes from God and seeks him. "Faith seeks, understanding finds; whence the prophet says, 'Unless ye believe, ye shall not understand.' And yet, again, understanding still seeks him, whom it finds . . . And man, therefore, ought for this purpose to have understanding, that he may seek after God."[83]

It is only John Scot Eriugena[84] in the ninth century who slightly challenges Augustine's position. On one hand, he admits that, "In no way divine authority deceives or makes mistakes,"[85] making clear that

---

79. 1 Cor 1:21–25; Eph 1:17; Col 1:9; Jas 1:5; 1 Pet 3:15.

80. Examples can be found in: Tertullian, "Flesh of Christ," V, 525; Tertullian, "Prescription," VII, 246; Clement of Alexandria, "Stromata," I.11, 311–12; I.13, 313; VI.5, 489–90; VII.10, 538–40.

81. Augustine, *Religione*, XXIV.45. Indeed, Augustine's position on this matter influenced profoundly all later developments of Western theology. Also, on a similar tone, Jerome's encouragement is to follow the intelligible meaning (*rationem*, that is, the "reason") of a Gospel passage, not just its authority. Jerome, "Letters," XIV.7, 16.

82. Augustine, *Trinity*, IX.12.17; XV.6.9.

83. Ibid., XV.2.2.

84. Not surprisingly, Eriugena is one of the least Augustinian of all the Western theologians, as he preferred the Greek Fathers to the Latin ones. It is important, here, to record Eriugena's position, as Richard of Saint Victor had certainly read his translations of Gregory of Nyssa's, Pseudo-Dionysius', and Maximus the Confessor's works, as well as Eriugena's own, original treatises. See Spinelli, *La Trinità*, 56.

85. "Divina . . . auctoritas . . . nullo modo fallit vel fallitur." Eriugena, *Divisione*, V.35, 959D. He also writes that, "Sacrae . . . Scripturae in omnibus sequenda est auctoritas, quoniam in ea veluti quibusdam suis secretis sedibus veritas possidet." ("The

while Scripture is *infallible*, patristic writings are only *helpful*, as they are human products.[86] On the other hand, he starts a parallel argument which tries to prevent the possibility of denying obvious, rational truths on the basis of faith claims, if they are discordant. "Any authority that is not confirmed by good reason should be considered wrong."[87]

Eriugena cannot be categorized as a mere rationalist, yet he appears to consider faith and reason almost as if they are on parallel yet independent journeys on the way to truth. Neither of them leads the other: both strengthen each other.[88] As he claims at the beginning of his main work, "I welcome nothing more gladly than reason strengthened by most firm authority."[89]

For the sake of the present study, it is important to remember that Anselm—sternly opposed to claims such as these—revived, in the eleventh century, a more traditional, Augustinian position. He sought to recognise the source and foundation of all truth exclusively in faith.[90] He also clarified, though, that as long as divine revelation maintains its pre-eminence its tenets are not necessarily to be considered *against* reason. Reason is granted full freedom of investigation inasmuch as this remains within the parameters imposed on it by the authority of faith. Nothing sums up this concept better than the Archbishop's great motto, "I do not seek to understand so that I may believe; but I believe so that I may understand. For I believe this also, that 'unless I believe, I shall not understand.'"[91]

---

authority of the Holy Scriptures is to be followed always, since truth dwells in it, almost as if it were in its very hidden places.") Ibid., I.64, 509A.

86. "Sanctorum Patrum *inconcussa probabilisque* auctoritas." ("The authority of the Holy Fathers [is] *firm* and *probable*.") Ibid., II.36, 617A, my emphasis.

87. "Omnis enim auctoritas, quae vera ratione non approbatur, infirma videtur esse." Ibid., I.69, 513B.

88. It is important, in fact, that he claims authority of faith to come from well inspired reason but no reason to come from faith. Ibid., I.69, 513B.

89. "Nil libentius accipio, quam rationem firmissima auctoritate roboratam." Ibid., I.64, 509B.

90. For a more in depth analysis of Anselm's *theologia fidei*, see Barth, *Anselm: Fides Quaerens*.

91. Anselm, "Proslogion," I.1, 87. Sadly, much of history of philosophy has not fully comprehended this very important aspect of Anselmian theology, betraying some sort of underlying, Cartesian bias in its description of the relationship between faith and reason in Anselm. Even Nietzsche was perhaps a victim of this reading, as his "madman" is closer to the heart of Anselm's thought than Gaulino's "fool" is (See

In direct opposition to Eriugena, Anselm argued against Roscelin of Compiègne, that,

> By always adhering to the same faith without hesitation, by loving it and by humbly living according to it, a Christian ought to argue how . . . [the things believed and professed by the Catholic Church] are, inasmuch as one can look for reasons. If one can understand, one should thank God; if one cannot, one should bow one's head in veneration . . . When beginners foolishly try to ascend intellectually to those things that first need the ladder of faith . . . they sink into many kinds of errors by reason of the deficiency of their intellect. For they evidently do not have the strength of faith.[92]

Later scholastic thinkers tended to follow Anselm's position. Hugh of Saint Victor claimed that although God is ultimately mysterious,[93] when we believe in the dogma of the Trinity, divine grace can enlighten our reason and show us by rational arguments that God's unity and triunity are ultimately not illogical, but almost necessary.[94]

Abelard, who shared Anselm's perspective on rational investigation stemming forth from the tenets of faith,[95] slightly changed Anselm's language in order to make his position even clearer, safeguarding it against abuse. Thus, whilst the Archbishop called the rational conclusion he could reach after believing "an *absolutely necessary* thing";[96] Abelard preferred to call it *honest*. As he wrote, "We want to use honest reasons

---

Nietzsche, *Gay Science*, III.125). Even in more recent studies, similar interpretations have still been advanced: Zino Zini affirmed that Anselm, in his scholastic understanding, reversed "Saint Augustine's *Crede ut intelligas* . . . into an *Intellige ut credas*" (Zini, "Anselm," 893–94), *de facto* denying any possible understanding of grace that enables human responsive, upward love. In truth, Anselm's thought starts in and is pervaded by a profound, background mysticism, which starts in the supra-rational contemplation of the revelation of God, which enlightens the mind, and opens the way to a degree of understanding.

92. Anselm, "Incarnation," 235–36. Affirmations that seem to echo Augustine's words can be found in another passage of the same treatise against Roscelin of Compiègne: ibid., 238–41. See also Anselm, "Why God," I.2, 267–68, where Anselm affirms that even if a certain claim can be formulated by means of logic, if it is not backed up by the authority of faith it should not be considered as a valid affirmation.

93. Hugh of Saint Victor, "Sacramentis," I.III.31, 234.

94. Ibid., I.III.4, 218.

95. See Abelard, "Teologia Christiana," III, 1226.

96. "Necessarium." Anselm, "Monologion," 11–12, my emphasis.

more than necessary ones, since the product of honesty amongst the faithful is always considered a more excellent thing."[97]

As it has been argued, Richard is certainly in line with traditional views. Yet, his peculiar understanding seems to stem also from an entirely original impulse. To him, "faith is the origin and foundation of all good."[98] But at the same time, "If faith is the origin of all good, knowledge is its consummation and perfection . . . Let us make our best effort to understand what we believe."[99] His double stress on faith first, and then on reason is probably to be traced back to the Victorine's spirituality, as his background mysticism highlights the element of contemplation as the goal of faith, even more strongly than Anselm or Augustine did.[100] In the Prologue, Richard's invitation to rational investigation is an encouragement to ascend in contemplation to the very place where God dwells so as to see him and live. As he writes, "Let us always strive, within the limits of what is right and possible, to comprehend by reason that which we hold by faith . . . If we are children of Zion, let us set up that sublime ladder of contemplation, let us assume wings like eagles, by which we can take off from the earthly ground and ascend to the heavenly places. Let us taste the realities of heaven, and not those of earth. [Let us taste the realities of heaven] where Christ sits at the right hand of God."[101]

The necessity of developing a mystical life and the characteristics of contemplation had already been extensively discussed by Richard in his mystical treatises.[102] Yet, the fact that in this dogmatic work he bases his typical *motum in Deum*—the spiritual journey towards God—on the christological model offered by the ascended Christ is significant. Faith, to Richard, teaches us those truths that are to be believed, inspir-

---

97. "Magis autem honestis quam necessariis rationibus utimur quoniam apud bonos id semper praecipuum statuitur quod ex honestate amplius commendatur." Abelard, "Introductio," III.2, 1090. The passage slightly echoes Anselm's words to Gaunilo, "My strongest argument that this is false is to appeal to your faith and to your conscience." Anselm, "Reply to Gaunilo," 111.

98. Richard of Saint Victor, *De Trinitate*, (PL 196) Prologue 889A.

99. Ibid., 889BC.

100. See Spinelli, *La Trinità*, 32, and Ethier, *Le "De Trinitate,"* 121. For an analysis of the "Mystique Spéculative," see Gilson, *Philosophie*, 297–309.

101. Richard of Saint Victor, *Trinity*, Prologue.

102. See Richard of Saint Victor, "Four Degrees," 213–33.

ing by grace in our spirit the desire for a rational investigation that may bring us close to God, where salvation is found.

> Let us ascend after our Head. Because if he has ascended to heaven, it is in order to stimulate and pull our desires after him. Christ has ascended and the Spirit of Christ has descended. It is for this reason that Christ sent us his Spirit, so that he could raise up our spirit after him . . . Why, after all, has [Christ] presented the Spirit as doctor and leader of our ascension, if it was not because he wanted our ascension, for the present time, to be spiritual? . . . Let us ascend in the spirit, then, let us ascend with our intellect to that place where at present we cannot ascend with our body.[103]

Petrarch would write about a century later that, "Eternal life is seeing God."[104] Richard seems to have defined eternal life in the same way.[105] Everything starts by the grace of God in the divine gift of faith, which enables rational investigation, leading the soul to the discipline of contemplation.[106] Contemplation, then, strengthens the very faith from which it originated, by reaching full sight of God's glory.[107] The attainment of this life-giving vision of the Trinity is ultimately what Christ's salvation accomplishes in us.[108] Salet summarises it best when he writes, "From faith, which is the foundation and origin of all good, we must rise up with all our fervor to the understanding of faith, by rising from the visible realities to the spiritual ones, and up to the Eternal One himself."[109]

The analysis of the problem of knowledge, then, is solved by Richard in the consideration of the restoring effect that the revealed

---

103. Richard of Saint Victor, *Trinity*, Prologue.

104. "Eterna vita è veder Dio." Petrarca, *Canzoniere*, CXCI.1.

105. As Richard quotes from John 17:3, "Eternal life [is] to know you, the true God." Richard of Saint Victor, *Trinity*, Prologue.

106. See Richard of Saint Victor, *Benjamin Minor*, 28–29, 44, 83–85, 97.

107. Richard of Saint Victor, *Trinity*, Prologue.

108. Richard describes three dimensions in our ascent to the divine (immortality, incorruptibility, and eternity). Ibid., Prologue. In a typical Augustinian fashion, he represents the initiating step by the image of the human spirit "com[ing] back to itself." Ibid., Prologue. See Augustine, *Religione*, XXXIX.72.

109. "De la foi, qui est le fondement et l'origine de tout bien, nous devons, avec toute notre ardeur, nous élever a l'intelligence de la foi en montant du visible aux réalités spirituelles et jusqu'à l'Éternel lui-même." Salet, *La Trinité*, 13.

truth of faith has on our intellectual abilities. Our faith seeks to understand by reason, so that reason can corroborate faith and lead the soul to the vision of God. Using the typical categories of Scholasticism, Richard of Saint Victor responds to the question of knowledge and the method of trinitarian investigation describing a search pattern that is profoundly Augustinian in its core.

De Trinitate: De Deo Uno

The Formal Structure of Richard's De Trinitate

Richard's *De Trinitate* presents a formal structure that is both lucid and elaborate. The work is divided into six books, and each book is subdivided into twenty-five chapters, each of which the Victorine provides with an original title. The internal partition is not merely due to practicality and editorial reasons; rather, it is an integral element in the construction of the theologian's argument. As Spinelli notices, "On the formal level . . . the *De Trinitate* is characterized by the harmony, balance, and symmetry that reign within it, as a whole, not less than in all its parts; in its articulated yet substantially solid and compact structure; in the orderly succession of chapters, titles, and topics."[110]

Starting from the analysis of physical reality,[111] the first book focuses on the demonstration of divine, substantial *unity*. Then, as benefits any mediaeval, Western analysis, Book Two produces a list of God's different *attributes*, providing through necessary clearness[112] a logical foundation for each of them. Once the simple and ineffable unity of the divine substance has been secured, Richard moves in Book Three to demonstrate the necessity of a real *plurality* within God's undividable unity. Whilst the fourth book is mainly constituted by a discussion on the concept of *person*, Book Five is the place where Richard proves the presence of *exactly* three persons in the divine substance. Lastly, Book

110. "Sul piano formale . . . il *De Trinitate* si caratterizza per l'armonia, l'equilibrio e la simmetria che regnano nell'insieme non meno che nelle singole parti, nella struttura articolata, ma sostanzialmente solida e compatta, nell'ordinata successione dei capitoli, dei titoli e degli argomenti." Spinelli, *La Trinità*, 31.

111. Richard of Saint Victor, *Trinity*, 1.VIII, X.

112. Ibid., 2.XXI.

Six examines the *names* of these persons, opting for an Augustinian terminology that calls them Father, Son, and Gift.[113]

As it has been said, the treatise is orderly and rigorous in its structure. Text geometry and architectural symmetries, as the typical tools of any twelfth-century work of rhetoric, are masterfully employed by Richard to convey the truth of his argument.[114] Nothing is left to chance: the entire theological system presented to the reader moves at a steady and rational pace, showing sophisticated attention to the details of structural choices. As the author affirms,[115] the goal of his work is to demonstrate the necessity of God's unity and triunity on the logical level, motivated by faith.[116] This is the reason why it seems fitting to say that the organisation of the treatise helps to reveal Richard's scholastic, Augustinian approach to the trinitarian subject. He *starts* with the demonstration of divine *unity* and *afterwards*, through the analysis of substantial attributes, he defines God's *Trinity*.[117] Correctly, Ribaillier observes that the most appropriate subtitle for Richard's *De Trinitate* should be *De Deo Uno* and *De Deo Trino*,[118] the two main sections into which this masterpiece is divided.[119]

The Substantial Unity of God

Richard's argument finds its starting point in the analysis of the division of nature. Quite predictably, the rationale for such a choice should

113. Ibid., 6.V, XIV. See Augustine, *Trinity*, XV.19.36.

114. Salet, *La Trinité*, 44–45.

115. Richard of Saint Victor, *Trinity*, 1.V.

116. In quoting from the Athanasian creed, Richard repeats the importance of *ratio* as an aid to faith. See Augustine, *Religione*, XXIV, XXV. Jerome, "Letters," XIV.7.

117. Richard's typical, scholastic procedure is also evident in the confutation method he employs, which is based on a rigorous application of the principle of non-contradiction.

118. Ribaillier, *Richard*, 15. This is the reason behind the subheading titles chosen.

119. The form of Richard's work is helpful in understanding the basic formulation of this study. Yet, one should not gain the impression that the author's *rational* and studied approach ever turns into arid *rationalism*. The goal of Richard's dogmatics is theological contemplation, not self-glorified rationalism. "Tout cet effort rationnel est identiquement mystique. Tout veut être humaine et bien appuyé sur la terre, mais pour mieux s'élever jusqu'à Dieu." ("This entire rational effort is at the same time a mystical one. Everything wants to be human and well grounded on earth, but only to better raise oneself up to God.") Salet, *La Trinité*, 45.

be found in the Victorine's speculative mysticism. As he writes, "From what we see, by a proper reasoning, we understand the existence of what we cannot see . . . *Ever since the creation of the world, the invisible realities of God are contemplated by intellects through the things that have been made.*"[120] However, the radical contraposition distinguishing eternal existence from temporal realities is quite common in Western, mediaeval, trinitarian speculations.[121] The reason for this lies in an attempt to account for the manner in which an eternal God could be connected to a temporal world whilst remaining free from *becoming*.

Plato and Neoplatonism had already dealt with the same issue, and found this connection in the doctrine of the Ideas:[122] the eternally existent, divine Ideas impose their form to the Chora, the formless matter, principle of chaos and irrationality, (through the action of a Demiurge) producing the sensible world.[123] Christianity, on the other hand, taught the existence of a single *arche* (origin) as the original source of being on the basis of the doctrine of *creatio ex nihilo* (creation out of nothing): reality in its entirety had been founded by God.

Patristic thought had already operated a progressive harmonisation of the two positions. Yet, Eriugena, whose writings Richard had read thoroughly,[124] had probably already reached the most radical conclusions in the ninth century.[125] He presupposed the existence of four types of substances:

- A substance, which creates and is not created;

- A substance, which creates and is created;

- A substance, which is created but does not create;

- A substance, which is not created and does not create.[126]

He considered the fourth to be impossible, and identified with the remaining three types of substances as follows: God the supreme cause

120. Richard, *Trinity*, 1.VIII.

121. See Reid, *Energies*, 20, 21.

122. Reale and Antiseri, *Pensiero*, 1:100–105, 259.

123. See Ibid., 106.

124. Spinelli, *La Trinità*, 56.

125. Indeed, it seems at times hardly possible to understand the rationale behind Richard's positions without careful study of Eriugena's claims!

126. Eriugena, *Divisione*, I.1, 441B.

(who creates and is not created), the Ideas (which create and are created), and the sensible nature (which is created but does not create).[127]

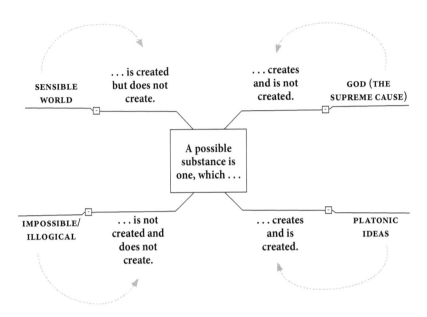

The use of a Platonic scheme allowed Eriugena to claim the eternal nature of the Ideas. To Plato, in fact, the Ideas that dwell in the Hyperuranium—the metaphysical place "beyond the heavens"—constitute the substantial, invisible realities, on whose model the Demiurge produces the sensible world. Scot Eriugena was thus able to affirm that eternity, as a substantial reality in the Ideas, could not be defined as a divine prerogative. To affirm this, he used theses derived from Dionysius the Areopagite,[128] whose works he translated.[129] By defining eternity as an ideal, substantial reality,[130] Eriugena, with the Areopagite,[131] affirmed that it could not be inherent to the being of God but that it must have been an independent property.[132] God, in fact, is absolutely simple and

127. Ibid., I.1, 442AB.

128. Ibid., I.13, 458AB.

129. See Eriugena, *Versio Operum*, 1025–194.

130. Eriugena, *Divisione*, I.14, 460.

131. Gilson, *Philosophie*, 81–82; 209–10.

132. Eriugena, just like the Areopagite, seems to speak of a time outside creation, as an objective entity even to God. Eriugena, *Divisione*, I.14, 460. See also: Eriugena, "Divinis Nominibus," X, 1163B–64C.

neither has nor can he have opposites within himself, as there cannot be substantial multiplicity in the one, divine substance.[133] Eternity, then, was described by the Areopagite and Eriugena as a logical, substantial concept to which temporality was opposed and that must have been, by necessity, foreign to the immensely simple, one substance of God. Since this substance by definition excludes from itself any opposition of contrary substances, it should be properly called *superessential.* As Eriugena writes, "God is said to be essence, but he, to whom nothing is opposed, is not properly an essence; then he is *hyperousios,* i.e., superessential . . . He is not properly called eternity, since temporal things are opposed to eternity; then he is *hyperaionios* and *hyperaionia,* i.e., more than eternal and more than eternity."[134]

Eriugena, then, moved to demonstrate the Ideas' subordination to God in an analogous way to the tradition of the Areopagite. As Gilson notes,

> Thus, here we encounter again the doctrine of the divine Ideas, but while Augustine [and] Anselm . . . identify them with God, Dionysius subordinates them to him, and the manner by which he does this deserves that one should pause, because his doctrine of the Ideas will rest as one of the permanent temptations of medieval thought. John Scot Eriugena will succumb to it . . . By saying that God is Being, Dionysius does not forget that here we are dealing with just a "divine name." In fact, God is not being, but is beyond being.[135]

However, if everything derives from the being of God, everything derives from his being-beyond-being: in Dionysius' system, then, nothing can be properly said to derive from *being.*[136] As Gilson points out,

133. Eriugena, *Divisione,* I.13, 458–59.

134. "Essentia ergo dicitur Deus, se proprie essentia non est, cui opponitur nihil; υρερουσιος igitur est, id est, superessentialis . . . Non enim proprie dicitur aeternitas, quoniam aeternitati temporalitas opponitur; υρεραιωνιος igitur est, et υρεραιωνια, plusquam aeternus et plusquam aeternitas." Ibid., 459D–60B.

135. "Nous rencontrons donc ici la doctrine des Idées divines, mais alors qu'Augustin [et] Anselme . . . les identifient à Dieu, Denys les lui subordonne, et la manière dont il le fait mérite qu'on s'y arrête, parce que sa doctrine des Idées restera l'une des tentations permanentes de la pensée médiévale. Jean Scot Érigène y succombera . . . En disant que Dieu est l'Etre, Denys n'oublie pas qu'il ne s'agit toujours ici que d'un 'nom divin.' En fait, Dieu n'est pas l'être, mais au delà de l'être." Gilson, *Philosophie,* 83.

136. If the sensible reality were originated by *being,* it would have its origin in the Ideas and not in God.

"Therefore, it is from a primitive non-being that everything comes."[137] Eriugena, who follows Dionysius' definition, clarified that the same reasoning could be applied to all the other, divine attributes. Thus, God is not good but he is beyond goodness; he is not powerful or knowledgeable, rather he is beyond power and knowledge.

Eriugena complained that the Greeks are able to express such concepts with extreme easiness due to the incredible flexibility of their language, while it is hard to express the same notions in Latin. However, he also specified that this divine *non-being* (and, by consequence, his *not-being good, powerful, wise,* etc.) is not the product of a shortage but it is the result of an exceeding surplus. As he argues:

> The same reason is to be observed in all divine names . . . He is not called essence, truth, wisdom, and all the other things of this sort in a proper way, but only so to speak. Rather, he [should] be called superessential, more than truth, more than wisdom, and so on for the rest. But do these [attributes] not seem almost other proper names? If we do not properly say that [God is] essence, should we properly say that he is supressential? Similarly, if he should not be called truth or wisdom, is he to be properly called more than truth and more than wisdom? Therefore, he does not lack proper names; for although these names are not generally articulated by the Latins in one single word and in one harmony of composition, apart from the word superessential, they are verbalised in one way by the Greeks.[138]

If this position is accepted, as Dionysius concluded, God reveals himself to be ignorant. Yet, his ignorance is a mystical one that is due to an excess of knowledge.[139] Following the Areopagite's lead, Eriugena also seemed to recognize, in a certain way, a true ontological status to

137. "C'est donc d'un non-être primitif que tout vient." Gilson, *Philosophie*, 84.

138. "Eadem ratio in omnibus divinis nominibus observanda est . . . Non enim proprie, sed traslative dicitur essentia, veritas, sapientia, ceteraque hujusmodi; sed superessentialis, plusquam veritas, plusquam sapientia, et similia dicitur. Sed nonne et haec quasi quaedam propria nomina videntur esse, si essentia proprie non dicitur, superessentialis autem proprie? Similiter si veritas seu sapientia proprie non vocatur, plus vero quam veritas, et plusquam sapientia proprie dicitur? Non ergo propriis nominibus caret; haec enim nomina, quamvis apud Latinos sub uno accentu, subque una compositionis harmonia usitate non proferantur, excepto eo nomine quod est superessentalis, a Grecis tamen sub uno tenore composita pronunciantur." Eriugena, *Divisione*, 460ACD. See also Gilson, *Philosophie*, 84, for a deeper analysis on Dionysius' thought.

139. Gilson, *Philosophie*, 84–85.

non-being, contrary to what Augustine had done. In summary, from Eriugena's perspective, any divine attribute cannot be identified directly with the divine substance. The *superessentialis*[140] (God) remains above any substance and any attribute, surpassing dialectically each attribute's substance and that of its *oppositum*[141] by an excess of being.

Augustine, on the contrary, had started his analysis by denying dualism as the source of reality. In his view, there could not be a Manichaean, cosmic contraposition between a principle of good and a principle of evil. Good is the only ontological principle: evil exists solely as a depravation of good,[142] just as dark exists as nothing but an absence of light. In the Augustinian perspective, God, the supreme substance, must necessarily coincide with *being* and with *good*. Evil, in fact, would only diminish God's substance making it less than supreme. As a consequence, since a substantial multiplicity cannot be found in God, all other substantial attributes must also coincide with the very divine substance. In God, then, *being* and *being good, being* and *being powerful,* etc. are equivalent.[143]

To Augustine, God is identified as *being* to the utmost degree and the very guarantor of the logical principle of non-contradiction. On the other hand, Eriugena's description tends to lead to the opposite solution: God can contradict the principle of non-contradiction, as he is above ontology, on which this principle is based.[144] In such a system, doing good or doing evil is a matter of indifference to God, because evil no longer stands as a depravation of good but merely represents good's *opposite universal*, which is dialectically overcome in God, who is greater than both principles.

In actual fact, Eriugena defended his schema by claiming that the shift he accomplishes in moving God's substance to a level beyond *being* ultimately secures the ineffable unity of God's substance over plurality and the limitations brought to it by any opposition.[145] In the Augustinian system, on the other hand, the very opposite would be true: God could

---

140. Eriugena, *Divisione,* 459D.

141. Ibid., 459–60.

142. Augustine, *City of God,* XIV.11.

143. See Augustine, *Trinity,* V, 8.9; XV, 5.8.

144. For an analysis of the principle of non-contradiction, see Reale and Antiseri, *Pensiero,* 1:35, 159–60.

145. See Eriugena, *Divisione,* 459.

be limited only if he was or did something *other* than good (i.e., something in opposition to his own self, something against that which he would otherwise do). By performing evil he would impose on himself something inferior (*depravatio*) to *being*. Evil, then, becomes the limiting factor of that supreme goodness that is proper to the divine nature.

Richard, as an Augustinian monk, understood immediately the dangers presented by the Greek theological system imported by Eriugena. However, he also understood that mediaeval, Latin terminology derived from Boethius had become equally dangerous in the hands of Gilbert Porreta. The Bishop of Poitiers, in fact, managed to develop a philosophical model that differentiated between *subsistens* (the subsisting being) and *subsistentia* (subsistence). Although he demonstrated that distinction between the two concepts does not necessarily deny the identification of what *(id quod – the thing which)* God is with his *divinitas (id quo – the thing by which)*,[146] this still sounds like claiming that the *subsistens* is such because of its *subsistentia*, that is its specific *quo est* (the thing by which he is what he is). In summary, God would only be God because he possesses as his instrument the idea of divinity, which makes him God.[147] Furthermore, if the Ideas are eternal, as they are the automatic consequence of God's original self-affirmation, the created, sensible world must be eternal as well. Its seeds, in fact, are already contained within the Ideas.

Although Richard mentioned "Power and wisdom . . . shared by . . . semi-divine [substances],"[148] he did not develop his theological system in line with Plato and the Areopagite and he also sought to develop a model outside the Boethian definitions spoiled by Gilbert. Defending the Augustinian position, he set forth to demonstrate that God coincides with *being* and with his substantial attributes. Richard's choices, also, take up a strong stance against Eriugena's theses. In considering nature, in fact, the Victorine distinguishes only between eternal realities and those that started in time.[149]

In this regard, Richard's argument shows careful precision. Since the original moment of temporal realities is by definition in time and

---

146. Gilbert Porreta, *Commentaria*, 1290B, 1296A.

147. Ibid., 1295–96.

148. Richard of Saint Victor, *Trinity*, 2.XIII.

149. Ibid., 1.VI–IX.

they obviously did not exist before that moment, they also prove to be contingent. On the other hand, eternal reality is revealed to be necessary. Its existence is the indispensable requirement for the origin of everything else that started in time. As Richard writes, "If everything is derived from this [power], this very [power] cannot exist if not by its own action, and it does not possess anything unless it is from itself . . . It is impossible, in fact, to give something greater than that which one possesses."[150] The eternal substance, in this perspective, is the actualizing factor that makes reality possible, the substance without which no other substance could ever be possible.[151] Similarly, if the possibility of all temporal realities is granted by the presence of the eternal substance, this substance coincides with God—the origin of everything. Eternity as God's attribute cannot belong to anyone else apart from him; everything else is a reality that has had its origin in time and from him.[152] In brief, the matter could be summarized as follows: any eternal reality is God and anything that God is must also be eternal.[153]

On the one hand, anything that belongs to the physical, temporal world and that is not God is known by means of experience.[154] On the other hand, we understand the eternal, necessary substance by means of faith and reason.[155] In fact, if this eternal substance is truly *necessary,* it can have nothing pertaining to it that is not likewise logically *necessary.* As Richard affirms, "I am absolutely convinced that in order to explain any of the realities whose existence is necessary, there are plenty of arguments not only plausible, but even necessary . . . It seems utterly impossible that all things that are necessary lack of a necessary reason."[156]

Before going further in his analysis, the Victorine provides his own definition of divine substance. As he writes, "We define as supreme over

150. Ibid., 1.XII.

151. Ibid., 1.XII. Following a process close to the one Richard uses here, Leibniz will say in the seventeenth century that, "If the necessary being is possible, it exists. But it is possible, therefore it exists." See Reale and Antiseri, *Pensiero,* 1:379; 2:351–52.

152. Richard of Saint Victor, *Trinity,* Prologue.

153. Ibid., Prologue. Richard's conclusion is diametrically opposite to Eriugena's. See Eriugena, *Divisione,* 459D–60B.

154. Richard of Saint Victor, *Trinity,* 1.IV.

155. Ibid., Prologue; I.VIII, IX.

156. Ibid., 1.IV.

all things, that of which nothing is greater, nothing is better."[157] Certainly, the Anselmian echo[158] that is immediately evident in these words is not there by chance. Again, Richard sets himself against Eriugena and his school as the one who continues the Augustinian theological system, identifying God with the most supreme being.

In basing his reasoning on the definition above, Richard notices that the supreme, eternal substance must also possess everything to the highest degree. In fact, since it is the prime cause of the sensible world, it must also be the source of those attributes that appear in the substances to which it gives origin. By necessity, then, the supreme substance must possess all attributes in a supreme way. If the opposite instance were true, the prime cause would end up donating to its creation more that it had in itself, which is absurd.

> If every being originates from that power, then that power is the supreme essence; if it gives origin to any other power, it is powerful to the highest degree; if any wisdom is derived from it, it is also wise at the supreme level. It is impossible, in fact, to give something greater than that which one possesses. One who has wisdom can entirely transmit it, just like one who communicates it can preserve it in its totality: yet, it is absolutely impossible to give a higher wisdom than that which one possesses.[159]

Additionally, this substance cannot but possess everything by virtue of itself, and this means that it must be identified with its own substantial attributes. If it received its highest properties from another substance, it would possess power and wisdom by means of participation, but any participating thing can never be said to *fully* or *supremely* possess power, or wisdom, etc. The divine substance, which is greater and better than any other (by definition), would thus result in being inferior to that very substance from which it receives its own properties.[160] Such an affirmation is clearly absurd. The only possibility is to say that the substance's being powerful "is derived from Power itself, its being wise, from Wisdom itself . . . [This supreme substance] possesses

157. Ibid., 1.XI.

158. Anselm, "Proslogion," II.1.

159. Richard of Saint Victor, *Trinity*, 1.XII.

160. Ibid., 1.XIV.

everything it has directly out of itself. Consequently, in order for it to have everything it receives by its own virtue from Power *per se* and those things it receives from Wisdom *per se,* it is necessary for Power and Wisdom to coincide absolutely with the supreme substance."[161]

Richard's argument allows a further analysis. If the supreme substance is the origin of everything, including its properties, then it must also be *the source of its own divinity.*[162] Richard's statement is clearly a polemical swipe at Gilbert Porreta and his theses, condemned a few decades earlier at the Council of Reims (1148). To the Victorine, *Divinitas* (divinity) cannot be seen as an instrument in which the supreme substance participates and by which it acquires divinity, but it has to be necessarily considered as an original property of the supreme substance, that in this way reveals itself to be God. "Now, the one who possesses divinity is God and anything that God is stems from divinity . . . Then it is certain that the very divinity and the supreme substance are identified."[163]

Richard's synthesis is almost mathematical: if Power, Wisdom, and divinity are to be identified with the supreme, eternal substance, it follows that Power, Wisdom, and divinity substantially coincide with one another and that in God everything is substantially one. "Finally . . . everything that is found within . . . true divinity is really, substantially and supremely one."[164] All divine attributes, then, are an exclusive, incommunicable, characteristic of God, with whose substance they are identified.[165]

The following diagram helps schematizing the logical rigor of Richard's argument to this point:

161. Ibid., 1.XIII.

162. Ibid., 1.XVI.

163. Ibid., 1.XVI. See also ibid., 1.XVII.

164. Ibid., 2.XVIII.

165. Ibid., 2.XII; XIII; XIX.

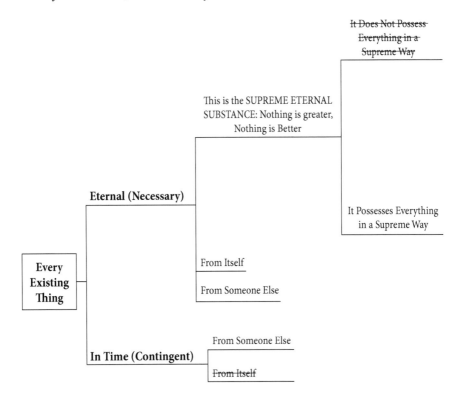

With such a premise, Richard sets out to demonstrate through *Rationes Necessariae*—the necessary logical reasons—God's oneness. Perhaps it is important to pause for a moment and analyze each of the different arguments that he uses.

ARGUMENT FROM THE DIVINE ATTRIBUTE'S SUBSTANTIAL UNITY

It is necessary that the eternal, supreme substance be incommunicable, coinciding with what it possesses at the highest degree. However, if all divine attributes are identified with God's substantial being, in whom everything is one, God is also *one* by necessity.[166] "So, it is necessary for the highest good to be supremely one, and not only supremely one, but also singularly supreme. Actually, it is not possible for two supreme goods to exist, just like [we cannot have] two absolute perfections."[167]

166. According to Richard, anything that exists and that reveals itself to be supreme will always end up coinciding with the substance of the Supreme Being. Substantial plurality is inconceivable.

167. Richard of Saint Victor, *Trinity*, 2.XIX.

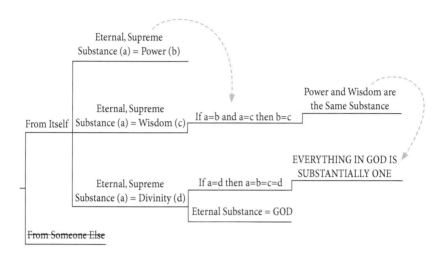

A *Priori* Argument from the Definition of God

By definition the eternal, supreme substance should be greater and better than everything else.[168] If we admit a multiplicity of eternal, supreme substances, each of them should also be greater than everything. Yet, they could not be greater than each other, as all of them would share the same prerogatives. They would be greater than everything else by definition and at the same time they would not be greater than each other. Such thought is absurd; thus God must be *one*.[169]

Argument from Power

As it has been demonstrated, the eternal, supreme substance coincides with the greatest degree of power. Since it is omnipotent, this substance also has the ability to prevent any other substance from being equally omnipotent. Yet, the fact that all remaining substances could be reduced

168. Ibid., 1.XI.
169. Ibid., 1.XV.

in their power by the supremely powerful substance demonstrates that the truly omnipotent substance can only be one. "It is impossible, that there be more than one omnipotent being. One who really is omnipotent, in fact, has no difficulty in acting in such a way as to leave anyone else powerless . . . Indeed, where is omnipotence in a being that can so easily become powerless! . . . The very nature of things admits only *one* omnipotent being."[170]

Argument from Divinity

As it has been shown before, the eternal, supreme substance, which possesses *divinitas*—the attribute of divinity—by virtue of itself coincides necessarily with God. A multiplicity of gods could be conceivable only if the divine, supreme substance decided to communicate its own *divinitas* to other substances also. In this case, however, together with his divinity God would also communicate his supreme substance, since *divinitas* is a substantial attribute of God. Multiple substances would then correspond to one and one substance would be identified with multiple ones. Ultimately, these substances would all coincide with each other while remaining different from one another at the same time, which is absurd. "The consequence is that God is necessarily only *one*."[171]

Argument from Immensity

God is the supreme being and nothing greater than him can exist: this makes him also immense.[172] If one hypothesised the existence of multiple divine substances, each of them should be equally immense. Yet, each immense substance would be in the condition of being greater than any greatness by definition, and at the same time it would be smaller, so as to allow the other immense ones to be greater. This is utterly illogical.

170. Ibid., 1.XXV, my emphasis. Richard's argument echoes Eadmer of Canterbuy's argument built on the concepts of *velle, posse,* and *facere.* See Eadmer, "De Excellentia," 557–80. Again, Richard demonstrates his debt to the Anselmian tradition.

171. Richard of Saint Victor, *Trinity,* 1.XVII, my emphasis.

172. Richard will demonstrate the logical necessity of the eternal, supreme substance's immensity in Book Two, while discussing God's substantial attributes, as will be examined later. As it is for now, it is sufficient for the reader to appreciate how the Victorine uses such an argument to confirm God's oneness. This is one of the reasons why Richard's *De Trinitate* should be read in its entirety, so as to recognise the value of its logical consequentiality.

"From these arguments we can conclude without a doubt that . . . only *one* immense being exists and could ever exist."[173]

OTHER ARGUMENTS

If everything that pertains to God is one in God, then the same reasoning argued from the analysis of one attribute can be reformulated and argued also from the analysis of another attribute. Indeed, each attribute coincides with all the others and with the eternal, supreme substance. To conclude, there are numerous other ways to prove that God is *one*.[174]

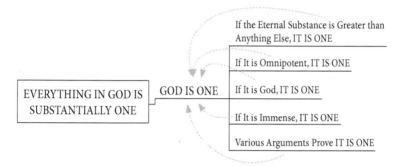

With this series of necessary reasons, Richard demonstrates the oneness of the divine substance. There *cannot* be more than one God.[175]

The Divine Attributes

Richard's attention in identifying God's attributes develops out of his demonstration of the necessity of divine unity. He had already identified the one God with *the supreme, eternal substance, source of being, origin of itself, fullness of power, and fullness of wisdom*.[176] His objective becomes investigating closely what power and wisdom imply in God.

173. Richard of Saint Victor, *Trinity*, 2.VI, my emphasis.

174. Ibid., 2.XIV.

175. As it has been noticed at the beginning, Richard's aim is to present the logical necessity of divine unity and triunity. By demonstrating the eternal, supreme substance's oneness, Richard has reached his first objective. At this point in his discussion, God's substantial unity *per se* neither implies nor excludes personal multiplicity that faith teaches (Ibid., 1.XVII). Plurality in unity will be the topic of the second half of this treatise.

176. Ibid., 1.XVI, XVIII, XX.

With respect to power, if God is *fullness of power* he is also *omnipotent*.[177] His omnipotence must necessarily manifest itself everywhere, without being limited in any way, by any place. In fact, if divine omnipotence were restricted to certain areas only, while being excluded from others, God would be only locally omnipotent. His substance would coincide with fullness of power only in certain locations but not in others, which is clearly illogical. "If he is truly omnipotent, he is also powerful everywhere."[178] The fact that his omnipotence is not limited by place clarifies that his essence also, with which its substantial attributes coincide, is not locally limited. God is not just *omnipotent* everywhere, but also he *is* everywhere, thus he is *omnipresent*.[179]

Such a state of being everywhere does not imply that God's substance is divided, in pervading the physical, space-dimensioned reality or spreading through the non-spatial world of the spirits. God, in fact, is one, as Richard has already demonstrated, and because of his unity his substance is absolutely simple. It admits no divisions, as these would correspond to a substantial multiplicity that has been already proved to be impossible in God. We cannot but affirm that God is present everywhere *in his entirety*, i.e., he is *undivided*.[180]

With respect to wisdom, on the other hand, if God is *fullness of wisdom*, he is revealed to be *omniscient*.[181] There is no possibility that the divine substance ever deceives itself. Ignorance and misjudgement come from imperfect understanding, but if God possesses the highest degree of wisdom there is nothing he can ignore or misjudge. As Richard writes, "This is a most certain thing: in the wisdom, which is God, there cannot be anything false . . . God is truthful, and this attribute comes to him from truth. Truth, then, is identical to God."[182]

By constructing his analysis according to the typical rules of an Aristotelian syllogism in the form known as *Barbara*,[183] Richard argues that by necessity all truth must be everlasting, since truth does

177. Ibid., 1.XXI–XXII; 2.XXIII.

178. Ibid., 2.XXIII.

179. Ibid.

180. Ibid.

181. I.e., supremely wise and knowledgeable. Ibid., 1.XXII.

182. Ibid., 2.II.

183. This choice shows how much pagan authors were appreciated at Saint Victor. For further analyses, see Spinelli, *La Trinità*, 18; Dumeige, *Richard de Saint-Victor*, 22–23.

not change with time. He adds to this the notion he has just proved: God and truth are identified. His conclusion is indisputable: God is *everlasting*.[184]

Conversely, God's immutability is proved as follows: "It is necessary to know that every mutation happens either from a [worse] condition to a better one, or from a [better] condition to a worse one, or from a condition to another of equal status."[185] Nonetheless, saying that God can move from a higher to a lower condition would be rather ludicrous. As argued, he is omnipotent, and omnipotence is—by definition—the ability to perform everything at the highest level, which is the very opposite of degradation. If God deteriorated, he would be omnipotent by definition but at the same time he would lose his ability to do everything at the supreme level. On the other hand, if God underwent a change for the better, he could receive this new, improved condition only by virtue of himself or by the action of some other substance. If he received it from himself, such a superior condition would already belong to him.[186] No proper change could be said to happen, thus no real mutation would take place. If he should receive it from someone else, God would cease to be the greatest being, source of everything: he would cease to be God. Mutation as improvement, then, proves to be in God just as preposterous as degradation. Lastly, if we say that the supreme substance mutates into a new but equal condition we would be forced to admit that in this change God has to lose something he previously had, and has to gain something else he previously did not have. Since it has just been demonstrated that God can neither gain nor deteriorate, he cannot mutate into a different-but-equivalent condition either. "In summary, he, who cannot become worse, is incorruptible. He, who cannot improve or mutate in any way, is absolutely immutable. Therefore, it is true and absolutely certain that God possesses *immutable* being."[187]

Moving on in his analysis, Richard affirms that since logical necessity requires God to be everlasting (i.e., without beginning or end) and

184. Richard of Saint Victor, *Trinity*, 2.II. As can be extrapolated from the passage, Richard's syllogism is:

> *Major Premise*: "All truth is everlasting;"
> *Minor Premise*: "God is truth;"
> *Conclusion*: "God is everlasting."

185. Ibid., 2.III.

186. In order to donate something to himself, God must have already had it.

187. Richard of Saint Victor, *Trinity*, 2.III, my emphasis.

immutable (i.e., without mutation), God must also be *eternal*.[188] The Victorine also points out that everything that lacks limits, having no beginning or end, can be properly said to be *infinite*. Yet, God's infinity cannot be pertinent only to his eternal lack of temporal limits: God must also be infinite with respect to all his other attributes. In fact, if the opposite were true, he would show himself to be unlimited concerning his eternity but at the same time he would be limited concerning everything else. Since the divine, substantial attributes coincide with the divine substance and with one another, he would be at the same time and with respect to himself both limited and unlimited. The nonsensi-

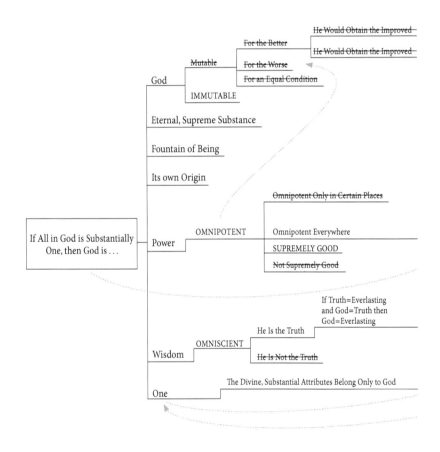

188. It is important to remind the reader here of the meaning that Richard gives to the word "eternal." As he writes, "Eternal . . . has the same meaning [as everlasting] but it also implies the impossibility of . . . mutation." Ibid., 2.IV.

cality of such a conclusion proves that God must necessarily be infinite in everything: he must be *immense*.[189]

The last divine attribute that deserves to be evaluated here is that which describes God's goodness. God's omnipotence presupposes the divine substance to be the centre of all fullness and every perfection. By necessity, then, God must be the supreme goodness. "Otherwise, if he, who is maximally powerful, were short even of one single element of any perfection—so not to be able to possess this [perfection]—he would not be omnipotent at all. That which is not short—and cannot be short—of any perfection is totally perfect."[190] It is clear, then, that by coinciding with the supreme good, God is also *supremely good*.

The following diagram schematizes Richard's argument:

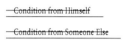

Condition from Himself

Condition from Someone Else

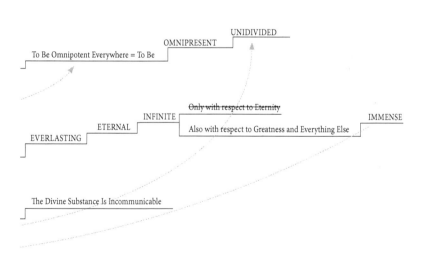

---

189. Ibid., 2.V. The argument from immensity that has been mentioned before to demonstrate the eternal substance's oneness is now fully intelligible. Multiple immense substances are inconceivable because immensity implies limitless greatness with respect to any other being. See Ibid., 2.VI.

190. Ibid., 2.XVI.

In summary, the divine, substantial attributes that Richard identifies are:

- Omnipotence (fullness of power);
- Omniscience (fullness of wisdom);
- Supreme goodness;
- Everlastingness (lack of beginning or end);
- Immutability;
- Eternity (everlasting and immutable);
- Infinity (without limits in time)
- Omnipresence;
- Indivisibility (supremely simple);
- Immensity (without limits of any sort).[191]

To conclude, by the end of the section of his treatise dedicated to God's unity, the Prior of Saint Victor has been able to demonstrate the existence of the one, unique God and to show his necessary properties.

De Trinitate: De Deo Trino

The Necessity of Plurality in Substantial Unity and the Concept of Caritas

As it has been briefly mentioned before, the divine, substantial unity *per se* neither implies nor excludes personal plurality.[192] "[The] examin[ation of] whether there is a real plurality in the true and simple divinity, and whether the number of the divine persons can go up to three, as our faith teaches us,"[193] becomes the focus of the second part of the *De Trinitate*—the most original portion of the entire treatise.

Richard has already shown that God is supreme goodness. As such, he must necessarily possess fullness of love, that the Victorine

191. Provided in parenthesis is a brief explanation of the particular meanings of Richard's terminology, when this is significantly different from common usage or when it is to be understood as technical language.

192. Richard of Saint Victor, *Trinity*, 1.XVII.

193. Ibid., 3.I.

calls *caritas*. As he defines it, "Supreme charity-love has to be absolutely perfect; in order to be supremely perfect, it must be so great that it could not be greater and . . . it must be of such . . . [goodness] that it could not be better."[194]

The term *caritas* was not new to trinitarian speculation. Augustine considered *caritas* the best of all possible definitions for the Trinity.[195] However, the use of love terminology in *City of God* is very wide: *amor*, *dilectio*, and *caritas* are all synonyms[196] and Augustine tends not to make distinctions between types of love on the basis of love's own object. While he describes the "love of God to the contempt of self" as the ultimate pursuit of a human being, he immediately complains that the city of men was founded by a self-destructive "love of self to the contempt of God," that keeps guiding the lives of its citizens.[197] This means that in Augustine's perspective even perverted love could be called true love.[198] Love of self is wrong, it leads to destruction, but it is nonetheless authentic.[199] Gregory the Great, on the contrary, seems to take the opposite stance. In his opinion, love cannot exist unless it is expressed *in alterum*.[200]

Although Richard was an Augustinian, in this case he shows a clear preference for Gregory's definition,[201] maybe because of Abelard's influence, as Bligh suggests.[202] To him, in order to be the greatest love and

194. Ibid., 3.XI.

195. Augustine, *Vecchio Testamento*, XXI.2; Augustine, *Trinity*, VIII.8.12; VI.5.7.

196. Augustine, *City of God*, XIV.7. See also Augustine, *Trinity*, VIII.7–8, where he accepts both "Deus dilectio est" and "Deus caritas est."

197. The "Amor Dei usque ad contemptum sui" and the "Amor sui usque ad contemptum Dei" are equally *Amor* to Augustine. Augustine, *City of God*, XIV.28.

198. Ibid., XV.22.

199. In his Hymn of the Paschal candle, Augustine argues that our sin consists of loving God's gifts instead of God. That is, our sin is not a lack of love but a misdirection of it. Ibid., XV.22.

200. Gregory the Great, *Omilie*, XVII.1.

201. Richard of Saint Victor, *Trinity*, 3.II.

202. As John Bligh demonstrates, "Abelard had led the way by his use of Gregory's dictum in the *Theologia 'Summi Boni'* and *Theologia Christiana*." Bligh, "Richard," 136. See also Abelard, *Theologia*, IV.117, 1299CD. Nonetheless, although it is very probable that Richard reused Abelard's application, his argument as set out in his *De Trinitate* is certainly original. Once more, Richard demonstrates his ability in using trinitarian material that the theological environment in which he operated offered him, reorganizing it into a new pattern.

exclude narcissism, *caritas* must have its own object outside of itself, otherwise it cannot subsist in God. "None is said to possess charity-love in the truest sense of the word if he loves himself exclusively. It is, thus, necessary that love be aimed at someone else in order to be charity-love."[203]

The concept of supreme *caritas* also excludes the possibility that the object of God's love be one of his creatures. In fact, any creature could never have the same dignity of God-the-lover, being inferior to him. It would transform God's supreme *caritas* into *caritas inordinata*. As Richard explains, "Even if there was one, single person in the very divinity, nothing would prevent it from having . . . charity-love aimed at one of his own creatures. However, [this divinity] could not conceive supreme charity towards a created person. Charity-love expressed by him who supremely loves someone else who should not be supremely loved, would be a disorderly charity."[204]

The Victorine, here, is not implying that God cannot love creation with supreme love. God's love for his creatures is indeed perfect. However, such *caritas* is called *inordinata* (disorderly) because while God loves creation with the highest degree of love, creation will never be able to love him in return with the same degree of supreme love. If this love, then, is *disorderly*, it is not the greatest conceivable love, which should be detectable in God. In the divine substance *orderly* love must also be found. *Caritas ordinata*, requires the lover to be loved in return with an equally supreme love.

Only another supremely perfect being can then reciprocate the immense, divine love it receives. "In reciprocal love, fullness of charity requires that each of the two [persons] be loved by the other at a supreme level, and that . . . both be worthy to be supremely loved, according to the abovementioned law of discretion. But if either of the two is equally worthy to be loved, both of them have to be equally perfect."[205]

The argument of *caritas* has a fundamental importance in Richard's theology. It proves the necessity of a plurality of persons in the one, divine substance[206] and also proves their equality. As Guimet comments, "It is because it [*caritas*] is supreme that it demands their [the persons']

203. Richard of Saint Victor, *Trinity*, 3.II.
204. Ibid., 3.II.
205. Ibid., 3.VII.
206. Ibid., 3.II.

equality . . . Thus, the demonstration of the divine persons' equality takes shape from the nature of charity . . . Charity-love does not attain its supreme level if he, who is the object of true love . . . is not also [the object] of love taken to its supreme level."[207]

Finally, Richard concludes that true, supreme love must also exclude selfishness. Divine *caritas* that is given as a gift must be such that lover and loved should desire also others to enjoy this most perfect love. "It is necessary that those who are . . . supremely loved seek with the same desire someone else to be included in their love and [seek] to possess [him] in absolute concord, according to [that very] desire [of theirs]."[208] Richard names this shared love *condilectio*, which has been translated here as "co-love," and by the same reasoning as above, he shows that it cannot be *disorderly*: the third, loved person must also be of equal dignity as the other two.

Condilectio, thus, is not simply a reciprocal *caritas*; rather it is *caritas* in harmony and communitarian spirit between *at least* three persons, who are united by the same circle of love. Triniatrian *condilectio* is the basis of divine relationality; it shows how the Trinity subsists because a communal love makes plurality-in-substantial-unity possible. As Richard writes, "We rightly speak of *co-love* when a third [person] is loved by the two, in harmony and with a communitarian spirit . . . when the two [persons'] affects are fused so to become only one, because of the third flame of love. From this, it is clear that not even divinity would have *co-love* if . . . a third [person] . . . was missing."[209]

In summary, the analysis of the concept of *caritas* allows the assertion that the supreme, divine substance requires *at least* three persons.

The Concept of Person

One should now move to analyse the meaning of "person." The Latin term *persona* indicates the mask actors wore in theatres to represent

---

207. "C'est parce qu'elle [la charité] est 'suprême' qu'elle exige leur égalité [égalité des personnes] . . . La démonstration de l'égalité des personnes divines a donc lieu à partir du caractère de la charité . . . La charité n'a pas atteint son degré suprême si celui qui est l'objet d'un amour vrai . . . ne l'est aussi d'un amour porté à son suprême degré." Guimet, "Caritas Ordinata," 229.

208. Richard of Saint Victor, *Trinity*, 3.XI.

209. Ibid., 3.XIX.

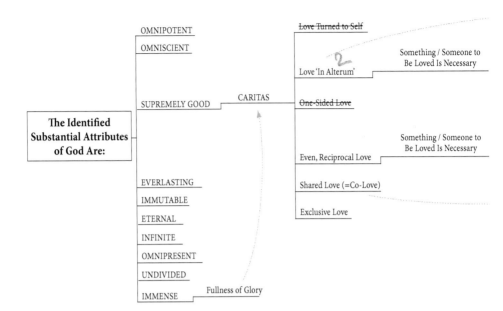

characters in plays. As Phaedrus shows,[210] a *persona* is pure appearance.[211] In classical understanding, a person is no more than a role player: the human being had to fulfil a function within society, acting according to his/her character's own requirements.[212] For this reason, classical philosophy prefers to concentrate its attention on defining distinctive properties of the human being, rather than analysing in detail the idea of person. According to Chrysippus, each human is a *zōon logikon*, i.e., an animal that is endowed with conscience, and able to

210. Phaedrus, *Fables* I.7.

211. See also Zizioulas, *Being as Communion*, 27–49.

212. Merlo and Moravia, "Persona," 768–69. For this same reason, in a strict sense, the concept of personhood could not be applied to the divine substance. "Neither Eraclitus' 'Logos,' nor Parmenides' 'Being,' nor even Plato's 'Idea,' nor Aristotle's 'Immovable Motor,' nor Plotinus' 'One' were personal, [divine beings] . . . The concept of Person began to be determined and clarified only with the beginning of Christian thought, which attributed personhood not only to man but also to God." ("Non erano [esseri] personali [divini] il 'Logos' di Eraclito, né l''Essere' di Parmenide e neppure l''Idea' di Platone, il 'motore immobile' [sic] di Aristotele e l''Uno' di Plotino . . . Il concetto di Persona venne determinandosi e precisandosi soltanto a partire dal Cristianesimo, il quale attribuì la personalità non soltanto all'uomo ma anche a Dio.") Ibid., 768.

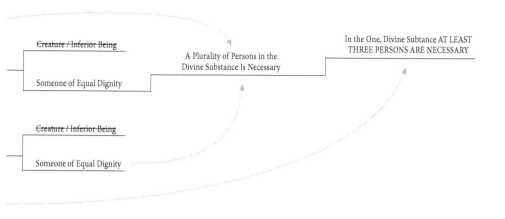

speak and think in an articulate and consequential manner.[213] Aristotle, highlighting the human characteristic of being *politikon* (social),[214] notices that human beings also have a nature destined to create inter-personal connections. Yet even these descriptions are ultimately very individualistic: it is the extrapolation of the individual from its context as a self-centred agent in the world (and not its *politikeia*, the human being's ability to create relationships) that is the object of inquiry.

Christian authors were the first to turn their attention to a new development of the concept of person, as they recognise personhood in God himself. In the East, the Cappadocian Fathers operated a redefini-tion of language terms. By distinguishing *hypostasis* from *ousia*, they defined the concept of person in a Christian sense, which would allow

---

213. Von Arnim and Adler, *Stoicorum*, 95 § 390.

214. Aristotle, *Politics*, 1.i, 9.

the notion of relationality.[215] Eastern theology has since insisted in following the Cappadocians on the hypostatic character of personhood.[216]

In the Latin speaking world, on the other hand, since *substantia*
and *essentia* are synonyms, an independent, trinitarian understanding
developed following Augustine's footsteps.[217] To Augustine, the classical definition of person defended by Quintilianus[218] was no longer
adequate:[219] he felt it necessary to develop Christian theology with a
different analysis of the meaning of *persona* rather than to continue to
describe the attributes of a human being. Personhood must necessarily
indicate relationship, as speaking of a "person" in the Trinity involves
describing its relationality.[220]

Augustine, then, strongly affirmed the *relational* aspect of the
divine persons.[221] However, with his distinction between the Trinity's
personal relationship *ad intra* and its perfect unity *ad extra*,[222] he emphasised divine unity of divine trinity—*Deus Unus* over *Deus Trinus*—
in a balance that is hard to maintain. In fact, between the fifth and sixth
century Boethius provided a definition of person that overstressed
oneness *without even mentioning relationality*, and his description of

215. "Father is not a name either of an essence or of an action . . . It is the name of
the Relation in which the Father stands to the Son, and the Son to the Father." Gregory
Nazianzen, "On the Son," XXIX.16. See also Basil of Caesarea, "Ousia and Hypostasis,"
1:197–227.

216. See Zizioulas, *Being as Communion*, 49–65.

217. Indeed, Augustine even claims to ignore the difference that Greek theologians
place between *ousia* and *hypostasis*, although he remains certain of their orthodoxy.
Augustine, *Trinity*, V.8.10.

218. Quintilianus, *Istituzioni Oratorie*, VII.3.15.

219. Augustine, *Trinity*, XV.7.11.

220. Ibid., VIII.1.1. Although Augustine did not produce a new, specific definition
and thus he uses *"persona"* also with an absolute meaning (ibid., VII.6.11.), it is plain
that to him, discussing Father, Son, and Holy Spirit entails describing their relationship. As he writes, "The Father is not anything, unless because He has the Son; that not
only that which is meant by Father (which it is manifest that He is not called relatively
to Himself but to the Son, and therefore is the Father because He has the Son), but
altogether that He is that which He is in respect to His substance, He therefore is,
because He begat His own essence." The structure of the period is complex, but its
meaning is clear: the subsistence of the Father is his being in relationship with the Son
(and vice versa). Ibid., VII.1.1.

221. Augustine, *Nuovo Testamento*, LXXI.20.33.

222. Augustine, *Trinity*, II.10.18; VII.3.6.

person as an "individual substance of a rational nature"[223] remained unchallenged in the West throughout a great portion of the Middle Ages.

Such an intensification of a suffocating character of individuality in the understanding of personhood offered the best environment for the flourishing of nominalist, trinitarian heresies between the ninth and twelfth centuries. Roscelin of Compiègne "denied that terms of universal character, indicating either genus or species had any other reality outside the very names expressing them and of the particular and concrete individuals to whom they point." [224] Human persons, to him, were nothing more than individual beings, and humanity could only be described as a gathering of those individuals together. Similarly, the Trinity could be acknowledged only by the description of the three individuals of which it is made, although these three are shown to possess together a single power and a single will.[225]

Anselm, in attacking Roscelin,[226] demonstrates how a less extreme individualistic understanding of person is necessary for theological analysis. As he claims, "In the case of God, although there are three persons, there is none the less one God; and although there is one God, the persons none the less never lose their plurality."[227]

This lengthy summary of the evolution of the concept of person is absolutely fundamental to understand Richard's choices. By examining Quintilianus', Augustine's, and Boethius' solutions,[228] he considered it indispensable to find a different definition of *persona*—one that might be suitable to the standard, Latin language[229] and applicable to both human beings and God. It is easy to see how Richard "[is] visibly more concerned with manoeuvring by artifices of language through that which he considers as heresies, than with building a positive notion."[230]

---

223. Boethius, *Liber de Persona*, III, 1343D.

224. Pietro Fedele, "Roscellino," *GDE* 17:790.

225. Gilson, *Philosophie*, 238–40.

226. "A certain cleric in France presumed to say this: 'If . . . the three persons are only one thing and not three things, each intrinsically separate, like three angels or three souls, such that they are none the less identical in will and power, then the Father and the Holy Spirit as well as the Son become flesh.'" Anselm, "Incarnation," 233.

227. Anselm, "Procession," 432.

228. Richard of Saint Victor, *De Trinitate*, (PL 196), 4.VI; see also ibid., 4.XXI.

229. Ibid., 4.IV.

230. "[Soit] visiblement plus préoccupé de louvoyer par des artifices de langage à

The Boethian tradition was not necessarily wrong, in his opinion:[231] it had just been misused and spoiled.[232]

Finally, on the basis of an extreme interpretation of Boethius' definitions, Gilbert Porreta had been able to formulate a doctrine which threatened the understanding of God's divinity and which had been recently condemned at the Council of Reims in 1148. The Bishop of Poitiers, in fact, had claimed that, "Of all the things that I have mentioned [before], what is said to be God is not referred *to the substance that is* [God], but [to the *substance*] *by which* [God is], that is, it is not referred to the *subsistent* but to *subsistence*."[233]

Boethius had noticed that substances and persons are always correlated.[234] Yet, "nature underlies person and . . . 'person' isn't used apart from nature. Both substances and accidents are natures, but 'person' is predicated of substance alone."[235] In Boethius' system, the difference between substance and person lies in the fact that substance, as a generic term, can include both rational and irrational beings and can be applied to describe both universals and particulars. "Person," instead, pertains only to particular substances that are part of the rational sphere. Person, in summary, coincides with the "individual substance of a rational nature."[236]

Richard followed a procedure analogous to that used by Boethius.[237] In fact, he affirmed that the term "person" always refers to a substance but with a narrower range.[238] In particular, the substance always indicates a *quid* (a "what") while a person always points to a *quis*

---

travers ce qu'il considère comme des hérésies, que de construire une notion positive." Ethier, *Le "De Trinitate*," 96.

231. Richard of Saint Victor, *De Trinitate*, 4.VI.

232. For example, according to Boethius, "The individual substance is called hypostasis because it stands under accidents, being placed under (*subposita*) and underlying accidents." McInerny, *Boethius and Aquinas*, 102–3. It is clear that Boethius is not saying that universals are a simple *flatus vocis*, but it is easy to understand how Roscelin could attack the Trinitarian dogma, by using Boethian expressions.

233. "Quod dicitur illorum . . . esse Deus refertur *ab substantiam*, non *quae est*, sed *qua est*, id est, non *ad subsistentem*, sed *ad subsistentiam*." Gilbert Porreta, *Commentaria*, 1290B, my emphasis.

234. McInerny, *Boethius and Aquinas*, 103.

235. Ibid., 100–101. See Boethius, *Liber de Persona*, I–II, 1341B–43C.

236. Boethius, *Liber de Persona*, III, 1343D.

237. Richard of Saint Victor, *Trinity*, 4.VII.

238. Ibid., 4.IV, VI.

(a "who").[239] As he writes, "With '*what?*' we inquire about a common property; with '*who?*' we inquire about an individual property."[240]

As previously noted, Richard's analysis is not aimed at finding a definition for the concept of person that allows the creation of a new philosophical system.[241] He simply wants to demonstrate that while the substance defines a *common property*, the person describes an *individual property*.[242] His definition of person is, "An individual, singular, incommunicable property."[243] Richard argues that although such a definition seems individualistic, it does not exclude plurality in the divinity, contrary to Boethius' formula.[244] In the same way in which no one is surprised by the fact that each human being is a person where multiple substances are found, no one should be surprised that God is a substance in three persons.

When we say "one person," we are certainly talking about someone who is only one, and yet who is a rational substance. When we are talking about three persons, we are doubtlessly referring to three "someones," each of them being a substance of a rational nature. But "[the fact] that more than one [person] . . . constitute one, single, and same substance has no importance with regard to the person's proper nature and its reality."[245]

All three *someones* in the divine substance share the supreme, supernatural, simple being, but as persons they must also present distinctions from one another. They are not *different*, as this would imply multiplicity of substances; rather they are *personally distinct*. As Richard claims, "Affirming that our God is one in substance and triune in persons is no contradiction at all."[246]

239. Boethius also makes an analogous comment. See McInerny, *Boethius and Aquinas*, 101.

240. Richard of Saint Victor, *Trinity*, 4.VII.

241. Ethier, *Le "De Trinitate,"* 95.

242. Richard of Saint Victor, *Trinity*, 4.VII.

243. Ibid., 4.VI

244. Ibid., 4.XXI. Richard wonders whether the Boethian definition could lead one to think that the divine, incommunicable (therefore unique and individual), rational substance could be considered to be a person in itself.

245. Ibid., 4.VIII.

246. Ibid., 4.IX.

In a very original way, Richard detects the distinctive, incommunicable properties of these persons in their method of procession. As Ethier comments, "There, Richard believes himself to be successful through the elaboration of his notion of person, which results in an ingenious decomposition of the term 'existence.'"[247] The Victorine argues that the Latin word *existere* (to exist) is in itself a compound made up by the preverbal preposition *ex-* (from) joined to a verbal root *sistere* (to be, to stay). Such etymological difference between the two words allows Richard to conclude that the verb *sistere* identifies a difference in the person's quality of substance, while *exsistere*[248] identifies a distinction in a being's origin.[249] This distinction can be applied to all rational substances that are capable of personal distinction, i.e., human beings, angels, and God. In human nature, persons' existences differ both in their quality (each is a different substance) and in their origin (each person has a different derivation). Amongst the angels, personal difference is only found in quality, as all angels have been directly created by God and share the same origin. In the divine nature, instead, the persons' difference *can only be sought in their origin.*[250] As he concludes, "Since the identity of the substance completely excludes any difference of quality, different persons' properties will have to be sought with regard to the sole origin."[251]

This detailed analysis on the concept of person in Richard's theology allows us to formulate a brief consideration. The definition the Victorine provides is ultimately not too different from that offered by Boethius, especially when one considers expressions that identify a person as, "One who exists only for himself . . . according to a certain, singular mode of rational existence."[252] His concept of person, taken in itself, does not even imply relationality; that is guaranteed instead by *caritas*. Richard's system, however, if considered *in its entirety*, de-

---

247. "Richard croit y réussir par l'élaboration de sa notion de personne, qui se résout en une ingénieuse décomposition du terme 'existence.'" Ethier, *Le "De Trinitate,"* 94.

248. From the Latin *ex-sistere*, "to be from."

249. Richard of Saint Victor, *Trinity*, 4.XII.

250. Ibid., 4.XIV–XV.

251. Ibid., 4.XV, XXII.

252. Ibid., 4.XXIV.

scribes a person as a distinct *quis* ("who") enabled by *caritas* to be in relationship.[253]

The Necessity of a Trinity

At the beginning of his treatise, Richard started by analyzing the division of nature, claiming that the sensible world constitutes the stepping-stone towards contemplation of God.[254] He also divided that which exists into two groups: one made of substances that had their beginning in time and one constituted by the prime substance, which is eternal,[255] and he claimed that eternity belongs to God alone.[256] It is now time to analyze the further distinction that Richard makes. The eternal being, at a personal level,[257] can receive its being *from itself* or *from someone else*. Any substance that had its origin in time, instead, must have been originated *ab alio*, (i.e., by something/someone else). In fact, if it had been its own origin, it would have necessarily existed before existing in time, which is illogical.[258]

The necessity of a plurality of persons in the one, divine substance has been proven earlier. Moving forward from this, Richard explains that it is necessary for at least one person to be *a semetipso* (i.e., from itself), otherwise there would be no logical cause to the being of all other persons. If nobody originated itself, nobody would exist at all. Thus, "one [person] must necessarily exist, who has its being by its own action and not by someone else's [activity]."[259]

This person gives being to all others; all others receive it in a timeless, causative sense—rather than temporally—since all divine persons share the eternal substance. Yet, if this person originates from itself *(a semetipsa)*, it also possesses everything it has to the highest degree *from itself*, rather than *by participation*. This means, for example, that it is

253. Again, we should realize how important it is to read Richard's treatise in its entirety. Samples and excerpts do not permit a full appreciation of Richard's arguments.

254. Richard of Saint Victor, *Trinity*, 1.VIII.

255. Ibid., 1.VI–IX.

256. Ibid., Prologue.

257. The same reasoning would not be applicable to divine substance, as this is incommunicable. Ibid., 2.XII.

258. Ibid., 1.VI.

259. Ibid., 5.III.

the origin of its own power at the highest level, i.e., fullness of power. Richard has already shown earlier that substance and attributes coincide with each other in God. Thus, saying that the person *a semetipsa* is the cause of all power and saying that it causes all beings is equivalent. If all beings—both eternal and temporal—have their origin in this person, this person can be *the only one* that gives rise to itself. In the opposite instance, in fact, it would not be the origin of everything. As Richard explains, "Everything that exists comes from him: every essence, every existence, every person . . . If all persons have their being by this person's action, it is absolutely certain that only [this person] has no beginning. It is also equally clear that no other [person] can exist if not because of this one, since it is from him that all *ability* comes. You can see that such an existence is absolutely incommunicable and cannot be shared by a plurality."[260] With such reasoning, Richard identifies the first divine person, as he demonstrates that *to be one's own origin* constitutes an incommunicable property.

All the other divine persons (at least three are necessary!) who receive their being *ab alio* (i.e., by something/someone else) can receive it only in one of three ways: *mediatedly, mediatedly and unmediatedly, or unmediatedly.*[261] If one of them proceeded in a mediated way from its prime source of being, it would not have fullness of wisdom, as it would know its causative origin *only* through another person mediating between them. Yet, if God is fullness of wisdom, this person would be both supremely wise—being God—and wise to a limited degree, since its knowledge would only be mediated. This scenario is clearly ludicrous, thus no mediated procession is possible in the divine substance.

Unmediated procession, instead, appears to be possible, as it permits full wisdom. However, only one person can *unmediatedly* proceed from the one that causes everything. If multiple persons proceeded in this fashion from the "ungenerated," they would all be fullness of wisdom but they would not have full knowledge of one another, as they would have no direct link between each other. This is incongruous. "In the divinity there is only one person who is from itself, likewise, there can be only one person originating from one, single [person]."[262]

260. Ibid., 5.IV.
261. Ibid., 5.VI.
262. Ibid., 5.X.

With this analysis Richard identifies the second divine *someone*, whose incommunicable property is his *unmediated procession* from the first.

It follows from the above reasoning that each remaining, possible person in the divine substance must necessarily proceed both *mediatedly* and *unmediatedly* from all the others, in order to have full knowledge of all the others. This means that personal procession always constitutes an incommunicable property for each divine person,[263] as the third proceeds *mediatedly* from the second and both *mediatedly* and *unmediatedly* from the first; the fourth proceeds *unmediatedly* from the third and both *mediatedly* and *unmediatedly* from the first and second, etc.

Richard points out that the chain of processions, which appears to continue without end, must actually have an end, otherwise God—the most perfect being—would never be complete.[264] The person who terminates this series, who is given origin but does not give origin to anyone, can only be one. In fact, by the same argument as above, if multiple persons were given origin without giving origin, they would have no immediate link between themselves. Since they would not know each other in an unmediated fashion, they would not be fullness of wisdom, which is absurd. In this way, another incommunicable property is isolated, thus the person who is *given origin without giving origin to anyone* is the last person in the divine processions chain.[265]

At this point, perhaps a summary is beneficial, in order to understand Richard's complex argument concerning the divine processions.

263. Ibid., 5.X.

264. Ibid., 5.XI.

265. Ibid., 5.XII. It is important to recognize this reasoning as the fundamental and ultimate point on which Richard of Saint Victor's defence of the *filioque* clause is based. In his perspective, there can only be one person ending the chain of processions if one wants to avoid the impasse of compromising the perfect and full wisdom and knowledge of the divine substance. If the Son and the Spirit were to be both described as proceeding from the Father alone, then they would both end the chain of processions and thus they would both know each other only through the Father, lacking an unmediated knowledge of each other. It is lamentable that the scarce availability of Richard of Saint Victor's dogmatic work as a primary source in English has allowed erroneous interpretations to arise also regarding this point. Indeed, such is the case in Dennis Ngien's recent research (Ngien, *Apologetic for Filioque*, 2005). Demonstrating only a partial knowledge of Richard's *De Trinitate*, Ngien misses this crucial passage in Richard's argumentative sequence and misconstrues Richard's apologetics, attempting to ground his defence of *filioque* in *condilectio*. Such lamentable misunderstandings only provide further evidence of the urgency, necessity, and importance of the present work of translation.

- There must be a person who does not derive its being from others but originates itself (first person).

- There must be a person who derives its being immediately from the first (second person).

- There must be one last person to conclude the procession series (last person).

- It is possible to conceive the existence of an indefinite number of intermediate persons between the second and the last one.

In order to demonstrate the Trinity, Richard employs again the notion of *caritas*. Since the *first person* does not originate from any other while it gives origin to all others, giving being to them, its love is *gratuitous,* as it donates itself with being.[266] The *second person*, who donates being to another one and receives its being from the first, demonstrates both *gratuitous* and *due* love.[267] Finally, the *last* person, who does not donate its being, as it interrupts the chain of processions, shows *due* love.[268] However, we know that substantial properties in God coincide with divine substance; therefore, *being* and *being supreme love* are equivalent. "In God . . . [every] person is nothing else than supreme love, distinguished by . . . a [distinct] property."[269] This means that each

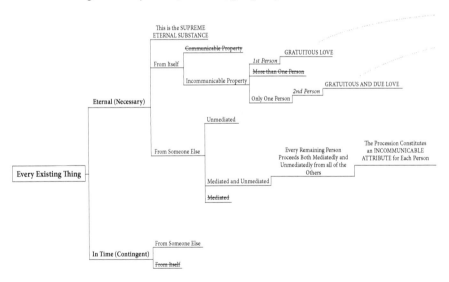

266. Ibid., 5.XVII.
267. Ibid., 5.XIX.
268. Ibid., 5.XVIII.
269. Ibid., 5.XX.

person is identified by its own, distinct love: the first by its *gratuitous* love, the second by *gratuitous and due* love, the third by *due* love, and all the other, intermediate, possible ones by *gratuitous and due* love.

Richard's analysis is brilliant: if other intermediate persons existed between the second and the last, their love would not be distinct from that of the second one. Indeed, all of them would show *gratuitous and due* love. Yet, as the property of their love is identical in all of them, all these intermediates would ultimately not be distinguished or distinguishable from one another by the property of their love. That is, their person, which should be identified by supreme love expressed by a distinct property, would necessarily overlap with that of the second person, as their property of the supreme love would not be distinct in any of the intermediates. In summary, one would have a series of persons with the same personal properties, i.e., a series of "identicals." As *identical* to one another, however, they are by definition no longer different. Indeed, they are not different persons, as they possess nothing that could make them non-identical with each other. The possibility of multiple, distinct, undistinguishable, identical persons is utterly absurd: by necessity there can only be one, single, intermediate person. *Thus, the divine substance admits only three persons.*[270]

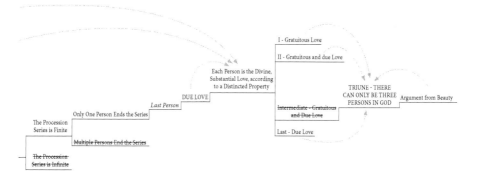

270. With a typical, mediaeval gusto, Richard sees confirmation of trinitarian necessity also in the argument from beauty. He underlines how supreme proportionality can only be found in a trinity rather than in a quaternity. Ibid., 5.XIV.

The Persons' Names

Once the persons' triunity in the unity of substance is proved, Richard pauses to examine the names by which Christian tradition distinguishes these three. Following Augustine's example,[271] he employs a criterion of analogy with human nature to find the reason behind divine names. The second person's immediate procession from the first, shows a direct and particular bond between these two. In human nature, the tightest and most immediate procession is represented by filiation (the production of offspring). Since in the eternal, supreme substance *to will* and *to produce* are equivalent, "It is right for one of the two [persons] in the Trinity to be called 'Father' of the other, and the other . . . to be called 'Son' of the same and only Father."[272] Richard warns that this is an *image*, and as such it is imperfect; yet, it is also the most accurate that could be found, and tradition has rightly used it.[273]

He finds it harder to produce a name for the third person. The designation "Holy Spirit," in fact, could suit any of the three.[274] Yet, this person cannot be called Son either, although it also proceeds from the Father. As Spinelli notices, "A priority of nature (and not of chronology) is found in the first procession with respect to the second one, as the one equal in dignity . . . is required 'before' the object of co-love."[275] He cannot be called "son" of the second person either. In fact, although he proceeds immediately from this one, he also proceeds from the Father. "Only the prior procession . . . which establishes a degree of closer kinship, deserves the name of generation, by which only the second person can be called Son."[276] Like Augustine, then, Richard names this third person *Gift of God.*[277]

---

271. See Augustine, *Trinity*, VI.4.6.

272. Richard of Saint Victor, *Trinity*, 6.V.

273. See Spinelli, *La Trinità*, 50.

274. See Ethier, Le *"De Trinitate,"* 100, 114.

275. "Si ha una priorità di natura (non già cronologica) della prima processione rispetto alla seconda, ché l'uguale in dignità . . . è esigito 'prima' dell'oggetto della condilezione." Spinelli, *La Trinità*, 50–51.

276. "Seule la procession prieure . . . fondant un degré de parenté plus prochain, mérite le nom de génération, d'où seule la deuxième Personne peut être dite Fils." Ethier, Le *"De Trinitate,"* 110.

277. Richard of Saint Victor, *Trinity*, 6.XIV.

Faithful to his mysticism, the Victorine highlights in the term *Gift* the sanctifying activity of the Holy Spirit. "What is the Holy Spirit's gift or mission if not that of infusing due love? The Holy Spirit, then, is given by God to man when due love residing in the divinity is inspired into the human soul. In fact, when this Spirit enters the rational soul it turns its sentiments on with divine ardor and transforms it by communicating to it a character similar to its own, in order [to enable] it to express back to its own Creator the love it owes him."[278]

Richard has thus identified the proper names of the three *qui*, the three "someones" of the Trinity: *Father, Son, Gift*. By this, he confirms their personal identity, since each person is always distinguished by a proper name, as he had claimed earlier.[279]

In closing, it seems appropriate to repeat the analogy with which Richard concludes and which seems to be a summary of his entire treatise. There is a teacher who discovers a science and teaches it to a student; this student learns it and writes it down; later, a person reads the book and learns it too.[280] "Three men, only one science. Three divine persons, only one and the same substance."[281] The truth that faith teaches us is reasonable: *God is one substance in three persons.*

Concluding Remarks

At the end of this analysis of Richard's trinitarian theology, it seems essential to evaluate the importance of the *De Trinitate*. The prime element that should be appreciated is Richard's profound, theological *Latinitas*. He is a convinced Augustinian who appreciates and uses very skilfully the wealth of the Western tradition and whose goal is that of expressing the meaning of Christian dogmas in an intelligible way to the average Latin reader.[282] His theology, in fact, responds and interacts with pecu-

278. Ibid., 6.XIV. For further analyses, see Spinelli, *La Trinità*, 51; Ethier, *Le "De Trinitate,"* 115–17.

279. Richard of Saint Victor, *Trinity*, 4.VII. The remaining chapters contain a discussion of the reasons behind certain verses that describe the Son as image of the Father. Ibid., 6.XI, XXII.

280. Ibid., 6.XXV.

281. "Tre uomini, una sola scienza. Tre persone divine, un'unica e medesima sostanza." Spinelli, *La Trinità*, 52.

282. Richard of Saint Victor, *Trinity*, 4.V, XX.

liarly Latin controversies. Yet, from within his own tradition, he is able to present a trinitarian model that could awake also the admiration and interest of Greek theologians, particularly through the wealth of insight that can be derived from Richard's exposition of love-bound relationality. Today, Richard's theology could represent a bridge for discussion with other traditions. Amongst the various trinitarian descriptions that twentieth- and twenty-first-century authors (such as Karl Barth, Joseph Ratzinger, John Zizioulas, and others) have offered or continue to offer, Richard of Saint Victor's insight can suggest a plausible point of common ground for interdenominational dialogue.

Secondly, it is unfortunate that Richard's dogmatics are so little known today, as they can be seen as the link between eleventh- and thirteenth-century Scholasticism. In fact, just as it is impossible to fully appreciate Richard's claims without analyzing previous developments of traditional concepts, it is likewise impossible to interpret thirteenth-century theologians without keeping in mind Richard's worldview.

For example, Thomas Aquinas, who certainly read Richard's works (he quotes from them),[283] held a definition of eternal life as a progressive contemplation of the divine that is not too distant from Richard's soteriology.[284] Justification, to Aquinas, is the movement of the rational creature towards God;[285] the process by which God not only justifies the human, but also makes him/her just. If Richard can offer the key to understanding the real meaning of Thomas' affirmations, then faith (the gift of grace) in both of their systems produces the desire of investigation. The product of this process is a strengthened faith, which contemplates God and increasingly approaches his unapproachable light.[286] The rational soul's movement towards God that Thomas advocates, then, is nothing other than Richard's sanctifying, rational search started by faith that brings one to the vision of God, revived to love by the action of the Holy Spirit. Rather than reading the *motum in Deum,* the spiritual journey of the rational soul towards God as the *root* of jus-

---

283. Thomas Aquinas, *Quaestiones*, q.14, art. 9, ad 1.

284. Refer to the above discussion on faith and reason in Richard's system.

285. Reale and Antiseri, *Pensiero*, 1:434–36.

286. Many scholastic theologians stress both the necessity of knowing God and the awareness that God is ultimately mysterious. See Hugh of Saint Victor, "Sacramentis," I.III.31, 234, where it is claimed that, "Deus . . . nec totus manifestus . . . nec totus absconditus." ("God . . . is neither totally visible . . . nor totally hidden.")

tification, one should consider it as its *application*. Any other interpretation would simply represent a distorted image of Thomas' theology that Richard of Saint Victor could help to correct.[287]

Lastly, in our postmodern world which questions absolute certainties but at the same time longs for spirituality, this mystical, twelfth-century author could become a helpful example to contemporary theology. He sees his faith as a journey, as a movement towards God, and develops a rational theology that starts from faith and comes back to it. It does this without despising reason, but restoring its value within the *context* of grace, as a gift from God. Richard deals with the question of knowledge according to the categories of his own time and elaborates a personal solution expressing it in a scholastic scheme. His flexibility should teach us to set our trinitarianism in dialogue with our contemporary theological and philosophical research on the problem of knowledge.

In summary, Richard's theological genius is such that contemporary debates can still benefit from its polyhedric approach to the divine mysteries. Perhaps, it is time that theology recognises, with Ethier, that with regards to Richard of Saint Victor, "We enter through an act of total faith into the most pure formulas of the Creed. One will never have the impression of 'dealing with the problem of a mixing of ideas in the concrete.'"[288]

---

287. Dante, who admired both Richard and Thomas, employs a similar theological model in his *Divine Comedy*. His *rescue* in the "dark woods" is described as caused and operated by divine grace. Grace moves Virgil (the symbol of reason) to lead the poet through Hell and Purgatory and triggers a journey, which culminates with Beatrice (symbol of pure faith and theology) taking Dante up to Paradise, where grace allows him to see God and live. See Dante, *Inferno*, I–XXXIV; Dante, *Purgatorio*, I–XXXIII; Dante, *Paradiso*, I–XXXIII.

288. "Nous sommes pénétrés par un acte de foi totale aux formules les plus pures du Credo. Jamais on aura d'avantage l'impression d'être 'aux prises avec le problème du mélange des idées dans le concret.'" Ethier, *Le "De Trinitate,"* 122.

PART TWO

On the Trinity

Translation

Prologue

My righteous one lives by faith.[1] This is at the same time an apostolic as well as a prophetic saying. In fact, the apostle tells that which the prophet had foretold, that the righteous one lives by faith.[2] If it is so, or better, because it is so, we absolutely must meditate with fervor and continually re-examine the mysteries of our faith. In truth, *without faith it is impossible to please God.*[3] In fact, where there is no faith, there can be no hope. *Whoever would approach God, in fact, must believe that he exists and that he rewards those who seek him.*[4] Otherwise, what sort of hope will be possible? But where there is no hope, there can be no love. For who can love something from which he hopes no good? Therefore, by faith we are lifted up to hope, and by hope we progress to love. After all, regardless of anything I possessed, *if I had no love, I gain nothing.*[5] In fact, you learn what the fruit of love is from the mouth of Truth: "*If someone loves me he will be loved by my Father, and I will love him and manifest myself to him.*"[6] Thus, love leads to manifestation, manifestation leads to contemplation, and contemplation leads to knowledge. When Christ our life appears, then we will also appear with him in glory,[7] and then *we will be like him,* for *we will see him as he is.*[8] You can see, then, the starting and the ending point, the steps by which we climb up through hope and love from faith to knowledge of the divine,

1. Hab 2:4.
2. Richard refers to St. Paul's use of Hab 2:4 in Rom 1:17; Gal 3:11 (cf. Heb 10:38).
3. Heb 11:6.
4. Heb 11:6.
5. 1 Cor 13:3.
6. John 14:21.
7. Col 3:4.
8. 1 John 3:2.

and through knowledge of the divine to eternal life. As he [the Lord] says, *"This is eternal life, to know you, the true God, and Jesus Christ whom you have sent."*[9] Therefore, life certainly comes from faith, but life also comes from knowledge: the inner life comes from faith; the eternal life comes from knowledge. From faith comes that life by which, at the present time, we live towards the good; from knowledge comes that life by which, in the future, we will live in beatitude. Thus, faith is the origin and foundation of all good.

How zealous we should then be in our faith, since from it all good derives its foundation and in it all good finds its completion![10] But if faith is the origin of all good, knowledge is its consummation and perfection. Let us try, then, to reach perfection, and by all degrees of possible progress, let us hasten to move from faith to knowledge: let us make our best effort to understand that which we believe. Let us think of how the philosophers of this world have applied themselves to such a knowledge and consider the point to which they have progressed. We should be ashamed to be found inferior to them in this regard. *"That which can be known about God is plain to them,"*[11] as the apostle testifies, *"For though they knew God they did not glorify him as God."*[12] Thus

---

9. John, 17:3.

10. The trouble in this sentence is the fact that both an *ad sensum* translation and a more literal and etymological translation are possible. *Firmamentum* can be understood in its more common meaning of sky/heaven—thus in this case, indicating the reaching of the highest summit—or as a derivative of *firmus,* thus shifting the attention to the unshakeable source of the faith. Possibly, this is to be understood as a clever play on words in the Latin and that both meanings are intentionally included by the author. Yet, rendering the full spectrum of evocative meanings in translation is a hopeless task. Salet, helped by a vague ambiguity in the French he uses, favors the less common, etymological reading of the sentence, thus his rendering tends to highlight the role of faith as the supreme source of good. Spinelli harmonises the two halves of this phrase and in his Italian text he translates that "From faith every good derives its origin and receives its sustaining." Although I understand the importance Richard assigns to faith—as *totius boni fundamentum* (the foundation of all good)—in full harmony with the most traditional Augustinian theology, I think it is important to emphasise also the goal of faith as a *terminus usque ad quem* (a target end to which it runs). In fact, later in this Prologue, Richard will encourage the reader to ascend by faith in contemplation to the heavenly places. In any case, the reader should realise that the original language of the sentence is much wealthier and thus mystically evocative, and no translation will ever be able to accomplish or replicate its strength.

11. Rom 1:19.

12. Rom 1:21.

they knew him. But how much more should we accomplish, who have received the tradition of the true faith from the cradle! In us the love of truth needs to bring forth greater results than that which the love of vanity was able to produce in them.[13] It should rightly be that on these topics we—who faith directs, hope leads, and love urges—demonstrate ourselves to be more capable [than them]. Therefore, it ought to be too little for us to hold by faith good and right ideas about God; we should rather make an effort, as it has been said, to understand what we believe. Let us always strive, within the limits of what is right and possible, to comprehend by reason that which we hold by faith. Yet, why is it surprising if our mind ends up finding the profound mysteries of God as obscure as darkness, when almost at every moment it is fouled by the dust of earthly thoughts? *Shake yourself from the dust*[14] virgin *daughter of Zion*. If we are children of Zion, let us set up that sublime ladder of contemplation, let us assume wings like eagles,[15] by which we can take off from the earthly ground and ascend to the heavenly places. Let us taste the realities of heaven, and not those of earth. [Let us taste the realities of heaven] where Christ sits at the right hand of God. Let us follow Paul in that place where he has gone before us, when he flew to the profound secrets of the third heaven, where he heard such mysteries that no mortal is permitted to repeat.[16] Let us ascend after our Head. Because if he has ascended to heaven, it is in order to stimulate and pull our desires after him. Christ has ascended and the Spirit of Christ has descended. It is for this reason that Christ sent us his Spirit, so that he could raise up our spirit after him. Christ ascended in the body; let us ascend in our spirit.[17] His ascent was bodily; let ours be spiritual,

13. The original Latin is tighter and much more effective. Yet, both Salet (in French) and Spinelli (in Italian) find it necessary to translate the sentence favouring a wordier rendering of the phrase's meaning to clarify it at the expense of its rhetorical force. Although the persuasiveness of a true mystic is found also in the images he is able to construct with his words, the present English translation too can possibly benefit from a loss of intense rhetoric in favour of clarity, albeit verbose and loose.

14. Isa 52:2.

15. Isa 40:31.

16. 2 Cor 12:4.

17. The word *mens* has been rendered with the term "spirit." The modern English usage of the word "mind," which would be the most literal translation, conveys a set of meanings that are completely alien to Richard and his mystical understanding. Richard is not a rationalist. To him, "mind" indicates rather the spiritual side of a hu-

instead. Why, after all, has [Christ] presented the Spirit as doctor and leader of our ascension, if it was not because he wanted our ascension, for the present time, to be spiritual?[18] In fact, at the ascension of our bodies, which for us is still to take place in the future, Christ himself will come in the body, in the same flesh that he assumed for us, according to the words: *He will come in the same way as you saw him go into heaven*.[19] Let us ascend in the spirit, then, let us ascend with our intellect to that place where at present we cannot ascend with our body.

Furthermore, it ought to be too little for us to ascend only to the mysteries of the *first* heaven in our intellectual contemplation. Let us ascend from the first heaven to the second, and from the second to the third. To those who ascend in their contemplation from the visible things to the invisible ones, and from the physical realities to the spiritual, the first thought that will occur will be that of immortality, then secondly of incorruptibility and thirdly of eternity. Such are the three areas: immortality, incorruptibility, eternity. The first one is that of the human spirit, the second that of the angelic spirit, the third that of the Spirit of God. In fact, the human spirit possesses immortality by right as a sort of inheritance, which no time or length of period can ever take away from him. In fact, the human spirit must forever either live in glory or face punishment. Thus, this spirit deserts itself, so to speak, and debases itself below its proper place every time it bends itself at present time towards the earthly and transitory things. To the spirit, then, ascending to the first heaven is nothing other than returning to itself and to orientate its thoughts and actions towards those things that belong to immortality and are worthy of itself. Incorruptibility, on the contrary, is far above the human spirit's condition: at the moment this [human

---

man person, which nonetheless does not exclude a person's rational abilities. See also: Spinelli, *Riccardo*, 78; and Salet, *Richard*, 55.

18. In his Italian translation, Spinelli confuses the accusatives *doctorem* and *ductorem* as nominatives referring to Christ our Head, whom Richard mentioned few lines above. Actually, the accusatives should be understood as appositions referring to the word *Spiritum*. It is very important to acknowledge the leadership role that Richard recognises to the Holy Spirit in our mystical ascension to God and the heavenly places. We should always remember that Richard is primarily a *mystic*: his systematic theology stems out of his intense mystical life. In Richard's mind it is the Holy Spirit (and it could not be anyone else!), who leads us to the vision of God, after the likeness of Christ our Head. In this regard, the Latin text is unequivocal.

19. Acts 1:11.

spirit] cannot possess it. However, the human spirit is capable to obtain by merit of its virtues this condition that right now it does not possess. Therefore, to the spirit, ascending to the second heaven is equivalent to providing for itself by merits the glory of incorruptibility.[20] On the contrary, the angelic spirit already possesses this incorruptibility almost by a hereditary right; it acquired it by the merit of its own perseverance on these terms—that it should never be able to lose it thereafter. The third heaven, finally, belongs only to the divinity; in fact, it is written in this regard that only God inhabits eternity.[21] All the other things that have had a beginning in time cannot possess eternity by the very fact that they have not always existed. Nonetheless, to be able to fly up to this heaven with the wings of contemplation and to be able to fix the eyes of the spirit[22] to the radiant light is a singular gift and one superior to all others. Consequently, we can ascend to the first heaven even now, we can ascend to the second one by virtue, and we can ascend to the third by spiritual contemplation.

Now, it is to this utmost heaven that the Spirit of Christ elevates the spiritual men, to whom the privilege of a revealing grace gives light in a more sublime and perfect way than the others.[23] It is up towards this heaven, in fact, that we are brought by the Spirit who lifts us up, every time that the grace of contemplation allows us to reach the comprehension of the eternal. Again, simply believing true statements on eternal realities should appear to us as too little a thing, if it is not also given to us to strengthen these faith truths by the witness of reason.

Let us not consider the notion of things of eternity—which we receive only by faith—alone to be sufficient, if we do not also learn that

20. Another possible translation is: "Therefore, it [the human spirit] has to ascend to the second heaven, in order to provide for itself by merits the glory of incorruptibility." Richard's Latin highlights, in its force, how this process of ascension is not only commendable but also a necessary duty of the soul enkindled by grace.

21. Isa 57:15.

22. See note 17.

23. It would be equally correct to translate the sentence as: "Now, it is to this utmost heaven that the Spirit of Christ elevates the spiritual men, whom He enlightens by the privilege of a revealing grace in a more sublime and perfect way than the others." In this interpretation, the agency of the Holy Spirit in the *ascensio nostra spiritualis* (our spiritual ascension), so dear to Richard's mystical approach, would be emphasised even more strongly.

notion, which our intellect can offer, since we are not yet capable to receive knowledge from direct experience.

We have included all these considerations in this prologue to our work, so to render our spirits more attentive and more passionate towards this study. We believe that there is a great deal of merit in being full of zeal in this investigation, even if its result is not as perfect as we had intended it to be in our desire.

Synopsis of the Topics of the First Book

Book One

I

If we want to lift ourselves up by sharpness of mind to the understanding of the sublime realities, it is helpful that we recognize what our habitual means to knowledge are. Now, if I am not mistaken, we have three ways to know things. We perceive some realities by direct experience, we attain to others by means of reason, and finally, we hold onto the last ones by faith. On one hand, it is by experience that we attain notions of temporal realities. On the other hand, we rise to the knowledge of the eternal things both by reasoning and by faith. Actually, some of these truths we are required to believe appear to be not just *above* reason, but rather *against* human reason, if they are not deeply and thoroughly investigated, or rather if they are not made manifest by divine revelation. Thus, in order to know or to affirm these truths, it is our custom to lean more on faith than on reason, on authority rather than on argumentation, according to the words of the prophet: *If you do not believe, you will not understand.*[1] However, it seems to me that in these words one should carefully notice also this: the authority [of the Scripture] does not deny us the intelligence of these truths in an absolute sense, but rather in a conditional way. In fact, it is written: *If you do not believe, you will not understand.*[2] Therefore, those who have well trained minds should not despair in acquiring understanding of these truths, provided, of course, that they feel assured in the faith and that they be of proved firmness before everything in the assertion of their faith.

---

1. Isa 7:9, according to the LXX's lesson, contained in an ancient Latin version.
2. Ibid.

II

Nonetheless, in all that has been said, this is a truly splendid thing: that those of us who are truly faithful hold nothing as more certain, nothing as more solid than that which we grasp by faith. In truth, the revelation made from above to our fathers has been divinely confirmed by signs and by prodigies so numerous, so amazing, so extraordinary, that doubting their truth even a small bit seems to be pure folly. Miracles so numerous and such that they could have not been performed, had they not been of divine origin, strengthen the faith and make it impossible to doubt. For this reason, as a testimony and also as a confirmation of those truths, we have used signs as [if they are] arguments [to us] and miracles as [if they are to us] experience. Oh, if only the Jews were to pay attention! Oh, if only the pagans were to take notice of it! With what security in our conscience in this regard we will be able to come forth to the divine judgment! [Is it] not perhaps [true] that in all assurance we will be able to reply to God: "Lord, if there is any mistake, we have been deceived by you. In fact, these truths have been confirmed before us by so many signs and prodigies of such nature that they could not have been accomplished if not by you.[3] Without doubt, they have been passed to us by men of outstanding sanctity, and they have been guaranteed by an authentic testimony of supreme value, since even you *worked with them and confirmed the message by the signs that accompanied it.*"[4] This is the reason why those who are truly faithful are more willing to die for the faith than to deny it. Then, without a shadow of a doubt, we do not hold anything more firmly than that which we grasp by a resolute faith.

III

To know these truths, then, about which we are rightfully told that *if you do not believe you will not understand,* one needs to enter by faith. Yet, one should not halt immediately on the doorstep, but should con-

3. An argument of a similar tone and nature can be detected in Dante, *Paradise,* XXIV, 89–111. The argument, so common in the mediaeval authors (e.g., Thomas Aquinas, *Summa contra Gentiles,* I, 6), is also of Patristic origin. Cf. Augustine, *City of God,* XXII. 5; Arnobius the Elder, "Adversus Nationes," II, 44.

4. Mark 16:20.

stantly press forward, towards a more intimate and more profound intelligence, persevering with the most intense and most insistent zeal, to progress day by day in the understanding of these truths that we hold by faith. The fullness of this knowledge and the perfect understanding of these truths give us eternal life. In this attainment we find supreme gain; in the contemplation of those realities, we receive supreme joy. These are the highest riches, these are the eternal delights; in tasting them we savor profound sweetness, by enjoying them we find never ending pleasure.

Now, then, it is with these truths, which the rule of the catholic faith requires us to believe, that we intend to deal in this work. [We do] not [intend to deal] with all the truths, but [only] with the eternal ones. In fact, in this present work, we have no intention to discuss the mysteries of our redemption that have unfolded throughout time and which we are required to believe, and which we actually believe. These two different types of truths, in fact, require different methods of approach.

IV

Therefore, as much as the Lord will allow us, our intention in this work will be to adduce not only plausible reasons to support that which we believe, but rather necessary ones, to corroborate the teachings of our faith by the clarification and the explanation of the truth. In fact, I am absolutely convinced that in order to explain any of the realities whose existence is necessary, there are plenty of arguments not only plausible, but even necessary, even though they may remain hidden to our attention at the moment. Everything that has received its existence in time, by the good pleasure of the Creator, may be and may not be: therefore and for this reason, its existence is not really deduced by reasoning but it is rather proved by experience. On the other hand, the eternal realities must necessarily exist: just like they have always existed, certainly they will also always exist. Indeed, they remain constantly that which they are and they cannot be something else or be in another fashion.[5] Definitely, it seems utterly impossible that things that are necessary lack of a necessary reason.

5. I.e., The eternal realities remain always immutable and equal to themselves, as they can neither change their substance nor their form.

It is just not within any spirit's capability to bring these reasons to light from the profound and mysterious bosom of nature, making them common knowledge after having pulled them up, so to speak, from the inmost recesses of wisdom. Many people are not deserving of this task; many are not suitable; many do not have the desire; and although, if it were possible, we should always keep these realities before our eyes, we barely and hardly ever think of them. With what ardent desires, I say, and with what passion we should set ourselves to that task and seek that contemplation, from which the highest beatitude of those who are to be saved depends! As for me, I believe I have offered some contribution, if it is granted to me to help the desiring spirits in this task even only a little, and to stir up, by my zeal, the lukewarm spirits to such a pursuit.

V

I have often read that there is only one God, that he is eternal, uncreated, immense, that he is omnipotent and Lord of everything, that everything that exists comes from him, that he is everywhere and that wherever he is, he is entire, not divided into parts. I have also read regarding my God that he is one and triune: one according to substance and triune according to persons. I have read all these things, but I do not remember having read anything on the evidences for these assertions. I have read that in the true God there is but a single substance, that in the unity of the substance there are multiple persons, each one of them being distinct from the others by its own properties. I have read that in God there is a person who is from himself and not from another one;[6] that there is a person who is only from one other person and not from himself;[7] and that there is a person who is from two other persons and not from one only.[8] Every day, regarding these three persons, I hear that they are not three eternal beings, but only one eternal being; that they are neither three uncreated beings nor three immense ones, but one single uncreated and one single immense being. I hear regarding the three persons that they are not three omnipotent beings but one single omnipotent being. Equally, I hear that they are not three gods

6. I.e., the Father.

7. I.e., the Son.

8. I.e., the Holy Spirit.

but only one God; and they are not three Lords, but only one Lord. I learn that the Father is neither made nor begotten, that the Son is not made but begotten, that the Holy Spirit is neither made nor begotten but that he proceeds. I frequently hear or read all these things, but I do not recollect having read anything about the reasons that prove them. Authorities are abundant over all these subjects, but demonstrations are not as copious. On all these themes, there is a lack of evidence and a rarity of arguments. Thus, as I have already said before, I believe I will have accomplished something if, in this research, I can offer even a little help to the searching minds, even though I will not be able to [fully] satisfy them.

VI

In order for the development of our reasoning to lay on a solid—and so to say—unmovable foundation of a clear and evident truth, it must start from an affirmation that no one could doubt or presume to contest. Every existing or potentially existing thing either possesses its being from eternity or it began to be in time. Similarly, every existing or potentially existing thing receives its being either out of itself or from another being, distinct from itself. For this reason, it is possible to identify in general three modes of being. In fact, every existing thing possesses its being either from eternity and out of itself or otherwise neither from eternity nor out of itself, or else, in an intermediate condition between these two, it possesses its being from eternity but it does not originate this from itself. There is finally a fourth possibility, which is the opposite of this third one, but it is completely irreconcilable with the very nature of things. In fact, absolutely nothing can exist, which [possesses its being] out of itself without existing from eternity. There was a time, in fact, when everything that started its existence in time was naught. But for all the time in which it was naught, it [also] had absolutely naught and could do absolutely naught; thus, it did not give existence or power of doing something either to itself or to another. Otherwise, it would have given out that which it did not have and it would have done that which it was not able to do. Therefore, understand from this, you, that it is impossible for something to exist completely out of itself without being from eternity. Here, then, we confirm with an evident argument that which we have already asserted before, [namely] that there are three modes of being.

VII

We must start from those realities that cannot be doubted in any way, and through that knowledge that we gain from experience, we must thoughtfully deduce that which is necessary to believe regarding those things that transcend experience. Now, this mode of being—that does not exist from eternity and that, because of this (according to the aforementioned argument) does not receive its being out of itself—is confirmed to us by the many-faceted, everyday experience. We constantly notice that certain beings depart, certain others replace them,[9] and those things that did not exist before come into existence. We ceaselessly observe this [pattern] amongst humans as well as amongst animals. Everyday experiences demonstrate the same regarding trees and plants. That which we can see in the work of nature is repeated even in the products of [human] activity. The fact that there are countless beings that did not exist from eternity is proven with certainty by everyday experience. The above reasoning, then, shows that everything that did not have its existence from eternity cannot originate from itself. Otherwise, it would be quite plainly evident that something has given existence to itself at the same moment when it possessed nothing and when it had absolutely no power. Now, how this is impossible cannot pass unnoticed to anyone who is sane in his mind! Therefore, all beings that have begun their existence in time share the fact that they do not exist from eternity, and for this reason—as it has already been said—they do not originate from themselves. Here, we have now dealt with that mode of being about which we can have no doubt, since we verify it in our daily routine.

9. It is so unfortunate that translations in modern languages are incapable of maintaining Richard's original Latin play on words between *secedere* and *succedere,* and his elegant phrase *in actum prodire* as counterpart to *non erant.* Once more, Richard shows his talent as an engaging lecturer, who employs all the tools of the finest art of rhetoric, of which he is a great master.

VIII

However, from this being, which does not exist from eternity and does not originate from itself, we deduce by reasoning also the existence of that being that is from itself and—because of this—that is also eternal. In fact, if nothing had originated from itself there would be absolutely no principle from which those beings who do not—or cannot—originate from themselves could have derived their existence. With no doubt, it is demonstrated that something originates from itself and, because of this—as it has already been said—also from eternity. If it were not true, there would have been a time in which nothing had existed; and then, even after that, there would have been nothing, because in this case there would have been no being, who would have given—or could have given—the beginning of existence to himself or to others. Now, the very reality [of facts] demonstrates—and the experience of the things that exist proves—that this is unmistakably false.

So, from that which we see, by a proper reasoning, we understand the existence of that which we cannot see; from the transient realities [we understand] the eternal ones; from the earthly ones [we understand] those that are above; from the human ones [we understand] the divine ones. *In fact, ever since the creation of the world, the invisible realities of God are contemplated by intellects through the things that have been made.*[10]

IX

Nevertheless, it should not appear impossible to anyone that there be an eternal being, which—however—does not originate from itself, just as it is necessary that the cause should always precede its effect and that every being, which derives from some other one, must always be subsequent to its principle. Doubtlessly, the sunray proceeds from the sun and originates from it; however, it exists simultaneously with the sun. Indeed, from the beginning of its existence, the sun has emanated its ray from itself and it has never existed without its ray. Then, if this physical light has a ray, which is contemporaneous to itself, why should that spiritual and unapproachable light not have a ray that is equally

10. Rom 1:20.

eternal to itself? In the created nature we see mirrored that which we need to believe regarding the uncreated nature. Every day we can observe how by the very work of nature, an existence produces another existence and from one existence another existence proceeds. What then? Will the work of nature be completely absent or result absolutely powerless in that supreme nature? Will that nature remain completely sterile in itself, after it has given the fruit of fecundity to this nature of ours? Will that nature, which gives generating powers to others, remain with no generation and sterile? Thus, from all this, it appears plausible that a being who is not originated from itself and who has existed forever should exist in that superessential immutability.

However, we will discuss this topic at a more appropriate time, with a broader and more effective argument.

X

Thus, in this work, we have set forth to discuss the two-fold mode of eternal existence, of which we have talked, and of the topics that seem connected with this consideration. In fact, we have no intention of dealing with temporal realities, which clearly belong to the third mode of being. We will deal with them only in the measure by which their analysis may prove to be necessary or useful to the examination of the eternal realities, just like the apostle teaches us and as we have already stated before: *the invisible realities of God are contemplated by intellects through the things that have been made.*[11] Therefore, every time that we elevate ourselves towards the contemplation of the invisible realities through the consideration of the visible things, what else do we do, if not to set up a sort of ladder, on which we mount up with our spirit to the realities above us? It is for this reason that in this work, the development of each of our reasoning starts from that which we know through experience. Therefore, the central theme of this work has to do with the eternal realities. On the other hand, the temporal things will be discussed only marginally.[12] In fact, the whole effort of this work of ours is aimed at [the analysis of] the two modes of being that exist from eternity.

11. Rom 1:20.

12. Note the rhetorical force of the Latin, *ex intentione* in contraposition to *ex occasione*. Again, it is a misfortune that such dramatic artifices are lost in modern language

XI

It is now the time to discuss more broadly about that being, which originates from itself and which—as it has been said—is eternal. Now, there is something that is definitely certain and—as I believe—no one can doubt: in the endless multitude of the existing things and in the many-faceted diversity of the degrees [of being], it is essential that something supreme should exist. We define as supreme over all things, that of which nothing is greater, nothing is better. Without a doubt, the rational nature is better than the reasonless nature. It is indispensable, then, that a rational substance be supreme above everything. It is clear that in the universality of things this substance occupies the highest position, and consequently, it cannot receive its being from that which is underneath itself. Thus, the existence of a substance possessing both of these characteristics—i.e. to be situated at the high point of the ladder of beings and to originate from itself—is fundamental. In fact, as we have already said and demonstrated before, if nothing had originated from itself, nothing would exist from eternity; in that case, things would not have had an origin and could not have unfolded. The evidence of experience persuades us of the need for a substance that originated from itself. If no substance had originated from itself, none of those things, which derive their origin from outside and which are incapable of originating from themselves, would exist at all. In summary, this substance, which has no existence unless from itself, does coincide with that being, who exists from eternity and [who is] with no beginning.

XII

However, that which has been affirmed regarding the supreme substance can be demonstrated with an even greater argument. This fact is absolutely certain: in the universality of beings nothing can exist if it has not received the possibility of existence either from itself or from outside. In fact, that which cannot exist corresponds to nothingness. In order for something to exist, then, this must receive the possibility of existing from the power of being. It is from the power of being that ev-

translations. See also note 5.

erything subsisting in the totality of beings receives existence. However, if everything is derived from this [power], this very [power] cannot exist if not by its own action, and it does not possess anything unless it is from itself. If everything exists by this power, then every essence, every power, every wisdom [derives its origin from this power]. If every being originates from that power, then that power is the supreme essence; if it gives origin to any other power, it is powerful to the highest degree; if any wisdom is derived from it, it is also wise at the supreme level. It is impossible, in fact, to give something greater than that which one possesses. One who has wisdom can entirely transmit it, just like one who communicates it can preserve it in its totality: yet, it is absolutely impossible to give a higher wisdom than that which one possesses. Consequently, it was necessary that the principle from which every wisdom derived its origin was wise in the highest measure. Nevertheless, where there is no rational substance, there can be no wisdom at all: wisdom, in fact, can only be found in the rational substance. Therefore, the substance that has supreme wisdom within itself is a rational substance and superior to everything else. I repeat: [this substance] is superior to everything else and every essence derives from it, every nature both rational and irrational. In summary, the power of being is nothing but the supreme substance. Then, just like the power of being is not, unless [it is] from itself, likewise also the supreme substance—which is nothing but the very power of being—cannot but be from itself. It is clear, then, that every existing thing is derived from the supreme substance. Yet, if all things are derived from it, nothing can exist by itself, except that one [substance]. Also, if every being, every power, every possession stems from that substance, there is no doubt that that substance possesses everything it has out of itself. Rightfully, then, this substance is called primordial, since every existing thing derives its principle and origin from it.

XIII

Now, let us ponder over that which has been said; that the supreme substance is powerful to the highest level. One fact is truly certain: its being powerful is derived from power itself; its being wise, from wisdom itself. It has also been demonstrated that [this substance] possesses everything it has directly from itself. Consequently, in order for it to have everything it receives by its own virtue from power *per se* and those things it receives from wisdom *per se,* it is necessary for power and wisdom to coincide absolutely with the supreme substance. Otherwise, without any power and wisdom, there could not [even] be a powerful and wise being, since [this being] would not receive that which is transmitted to it by power and wisdom from within itself but from without. In conclusion, if it is true that both power and wisdom are identified with the supreme substance, then each of these two are identified with the other.

XIV

Now, this is what must be underlined with the greatest energy: since the supreme substance coincides with power, we cannot have any different substance [from that one considered]. Otherwise, different substances would constitute a single substance and one single substance would correspond to different ones: this is absolutely impossible. However, you could perhaps object to this: "Can another substance with supreme power exist, even if it cannot be identified with this one? And should [these two] not have the same power, since both of them have supreme power?" With no uncertainty and with no hesitation I answer that if one of these substances possesses supreme power without being identified with it, then it is not as powerful as the one that fulfils both these conditions. Indeed, being able (on one hand) and not being able (on the other) to do that which to others is totally possible, is not the same as to enjoy the fullness of the very power, but rather it is to participate in it. And enjoying fullness is significantly superior and much higher than sharing in the participation of something great. Therefore, from this it is clear that the primordial substance cannot have [another] equal [substance]. Likewise, from that which has been demonstrated before, it is evident that it can [also] admit no substance superior [to itself].

XV

It seems that the primordial substance has the natural property of being superior to all things and of being unable to admit any [other substance] equal to itself or above itself. That which belongs to the substance, in fact, certainly belongs to nature. Since primordial substance corresponds *per se* under every aspect to the highest power, it is proper to its nature to be powerful at the highest degree and to be unable to admit anything more powerful or with its same power. Let us see, then, if this can at least have an inferior [substance], which might share its nature. But, how is it possible—I wonder—that some substance be inferior to the primordial essence, if by nature it holds in common with this one that very thing, which cannot admit anything either equal or superior? If it were so, one of the two substances with respect to the other—or better, each of them with respect to itself—would be superior and inferior, greater and smaller. Therefore, it is impossible that the primordial substance should have [another substance] sharing its own nature.

XVI

By our previous demonstration, we consider certain that every existing thing is derived from the supreme and single substance and that this substance possesses everything it has in itself. Yet, if everything is derived from it, even divinity is derived from it. Then, if this substance has transmitted [divinity] to another [substance] without retaining it for itself, it would have a substance superior to itself. However, as it has been demonstrated before, the supreme substance cannot admit another, superior one. It is evident, thus, that [the supreme substance] has preserved divinity for itself and still holds it. Now, the one who possesses divinity is God and anything that God is stems from divinity. But if the supreme substance possesses that which in fact is God—thanks to its divinity, which it derives from no other origin but itself—then it is certain that divinity itself and the supreme substance are identified. Therefore, this [substance] could not have communicated to another substance the possibility of having divinity nor even to be divinity itself. In the opposite instance, the supreme substance would have [another substance] equal to itself, which is impossible.

From this we can conclude, then, that true divinity resides in the unity of substance and true unity of substance is realized in divinity itself. In summary, God cannot be but one in substance.

XVII

See, now, how easily we can demonstrate that God is necessarily one. Everything God possesses comes to him from himself; consequently, it is clear that even divinity is one with him. Thus, it is unfit to think that he receives that which he owns by the effect of divinity from without rather than from within himself.

Regarding the divinity, either this is incommunicable or it is shared by a number [of beings]. If it is incommunicable, the consequence is that God is necessarily only one; on the other hand, if it is shared by a number [of beings], then even that [supreme] substance, which coincides with the very divinity, will also be in common.

One single substance, however, cannot be common to multiple substances; otherwise one single and identical substance would correspond to many [substances], and many [substances] to one only. This is manifestly false, as reason demonstrates.

Instead, if we affirm that [divinity] is common to more than one person, according to what has been said, even the substance that is identified with divinity itself will certainly be common to all of them. In that case, there will indeed be more than one person in the single divinity, but the substance will remain only one.

Thus, in spite of whether one says that in the single divinity there is only one person or whether one claims that there is a plurality [of persons], God cannot be but only one in the substance.

So, one single and only God exists from himself and—because of that—from eternity. Furthermore, according to that which we have demonstrated regarding the supreme substance—which coincides with God—it is from him that every existing thing is derived, it is because of himself that he owns everything that he has, and it is God who identifies with power and wisdom.

XVIII

If the wisdom and power of God constitute in everything a single and identical reality, there will be no perfection, no excellence, contained in one that is not contained also in the other, in the same measure and equally in full. Consequently, in God's wisdom there is nothing greater, nothing really better, than that which is in his power, and thus in his essence—since power and being are in him one single thing. Thus, any conquest or extraordinary or finest definition of divine wisdom is entirely contained with absolute fullness in his power, totally comprehended in his essence. Indeed, if God reached by [sole] intelligence a part of his eminent perfection without being able to realise it by his own efficacy, then he would certainly result higher in wisdom than in power. The effect of this would be that the one and same substance would be at the same time greater and smaller than itself. Then again, the divine substance fully corresponds to its own power and wisdom. Thus, in God, if wisdom were more developed than power—if ever things could have been set up in these terms—then the one and same substance would be greater than itself regarding wisdom, in comparison to power, while this same [substance] would clearly be lesser than itself regarding power, in comparison to wisdom.

In conclusion, nothing greater, nothing better than God can be conceived by God himself, nor can it be comprehended by his intelligence.

XIX

Therefore, divine knowledge cannot conceive anything on the intellectual plane more perfect than God. Even less, then, human understanding can imagine something greater and better than God. In fact, that which human thought comprehends by intelligence cannot pass unnoticed by the divine intelligence. To presume that humanity, with its thought, could bring itself above God would be folly. In spite of its investigations, humanity is not even able to understand who God really is! Therefore, the better and the higher the result of human thought, the more it comes closer to God, but it never reaches him.

XX

It seems certain, then, that all people, whether more or less educated, almost by a sort of gift of nature, are naturally persuaded and consider undeniable the fact that anything that is judged to be the best, should be attributed to God without hesitation. And if some do not accept this principle on the basis of the evidence of reasoning, they are convinced with no doubt by devotion. This is why even those who do not know how all of this can be demonstrated recognise that God is immense, eternal, immutable, wise to the utmost degree and omnipotent. Therefore, to those who are learned, the attribution of every highest conceivable thought to God constitutes a fundamental assumption, and to everybody this is a universally accepted concept. It is from this solid foundation of certainty, and almost of intimate truth, that even the greatest teachers generally start with their speculations, when they set forth to discuss with greater depth and more fervently the divine attributes.

XXI

The fact that God is powerful to the greatest degree, has already been sufficiently demonstrated. Nonetheless, one can still ask this question: is God defined as powerful at the highest degree because none is superior to him in power, or is he powerful at the highest degree in the sense that he can do everything and he is really all-powerful? Now, if we deny that God is all-powerful, we demonstrate believing that something superior to God can exist. Superiority, in fact, consists of possessing omnipotence, rather than any power that lacks something of the fullness of omnipotence. But that which man can easily understand cannot pass unnoticed to the divine wisdom. Then, if God understands that he cannot entirely possess the fullness of power, in him wisdom would be superior to power. But wisdom and power are nothing else than the very being of God. Consequently, on the basis of the above considerations, the one only and same essence would be both superior and inferior to itself, and nothing is more impossible than this.

To conclude, then, we deduce that God can do everything, with regard to those things in which power [actually] corresponds to ability. In many cases, in fact, we talk about ability whilst it would be more appropriate to talk about inability rather than ability. [When we say] to be able to diminish, to be able to fail, to be able to be destroyed and annihilated, and so on with similar things, it is certainly better [to say] "not-to-be-able" than "to-be-able," since these are expressions of weakness rather than greatness. Thus, all those things mentioned—and only those—are in the power of him in whom power constitutes a real ability, as we have already observed. Even more rightly and objectively, we affirm that he is omnipotent, because we subtract from his power anything denoting weakness.

XXII

The question that we have posed regarding the divine power can also be posed regarding the divine wisdom. Is this called supreme because there will never be any other superior to it, or is it really supreme in a way so to be perfect under every aspect? Yet, this is utterly certain: where there is omnipotence, fullness of wisdom cannot be lacking. In fact, if God lacked an unattainable level of perfection from the fullness of wisdom, he would certainly not be omnipotent. It is clear that the wisdom of God cannot lack anything of perfect science and prudence, the addition of which could make him greater or better.

We must underline that it is from the consideration of the divine wisdom that the fullness of his power is also deduced, just as [his] fullness of wisdom is manifestly demonstrated by the reflection on [his] omnipotence.

XXIII

We can demonstrate also in another way that which we have already affirmed regarding the divine wisdom. It is clear that whoever is wise either possesses the fullness of wisdom or participates in wisdom. Nonetheless, according to the previous considerations, we already know that wisdom coincides with the divine substance. Then, who could claim—unless he is foolish—that the divine substance possesses wisdom (i.e. itself) only in part and that it is not able to possess it in its fullness? Consequently, just as it is impossible that the divine substance does not possess itself entirely, it is likewise absurd that it lacks fullness of wisdom.

XXIV

We can demonstrate through a similar reasoning that which we have already said regarding omnipotence. Just like any wise man is such either through fullness of wisdom or through participation in it; likewise whoever is powerful is so either because of the fullness of power or by participation in it. It is impossible, however, for something to participate in itself.

Thus, since God is powerful, he cannot be such by the effect of participation in the power: the fullness of power is identified with God. It is clear, then, that God is powerful through fullness of power. But where there is fullness of power no power can lack. To conclude, then, God possesses omnipotence and he really is omnipotent, because in him all power resides.

XXV

Furthermore, it is impossible that there be more than one omnipotent being. One who really is omnipotent, in fact, has no difficulty in acting in such a way as to leave anyone else powerless. Otherwise, that one would not really be omnipotent. Indeed, where is omnipotence in a being that can so easily become powerless! Here, how easy it is to demonstrate that the very nature of things admits only one omnipotent being. Moreover, it is on the basis of an undeniable argument that we conclude that God is omnipotent, and we can never doubt it again. Just like the omnipotent being can only be one, there can only be one God.

Then, that which we believe and that which we have discussed previously is unquestionable: the true divinity dwells in the unity of substance and the unity of substance dwells in the true divinity.

Here, we have already sufficiently examined the theme of the unity of divinity. At this point, we are left to say something regarding its peculiarity.

Synopsis of the Topics of the Second Book

XV. There cannot be but one single Lord, just as there cannot exist but one God.

XVI. God is in himself his own good; he is the highest good and the highest good is absolutely perfect.

XVII. In this highest and absolutely perfect good there is true unity and highest simplicity.

XVIII. A second argument to confirm that which has been asserted regarding the simplicity and unity of the highest good.

XIX. The absolutely perfect good is most highly one [and single] and singularly highest.

XX. The simplicity of that true and highest unity is incomprehensible.

XXI. On the basis of one's own knowledge, one can deduce by analogy that which one should think regarding that super-eminent incomprehensibility.

XXII. More correct definitions of the divine substance. God is great with no quantity and good with no quality.

XXIII. God is in every place without being contained and in every time without undergoing mutations. The manner in which he is uniform and the manner in which he is multiform.

XXIV. In God, acting corresponds to willing that things be done by him, and allowing is equivalent to not-opposing that things be made [by others]. He equally possesses both that which exists at the moment and that which does not exist at the moment.

XXV. Everything affirmed up to this point regarding the divine attributes seems to refer to that being who exists from eternity and originates from himself.

Book Two

I

After having dealt with the topic of the unity of God in the manner we thought fitting, we still have something left to say regarding the attributes of his nature, especially regarding those that we repeat daily in the divine praises.

Now, among these attributes, some are such that the spirit accepts them with no objections and recognises [them] spontaneously, even if it does not know how to demonstrate them. Conversely, it would not assent to others or it would assent with less confidence, if it were not encouraged to do so by the very tradition of the catholic faith. For example, the human spirit willingly assents and freely admits that God is uncreated, eternal, immense. However, it would not easily believe that the existence of multiple eternal and immense beings is impossible, if the rule of faith did not enlighten it in this regard, especially as this reveals to us that three beings possess both eternity and immensity, as every mouth confesses.

After all, from the previous considerations, it appears sufficiently clear that God is uncreated and this does not require a new demonstration. If he had been created, in fact, he would have had a creator. Yet, the being, who is not but out of himself, cannot have a creator. In fact, what do we mean by the word "created," if not "made out of nothing?" Well, it is impossible that he who has never been nothing[1] could have been made from nothing, since he has possessed *being* from himself and from eternity.

---

1. Or, "that the ever-existing one."

II

Therefore, it is already established that he who has existed from eternity and who lacks a beginning is uncreated. Now we need to investigate whether, besides having no beginning, this [being] also has no end and has an everlasting existence. In fact, being everlasting means having no beginning and no end. Therefore, on the basis of that which is absolutely certain, let us try now to demonstrate that which one could doubt. And this is a most certain thing: in the wisdom, which is God, there cannot be anything false. Otherwise, he would not be maximally wise, as he could have either deceived someone else or himself. It is clear, then, that God is truthful, and this attribute comes to him from truth. Truth, then, is identical to God, since it can be truly demonstrated that he receives from himself—and not from others—that which in any case he receives from truth itself. Truth, on its part, will always exist just as it has always existed. It has been true from eternity and it will be eternally true that this universe could have existed; if it could have not existed, in fact, it would have not existed at all. Thus, truth has always existed [and] from it, that which was true from eternity has [always] been true; and truth will exist forever [and] from it, that which will be eternally true will be true. Therefore, if that which has always been true [and] will always be true has received true *being* from the truth, which is God, certainly God, who is the truth, will lack both a beginning and an end. God is thus everlasting, since he owns an everlasting being, lacking both beginning and end.

III

Since it is now established that God owns an everlasting being, it is logical to wonder whether his being is also immutable. It is necessary to know that every mutation happens either from a [worse] condition to a better one, or from a [better] condition to a worse one, or from a condition to another of equal status. When nothing like this can happen, we there have a real immutability. Thus, let us diligently examine one by one the hypotheses we have considered.

Yet, how could he who is omnipotent deteriorate? What does "deteriorating" mean if not "corrupting"? But he who is truly omnipotent—or rather, he who is omnipotence itself—cannot be prey to any corruption.

Then, let us see, now, if he, who—as we already know—cannot decrease, can at least improve. Well, every growing thing receives a certain increase in good by whose effect it can become better. Yet, where would this additional good come from, in him who has—and cannot but have—everything from himself? In fact, if he already owned this good, how could it come to him through growth? If he did not have this before, it is clear that he could not transmit to himself or others that which he did not have. From this, then, we can conclude that God can neither grow nor diminish.

At this point, it is left to consider whether at least he can move from one condition to another [of] equal [degree]. However, moving from one condition to another [of] equal [degree] necessarily includes losing in some way something that was owned before. As a compensation for this loss, he would acquire something that he did not possess before. In this case, through just one transformation, God would undergo the two mutations described above, which are both excluded by the reason previously shown.

In summary, he, who cannot become worse, is incorruptible. He, who cannot improve or mutate in any way, is absolutely immutable. Therefore, it is true and absolutely certain that God possesses immutable being.

IV

Yet, if we integrate in one single conclusion the three we have formulated above, we obtain the demonstration that God is not only everlasting but also eternal. [The word] "eternal," in fact, [means] one thing, [whereas] the word "everlasting" [means] another. Namely, as it seems, "everlasting" indicates something that has neither beginning nor end. "Eternal," on the other hand, has the same meaning but it also implies the impossibility of any mutation. Perhaps, it is not possible to encounter either of the two separately, but it is proper to distinguish the meaning of these words. Then, what is eternity but a period with no beginning and no end, unsusceptible to mutation? Now, he who is uncreated and everlasting has neither beginning nor end. His condition is immutable and for this reason it undergoes no change. These three [attributes][2] demonstrate that God is eternal. In fact, undoubtedly, these three [attributes] allow him to possess eternity and to be eternal.

V

Without a doubt, the [being] that neither has beginning nor end is certainly infinite. Then, one can ask whether [God], who is infinite by virtue of eternity, is also infinite by greatness.

Towards the beginning [of this work], we have demonstrated that the divine substance coincides with power and wisdom *per se*. Well, in the same way, regarding that substance that we are studying—which receives everything it has out of itself only—one can demonstrate that eternity (by which means it is eternal) and greatness (which makes it great) are identified with this substance. Therefore, if we demonstrate that God's eternity is infinite, we cannot but affirm with certainty that his greatness is also infinite. Otherwise, evidently, we would be forced to admit one same substance to be at the same time both greater and lesser than itself. Actually, if its eternity was infinite and its greatness limited, then one and the same substance would be greater than its greatness—i.e. than itself—with regard to its eternity, and lesser to its own eternity—i.e. to itself—with regard to its greatness. It is clear that we must deduce that if eternity is infinite, greatness too will be infinite. Consequently, God has an infinite and—for this reason—immense greatness.

In fact, that which is infinite cannot be comprehended by any measure. Rightly so, then, God is said to be immense, since his greatness is not measurable in any way.

VI

Thus, we would also like to consider whether it is possible for more than one immense being to exist.

Rightly, one defines as "immense" that which cannot be comprehended by any measure. One calls "immense" that which shows no

2. I.e., "Uncreated," "Everlasting," and "Immutable."

equality or proportion with any magnitude. Therefore, if we suppose the existence of multiple immense beings, each of them would be incommensurable with respect to anyone else, and incomprehensible to anyone else. Then, with reference to dimensions, none [of these beings] will be able to be understood by anyone else. The consequence will be that each of them is superior to everyone else, and the result will be that the measure of each of them is—at the same time—greater and smaller than that of anyone else. If this is impossible—or rather, since this is impossible—it will also be impossible that a plurality of immense beings exists. If none of these beings is greater or lesser than the others, just like each of them is comprehensible and measurable *per se*, then it will also be comprehensible and measurable before the others.

From these arguments we can conclude without a doubt that absolutely only one immense being exists and could ever exist.

VII

We already know that the existence of a multiplicity of immense beings is impossible. Let us see now if it is possible for more than one eternal being to exist.

From [our] previous considerations, we have recognised and we acknowledge as certain that the divine substance is identified with its own immensity, with the eternity itself. Thus, it is clear that eternity and immensity are identical to each other. Therefore, it is evident that whoever possesses eternity cannot not-have immensity. Yet, if he who is eternal cannot lack immensity, there is no doubt that he will be both eternal and immense. Thus, since there cannot be multiple immense beings, there cannot be a plurality of eternal beings either.

At this point, then, we should seriously notice and draw careful attention to this fact: in these argumentations and deductions of ours, we derive some conclusions by examining a particular [divine] attribute that we are analyzing; conversely, we reach some other conclusions by considering another attribute and understanding the reciprocal relationship between the two [attributes]. In effect, we infer the deduction on the possibility of existence of one—only—immense being from the very attribute of immensity. On the other hand, we deduce the impossibility of the existence of multiple eternal beings both from the examination of the very attribute of immensity and from the reciprocal relationship between immensity and eternity.

VIII

We hold certain that only the divine substance originates from itself, and that all the other things are derived from this substance. However, anything that is derived (or even could be derived) from that substance exists either because of the activity of the divine nature or because of a bestowal of grace. Now, just as it is certain that the divine nature cannot deteriorate and omnipotence cannot be corrupted, it is necessarily also certain that the divine substance could not produce a being who is not God, by an operation of his own nature. Nonetheless, as we have sufficiently demonstrated, God cannot but be only one in his substance. Consequently, concerning God, with regard to that unique and exclusive substance of his, there cannot be another God, or rather, there cannot be any other being who is not God. Clearly, then, everything that is other than God has its origin in him after a gratuitous act.

In any case, anything that derives its origin from God—not really as a result of a requirement of nature, but rather by a gratuitous act [of God], according to his own good pleasure—could have been made by him, but equally it could have not been made. Thus, that which is realized by God cannot be made of that incorruptible and unalterable substance, which belongs to God. Consequently, it is clear, that all the other things are either made out of nothing or have a mutable component as their matter—with the sole exception of the divine substance. Then I wonder: where did the primordial matter originate from? Since in no way could it have existed out of itself and could it have not possessed the divine substance as its matter. And if we affirm that the primordial matter has a matter, we assert and deny at the same time that this [matter] is primordial. Then, the conclusion is evident: the primordial matter, all the material beings (constituted by this matter), all the immaterial beings, and finally all beings, have been created out of nothing.

Thus, we have clearly confirmed the truth of what we believe, i.e. that only God is uncreated. In conclusion, just as God alone originates from himself, likewise—undoubtedly—he alone exists from eternity.

IX

There has certainly been a time in which everything that has received its being from creation was absolutely naught. Otherwise, this could not have been created out of nothing. Every created thing, then, started existing in time. Let us now ponder over the uncreated. This one has preceded any time. However, anything that was in existence when there was no time could not have been susceptible to mutation. In the opposite instance, it would have been conditioned by time while time did not exist. And this is absolutely impossible. That which is subject to change is also subject to time. Time is always moving and cannot stop, not even for a while. After all, it is absolutely certain that, if there were no mutation, time would not exist. That which we have said before regarding the fact that anything that is subject to mutation is also subject to time is now clear. Yet, nothing could have undergone mutations when time was not. Consequently, having existed before all times, the uncreated being could not have undergone mutations. Now, just as that which is immutable cannot move from "being" to "not-being," likewise it cannot move from "being in a certain fashion" to "being in another fashion." However, anything that cannot move from "being" to "not-being" lasts eternally and anything that cannot move from a fashion of being to another one subsists with no mutation. Not only, then, the uncreated had no beginning but it also lasts with no end and with no possibility of mutation. Lacking beginning or end and any type of mutation means being eternal. Therefore, the necessary conclusion is that the uncreated is also eternal, and vice versa, that the eternal is clearly also uncreated. In fact, anything that is eternal exists from eternity and because of this it cannot have been created.

Finally, these arguments encourage us to conclude that if there is but one single uncreated being, there is also but one single eternal being. Similarly, on the other hand, if there is but one single, eternal being, there is also but one single uncreated being.

X

We can demonstrate that which we have affirmed before concerning God's immensity with a further argument, pondering over that which is characteristic of immensity itself. In fact, everything that has a determined measure would be greater if its dimensions were doubled, and it would be much greater if they were increased by ten times or even by one hundred. Again, if it were multiplied a thousand-fold or rather, a million-fold, it would continue to grow. Then, I think, from this we can understand the following: to possess a determined magnitude means to participate in it, and not necessarily to be identified with "greatness." God, however, as the previous argument showed, is greatness itself and there is absolutely no reality that can participate out of itself or that can partly be and partly not-be that which it properly is. Therefore, God, who is greatness, cannot have a limited magnitude. It is ascertained, then, that he transcends every limit and that because of this he is immense. He is not circumscribed by any measure, and he cannot even be conceived as measurable. Thus, that which we believe, that which we confess and proclaim every day, stands undeniable. God is immense.

We can reach this same conclusion by considering omnipotence. However, since it is very easy to formulate such a consideration, we do not see dealing with it as necessary. After all, on the basis of the expounded arguments, we know that omnipotence coincides with immensity itself and eternity itself. By necessity, then, he who owns immensity and eternity also owns omnipotence. Thus, just as only one can be omnipotent, only one can be immense and only one can be eternal.

XI

Initially, we have demonstrated that the divinity is absolutely incommunicable and cannot consist of multiple substances. That which has already been said there with regard to the divinity can similarly be affirmed regarding God's immensity and finally also regarding his eternity. Actually, just as it is impossible for one single substance to be communicable to multiple substances, likewise eternity and immensity cannot be communicable to multiple substances, since they are fully identified with the divine substance. Therefore, none is immense but the sole and only God; none is eternal apart from the sole and only God.

At this point, however, a great problem arises which could trouble the less prepared readers if it were not resolved in a clear manner. It has already been demonstrated that the divine substance coincides with power and wisdom themselves. Now, who could affirm that power is incommunicable and that wisdom could not be shared by a multiplicity of substances? If immensity and eternity are recognised as incommunicable, by the fact that they are identified with the divine substance—as it has been proven—why are power and wisdom, by the same reason, not said to be incommunicable and impossible to be found in multiple substances? Since the premises have the same reasons, why should the conclusion not be analogous? Nonetheless, in order to solve more easily this intricate knot, let us examine with a deeper investigation that which we have already claimed about the singularity of divinity.

XII

It should be kept in mind that each substance possesses its being by virtue of its own substantiality. If there is no substantiality, in fact, it is not possible to properly speak of substance, as we define "substantiality" as that property of subsistence which allows a substance to be called as such and to actually be such. The substantiality of the human substance is the very humanity, since a substance that does not possess humanity could not be reasonably defined "human." We can notice in a similar manner in all the other substances that which has been said regarding this [substance]. Furthermore, substantiality can either be general, or particular, or individual. The substantiality that is common to several species is general. Corporality is an example of it, which is proper to all bodies, both the animate and the inanimate ones. The particular [substantiality], on the other hand, is that which concerns all the individuals within one single species, as in the case of humanity, which is common to all humans. Finally, the individual substantiality is that which distinguishes only one single individual and cannot concern in any way a plurality of substances. As an example of individual substantiality we have no available vocabulary. However, in order for this reasoning to be clearer, we can think of a proper name. Thus, we derive "Danielity" from "Daniel," just as we derive "humanity" from "human." "Danielity," therefore, must be interpreted as the substantiality—or, if preferred, that subsistence—that allows Daniel to be that substance, which he is in himself, and which no other substance can share. Then, whilst humanity and corporeity are common to many,

"Danielity" is absolutely incommunicable in the sense that it belongs to him in such a way that it cannot be anyone else's. Actually, whoever possesses this substantiality with no doubt will be Daniel, while the being who does not possess it will not be the same Daniel. It is the difference of substantiality that determines different substances. Conversely, one, singular, distinct [substantiality] cannot but give rise to one, single substance. "Danielity" is thus incommunicable, as this is the subsistence of a unique substance in a manner that it cannot belong to another. Consequently, if [the individual substance] is defined as incommunicable—because it cannot belong to another substance—it would be even more [incommunicable] if Daniel's substance coincided with his own substantiality in every way! Now, divinity is identified under every aspect with the divine substance—i.e. with that singular substance which is unique and exists out of itself—and this [substance] alone is the origin of everything else. Just as it is impossible that different substances be one, and that one, single substance be different substances, likewise the very divinity cannot be communicable.

There, then, we have demonstrated the incommunicability of the very divinity in such a way that the reader, who is still not persuaded, would appear not just blind but obtuse.

On the ground of the above reasoning, immensity and eternity are proper to only one being, in such a way that they cannot belong to others. For this reason we conclude that they are incommunicable.

We add that they coincide—under every aspect—with the divine substance and their incommunicability emerges also from this fact.

XIII

But if we go back to the argument at the origin of this digression, why should we not define also power and wisdom as incommunicable, by the same reason, since they are identical to the divine substance? We need to remember that we abuse both the term "power" and the term "wisdom," when we use them to speak at times of human things and at times of divine things, giving the impression that our words do not have a single meaning but are rather ambiguous. Concerning God, we affirm that he is wisdom; with regard to humanity, we do not say that it is wisdom, but rather that wisdom is in it. In the first instance, the word "wisdom" points to something that is a substance—and even more than a substance. In the second one, the term "wisdom" means something that is not a substance at all. In both cases, the expression is the same but the significance of the word is different. If confusion arises when the same word indicates different substances with different meanings, even more [confusion is generated] when one single term is divided to signify both that which is defined as a substance and that which we deny being such. For example, we claim that humanity has wisdom, but we also say that God has wisdom as well. This is evidently an affirmation that generates confusion and that can only be formulated in an improper way with respect to God. An abuse as great as this would be to claim that Abraham *is* not a man, but *has* a man. This impropriety of language and these unclear expressions confuse the judgment and do not allow declaring either power or wisdom as incommunicable. Then, let us use a term that can be suitable only to the divine power or divine wisdom, and we will see how both of them are incommunicable. In fact, the very term "omnipotence"—which is suitable only to the divine power—is absolutely incommunicable as only one can be omnipotent, as we have already demonstrated. We do not have a word analogous to "omnipotence" to indicate "divine wisdom," but often we define that by adding [other terms to it], just like when we talk about "highest wisdom," "wisdom itself" or "fullness of wisdom." In any manner in which we want to define these divine and uncreated power and wisdom—i.e., in such a way that [such a definition] could not be applied to any other [power or wisdom]—both of them will be incommunicable and impossible to be shared by a multiplicity of substances, not just angelic and human substances, but even semi-divine ones.

XIV

Without considering that which we have already said about the singularity of the divinity, we can observe—then—the many ways that we have to demonstrate that there is only one God. "Only one uncreated being," "only one eternal being" and "only one immense being:" each of these [definitions] proves and convinces without doubt that there is but one single God. If we ponder well, we can conclude the same by considering [the theme of] unity. Actually, if we affirm the existence of a multiplicity of gods, this consideration will allow us to believe that any one [amongst them] derives his existence from any other one [of them], while it is proper to each one of them to exist by his own virtue. Yet, since we know that this can be examined and demonstrated on the basis of that which has been affirmed before, we will willingly omit this argument of reflection, leaving it to the reader's acumen.

XV

Let us see now if there can be but one single Lord, just like we confess every day.

Rightly, we call him "Lord," whose freedom is not subject to any authority and whose power or dominion is without limits. Conversely, we cannot really call "Lord" one who unwillingly obeys and yields to another being's will. It seems impossible, then, for multiple Lords to exist. In fact, if it were so, just think of the many inconvenient consequences that would arise! Let us imagine, for example, that one of these Lords wants to subdue another one. Well, if the assailed one is not able to repel the violence of the assailer, would he not be a servant rather than a Lord? On the other hand, in case the promoter of the aggression—repelled and overwhelmed by force—should surrender, could he really be considered Lord? He obeys the will of his vanquisher; unwillingly—that is true—yet still submitting! Consequently, if we say that there are multiple beings of equal power and multiple Lords, the unquestionable result we obtain is that there is no real Lord.

Yet, that which convinces us from the examination of the characteristics of power is confirmed by the consideration of omnipotence. Actually, just as it is impossible for more than one omnipotent being to exist, it is also impossible for more than one single Lord to be. After all, who could resist the strength of him who could really do everything?

To summarize, we should hold as certain that there is not—or rather, that there cannot be—more than one Lord, just as there is not more than one, only God.

XVI

He who really is omnipotent cannot lack any of the desirable attributes. Where omnipotence resides, no fullness and no perfection can be absent. Otherwise, if he, who is maximally powerful, were short even of one single element of any perfection—so not to be able to possess this [perfection]—he would not be omnipotent at all. That which is not short of—and cannot be short of—any perfection is totally perfect. Nothing can be better, nothing can be greater than that which is full and perfect under every aspect. Regarding the omnipotent being, then, it is clear that he is the highest good and thus he is—for himself—his own good. In fact, just like the person holding the highest position cannot have anyone above him, similarly he who is superior to all cannot receive his own goodness or his own blessedness from someone below him. After all, how could he who owns everything out of himself even become good or blessed by someone else's action? He is, thus, good because of himself and blessed because of himself. He is his very goodness, he is the very highest good; he is his own happiness, he is the highest happiness. We demonstrated, then, that which we had affirmed, i.e. that he is the highest good and that because of this he is totally perfect. In fact, what is beatitude if not fullness and perfection of all goods? That highest and totally perfect being, clearly, does not lack anything that [could be] added to him to make him better.

XVII

If the fullness of all goods resides in that true, highest, and entirely perfect good, does this mean that goodness—perfect under every aspect—is made up by many goods? Yet, that which is made up by multiplicity is also naturally dividable, and that which is dividable by nature, is also naturally mutable. And where there is mutability, there cannot be eternity and not even true happiness. Yet, the totally perfect good cannot be deficient of either of these [two].[3] In fact, apart from the other considerations, mere reflection on omnipotence demonstrates that this cannot lack any perfection and consequently any of these [two goods]. Thus, it is evident that true immutability—and, by consequence, authentic and

3. I.e., "eternity" and "happiness."

supreme simplicity—resides in that eternal happiness and truly happy eternity.

On the other hand, where there is supreme simplicity, there is also true and highest unity. Therefore, everything that dwells in the highest good is truly and supremely one. It cannot admit any distinction within itself, rather it is in itself everything that it is.

XVIII

We are even able to demonstrate in another way that which we are affirming here regarding the simplicity and unity of that supreme and highest good. We will reach, in this way, the same conclusions we have already expounded. In fact, our reasoning has previously demonstrated that the divine substance is identical to power itself, identical to wisdom itself. From this, we deduce that each of these coincides with the other. Regarding this substance we have already said—rather, we have also demonstrated with an analogous reasoning—that this is immensity itself and that this is identical to eternity itself. Observe, then, how these [attributes] constitute a single and same reality and can be reciprocally predicated. That which we say regarding [God's] goodness can be deduced—with a similar criterion—also with regard to his blessedness. In fact, just like the previous characteristics, these ones can be defined from each other and from those already described. Absolutely everything that we claim to exist in the divine substance or that communicates to it that which it possesses, proceeds from the same reasoning.

Consequently, since everything existing in the supreme substance—or rather, everything that the supreme substance is—is truly and most greatly one, in it there is no difference between "being" and "living" or between "living" and "understanding," and there is no [difference] even between "being powerful" and "being wise." Lastly, [in it,] goodness and blessedness do not seem to be something distinct from each other nor from the previous characteristics.

Finally, such reasoning allows us to conclude that everything that is found within the highest good and true divinity is really, substantially, and supremely one.

XIX

So, it is necessary for the highest good to be supremely one, and not only supremely one, but also singularly supreme. Actually, it is not possible for two supreme goods to exist, just as [we cannot have] two absolute perfections. If we admit the existence of two equally perfect beings, in fact, we must admit, as a consequence, that all fullness, all perfection that is present in one [of them]—in an identical way and measure—should be entirely present in the other one as well. Thus, both of them will possess one single and same fullness; both of them [will possess] one, single and same perfection. However, where we cannot record any difference, we cannot logically affirm or record plurality of any sort. Therefore, multiple, absolutely perfect beings do not exist, and they cannot possibly exist in any way. After all, as others have claimed before us, if a totally perfect being exists, this being is sufficient for everything. In the opposite instance, this would not be a totally perfect being. And if only one [perfect being] is totally sufficient, a second one would be superfluous. And if this [second, perfect being] is superfluous, how could it be useful? If it is useless, how could it be good? Then, as it has been said, that absolutely perfect good, will not only be supremely one, but also singularly supreme. Therefore, as we can observe, our affirmations concerning the supreme good lead us to the same conclusion of our previous enquiry on the unity of the divine substance. In fact, since it is impossible for the highest good not to be only one, if God is truly the highest good, then it is certain that there is only one, single God, in line with that which our faith affirms.

Therefore, supreme and substantial unity—I conclude—resides in that true and supreme blessedness and in that supremely blessed divinity, and true and highest simplicity [resides] in unity itself. There, in fact—as we have already demonstrated—every existing thing is identical to itself.

XX

If there is authentic and highest simplicity in this [divine] unity, this [unity] has no relationship with the [unity] of [another] substance, which—although is one altogether—is [actually] made up of various parts. If everything that is in this [divine unity] is identical to itself, [this divine unity] is not comparable to the unity of multiple substances concurring to form one, single nature. If this [divine unity] is truly and supremely simple, what type of analogy can there be between it[self] and the aggregation of heterogeneous substances in one, single person? If there is absolute identity in this [divine unity], what does this [unity] have to do with the combination of subsisting and subsistence? In spite of this, [that divine unity] is also much greater than that union, which derives from the composition of multiple substances in one, single form. It is clear, then, that this [divine union] will transcend in an incomparable and incomprehensible way all the other [unities], since it possesses the supremely simple and unalterable being, in the identity of infinity.

We find true unity, we find supreme simplicity, we find real and supremely simple identity in that supreme and totally perfect being. There—and this is even more extraordinary—one finds true unity with absolute fullness; there, [one finds] highest simplicity together with an incommensurable perfection; there [one finds] a supremely simple identity with the infinity of every excellence.

Therefore, notice how incomprehensible and absolutely immeasurable is the simplicity of the authentic and supreme unity.

XXI

In any case, [I want] to avoid that some less expert [reader] might think that I am making contradictory and irreconcilable affirmations, almost as if the things that have been stated could not be claimed together at the same time. For this reason, I will show [my reader] the way in which he can see—as in a mirror—and verify by analogy within himself that which he should think regarding that super-eminent incomprehensibility. If one had a grain in his hand, should he certainly not think and claim without hesitation that no other [grain] is numerically identical to this one? Thus, if later he were asked about each single grain of any pulse or cereal, should he not invariably respond that this is distinct from each and every other one? He would be persuaded in the same way regarding each single hair; he would say the same regarding the whole of [his] hair. What would he say regarding each drop in the sea?

What would he claim with regards to any leaf on a tree? If the whole earth were reduced to dust and we could ask [this person's] opinion on each of [the earth's] particles, he would answer in the same manner to each question, resolutely and with confidence. If the earth's dimensions grew exponentially, [this person] would hold the same opinion on this earth's most minuscule portions.

I have tried to expose these topics with clarity, in order to allow anybody—as unprepared as [a person] may be—on the basis of his knowledge, to observe and comprehend that one, single, and simple truth hides an infinite number [of other truths]. What is so surprising, then, if in that wisdom—which is God and in which all truth resides (otherwise, if some truth were hidden from it, it would not be perfect)—what is so surprising—I repeat—if in that [divine wisdom] we can find highest simplicity, on one hand, and supreme and infinite multiplicity, on the other? What is so extraordinary—I ask—if [in that divine wisdom] both identity and infinity of multiplicity, both simplicity and immensity of greatness, both true unity and universality of all fullness are harmonised and unified? Therefore, each one is able to understand from his own knowledge that which he should believe regarding that super-eminent incomprehensibility.

XXII

On the basis of our previous considerations, we have concluded that in that nature—which is God—we find both supreme unity and true simplicity: there is no composition there; there is no aggregation. [That nature] is not inherent to any subject, and nothing is inherent to it as to a subject. It is defined—and it is—the supreme power; it is defined—and it is—the highest wisdom. And in order to avoid thinking of it as existing in a subject, we call it "substance." However, contrary to the nature of substances, we see how nothing is inherent to it as to a subject. For this reason, we conclude that we are not dealing here with a substance but with a supra-substantial essence. Our previous considerations—if they have not been forgotten—have demonstrated that in [this essence] both goodness and immensity are identified with each other. Then, what? Does the fact that its immensity coincides with its goodness mean that God is good because he is immense? If his goodness is identical to his immensity, then will God be great because he is good? Yet, as it seems, goodness relates to quality, while immensity refers to quantity. Then, what? Is [God] great with regard to his quality and good with regard to his quantity? And who is able to [understand] this? Or rather, since his immensity and goodness are identical to his substance, will God be good with no quality and great with no quantity? Again, who is able to [understand] all this?

From these arguments—I believe—one can very easily understand how everything that rational evidence makes us believe regarding our God is [ultimately] unspeakable, and even incomprehensible.

XXIII

From that which has been said before, we are persuaded that God is omnipotent and that everything is certainly possible for him. Now, if he is truly omnipotent, he is also powerful everywhere, as a consequence. If he is powerful everywhere, he is also present everywhere in his power. If he is everywhere in his power he is also everywhere in his essence, since power and essence in him are identical. Furthermore, if he is everywhere in his essence, this means that [God is present] both where there is space and where there is no space. Therefore, he will be in every place, just as he will be outside every place. He will be above everything and underneath everything. He will be both inside and outside everything. However, since God's nature is simple, he will not be here and there—divided into parts, but [he will be] all together everywhere; therefore he will be whole in each smallest part of the whole, all in all and all outside all. Then, if [God] is entire outside of any place, no place can limit him. If he is entire in every place, he cannot be excluded from any place. Finally, with regard to place, he is nowhere, since he is neither enclosed in nor excluded from any place.

And, just as [God] is in every place with his presence, but in no [place] locally, likewise he is also in every time with his eternity and in no [time] temporally. In fact, just as he who is simple and not composed [by multiple elements] cannot be distended in space, similarly, he who is eternal and unalterable cannot mutate in time. Thus, no reality that is still non-existent is future to him; in a similar manner, no reality that is no more is past to him; finally, no reality existing in the present is transitory to him. As a consequence, he is in every place without being limited and in every time without undergoing mutations.

Also—and this is extraordinary—he is multifaceted in the multiplicity of beings, although he is always uniform with regards to himself. In fact, if you look for the mode of being of him who is without a mode of being, *in se* and *per se*, according to the multiplicity of his nature, he shows himself to be uniform everywhere. And yet, considering the gifts he gives, in these beings and in those others, he manifests himself to be multifaceted.[4] He is present in some [beings] because he allows them to participate in his power—and not in his life! He is present in others because he allows them to participate in his life—yet not in his wisdom! He resides in some by transmitting his own goodness—yet, not his own blessedness! On the other hand, clearly, his presence allows others to participate both in his goodness and in his blessedness. Thus, [God], who is uniform *per se* and cannot change, is tight-fisted in his generosity towards some beings, whilst he opens his hand more generously towards others, and towards yet others [is] even more generous.[5]

XXIV

Since God is really omnipotent, every existing thing subsists either by his action or by his permission. In fact, if everything that happens were not the result of his will, he would certainly not be omnipotent. His acting, then, corresponds to willing things to happen because of him; his permitting, instead, means not preventing them from happening by someone else's activity. Just like his sufferance is without passion and his compassion is without sympathy, each of his actions is without turmoil and his acting is always without fatigue.

However, if acting for him is identical to willing something to happen by his work, does this mean, perhaps, that when [God] produces that which before was not—perhaps, I say—[God] wills something that he did not will before? Yet, one who is truly immutable cannot change his will. Then, [God must have] always willed that which he once willed. Then, has he accomplished from eternity that which he has produced with his will because he has always willed for this to happen?

4. Eph 3:10; 1 Pet 4:10.
5. Ps 144:16; cf. Ps 103:28.

And if he has already made those things that will be, does this mean that he is still making and will he continue to make those other things that have already past or those that will be no more in the future? Is his acting as constant as his will? And does he cease to have that which he had before when something ceases to exist? Or rather, does he start possessing [that which he lacked before] when something, that before was not, starts existing? Indeed, when something ceases to exist or has not yet started existing it is naught. Yet, that which is naught cannot be possessed. The omnipotent possessor, however, can neither increase nor diminish his wealth. Then, what? But think: [can you not say that] that which is existing at the moment is superior there, where it does not exist in its actuality, rather than [here,] where it exists in its actuality? In fact, it is ephemeral here, [while] it is eternal there. That which has been made—even when it did not exist in its own actuality—was life, there.[6] To summarize, he, who can neither gain nor lose anything, possesses in the same measure both that which exists in its own actuality and that which does not exist in act.

XXV

Regarding God's relative attributes, we would like to finish here, since their meaning is too broad to be discussed in a brief outline. Actually, in my opinion, their significance is connected to all the predicaments. In fact, in addition to the relationship that they express, [these attributes also] indicate that which ordinarily pertains sometimes to certain predicaments, sometimes to certain others. For example, we talk about substance to affirm that one [attribute] is consubstantial to the other; we talk about quantity to say [that one] is either equal or unequal; we talk about quality to say [that one] is either similar or dissimilar; [we talk about] place to say [that one] is either superior or inferior; [we talk about] time to say [that one] is either anterior or posterior; [we talk about] position to express sitting next [to another] and sitting together; [we talk about] condition to indicate the possessor or the possessed; [we talk about] action and passion to say generator and generated, lover and loved. It is better to leave out these topics at the moment, in order not to face a theme that we could not outline with necessary brevity.

6. John 1:4.

In addition, it needs to be noted here that everything that has been said regarding the divine properties, applies to that being who exists by virtue of himself, and who, because of this, is eternal. In fact, every affirmation made in this regard up to this point would be valid, even if there was nothing eternal receiving its origin from outside itself.

Synopsis of the Topics of the Third Book

Book Three

I

In the topics we have covered up to this point, we have discussed the unity and the attributes of the divine substance, according to our understanding. Yet, from this point onwards, we set forth to investigate that which is to be thought regarding the plurality and property of the divine persons.

First of all, then, it seems we should examine whether there is a real plurality in the true and simple divinity, and whether the number of the divine persons can go up to three, as our faith teaches us.

Afterwards, [we will examine] the way in which the unity of substance can be reconciled with the multiplicity of persons.

Thirdly, then, we will have to verify whether—in harmony with the dogmas of our faith—there is a single person originating from himself, while each of the remaining ones would originate from outside. We will have to consider also the other eventual questions, related to this. If we are able to demonstrate all of this on a rational level, we will still have to examine the following: whether in the two persons who originate from outside of themselves there are two different ways of acting; which [mode] is proper to each of them; and which names are appropriate to them, according to their individual characteristics.

Yet, the fewer the arguments we find in the writings of the Fathers—from which we could deduce conclusions in these investigations that we still have to complete, not according to scriptural texts, but with a rational demonstration—the greater the effort we have to produce and the deeper the passion [by which] we must endeavor.

On the other hand, if someone wants to, he has all the right to laugh at the aim of this quest of mine and tease [me for it]. To be honest, in fact, knowledge is not that which pushes me to set forth in this attempt, but rather it is the fervor of my burning soul that impels me. What will it matter if I do not arrive where I desire and if my strength abandons me while I run? I will still be happy to have run, made an effort, sweated, always looking for my Lord's face. Even if I faint because of the path's length, roughness, and difficulty, I will have obtained something if I can say in good faith: "I have done that which I was able to, *I sought him, but did not find him; I called him, but he gave no answer.*"[1] Here, Balaam's well-known ass, which delayed its knight while on a trip,[2] hurries me and pushes me—I do not know how—to continue running the road on which I started. I also hear her speaking to me and saying: "He who enabled me to talk, will enable you as well." Let us dedicate ourselves with all our effort to accomplish our goal.

II

The arguments discussed previously made clear to us that fullness and perfection of all goodness reside in the supreme and totally perfect good. After all, true and highest love cannot be absent where fullness of all goodness is found, since nothing is better or more perfect than charity-love. Yet, none is said to possess charity-love in the truest sense of the word if he loves himself exclusively. It is, thus, necessary that love be aimed at someone else in order to be charity-love. If a multiplicity of persons is absent, there can be no place for charity-love.

Perhaps, one can object: even if there was one, single person in the very divinity, nothing would prevent it from having charity-love aimed at one of its own creatures—indeed, it would certainly have it. However, [this divinity] could not conceive supreme charity-love towards a created person. Charity-love expressed by him, who supremely loves someone else who should not be supremely loved, would be a disorderly charity-love. And it is impossible that disorderly charity-love be found in that highly wise goodness. Finally, a divine person could

1. Song 5:6.
2. Num 22:22–35.

have not shown supreme charity-love towards another person, who was not worthy of supreme love.

Besides, in order for charity-love to be supremely perfect and the highest [possible], it must be so great not to be able to admit another greater love, and [it must be] such not to allow a better one. Now, as long as one loves no one else as himself, his personal love aimed at himself demonstrates that he has not yet attained the highest level of charity-love. A divine person, however, would have no one to love as worthily as himself, if he had absolutely [no other] person with his same dignity. No person apart from God would be gifted with the same dignity of a divine person. Consequently, in order for fullness of charity-love to reside in the very divinity, a divine person had to be united with another person of his same dignity, and thus, also divine.

Therefore, see how easily reason demonstrates that a plurality of persons cannot but be present in the very divinity! It is certain that God alone is supremely good; so only God must be supremely loved. Therefore, a divine person could not show supreme love towards another person lacking divinity. Besides, fullness of divinity could not have subsisted without fullness of goodness. Fullness of goodness, on the other hand, could not have been present without fullness of charity-love; and fullness of charity-love [could] not [have existed] without plurality of divine beings.

III

That which the fullness of goodness demonstrates in a convincing way regarding the plurality of the [divine] persons is also proven, via analogous arguments, by the fullness of happiness. That which one [of them] declares is confirmed by the other, and both [of them] loudly proclaim witness to one, single truth.

Let each person ask his own conscience and—without a doubt or a discussion—he will notice that just as there is nothing better than charity-love, similarly there is nothing more joyful than charity-love. And this is that which nature teaches us, and the many-fold experience reveals to us the same. Thus, just as it is impossible for something than which nothing is better to be absent in the fullness of true goodness, it is likewise impossible for something than which nothing is more joyful to be absent in the fullness of supreme happiness. It is necessary, then, that in supreme happiness charity-love is also present. However, in order for charity-love to be present [also] in the supreme good, there must be someone who can demonstrate [this charity-love] and someone to whom this [charity-love] can be shown. To want to be much loved by him who is much loved is typical of love. If this is not possible, there absolutely cannot be [love]. Therefore, there can be no joyful love that is not also reciprocal. Thus, in that true and supreme happiness, neither joyous love nor reciprocal love can be absent. Absolutely, both he who donates love and he who returns it must be present in reciprocal love. Then, he who donates love is other to him who returns it.[3] But there, where one and "an-other"[4] are certainly present, true plurality is detected. Consequently, in that fullness of happiness a plurality of persons cannot be absent. It is clear, though, that supreme happiness is nothing else but divinity itself. Therefore, the manifestation of gratuitous love and the returning of due love demonstrate without a doubt that there has to be a multiplicity of persons in divinity itself.

IV

Clearly, if we claim that in divinity itself there is one, single person, just as [there is] one, single substance, with no doubt, [the consequence is that this divinity] has no one to whom it can transmit the infinite richness of its fullness. But why should this happen, I ask? Perhaps, because even if [this divinity] wills, it cannot have anybody with whom to enter into a communion? Or maybe because even if it could, it would not will

---

3. The immediate sense of the Latin is much plainer: "He who donates love is different from the one returning it." However, the deeper meaning that Richard wants to convey here and that he introduces in this case, in a very subtle and almost furtive fashion, is the fact that otherness as "distinction" is detectable in the one essence of God. Helped by the relative flexibility of the Italian and French languages, both Spinelli and Salet tried to maintain both levels of significance in their translations. Unfortunately, the needs of modern English are such that in order not to lose the more fundamental reference to the idea of *"the Other"* in God, the rhetorical and linguistic force of Richard's original is somewhat lost.

4. Again, the Latin of this sentence should be translated as "where two are present." However, for the reasoning presented in the above note, it might be appropriate to draw attention to the concept of distinction/plurality that here Richard tries to introduce in the Trinity.

to do so? Yet, certainly, the omnipotent one cannot use impossibility as his excuse. Then, perchance, does that which does not result from lack of power result from lack of benevolence? Consider, please, the quality and seriousness of such a lack of benevolence in a divine person, if he were to refuse to have someone with whom to share communion, although he could have someone if he wills it so.

As it has been said, it is certain that nothing is sweeter than charity-love, and nothing is more joyful [than it]. Spiritual life cannot experience anything more pleasant than the delights of charity-love. It will never be able to enjoy a more desirable pleasure. Then, if the [divine person] remains with no company, alone on the throne of his majesty, he will be forever excluded from these delights. From this, we can understand the nature and seriousness of this lack of benevolence, if [God] had egotistically preferred to retain for himself alone the abundance of his richness, even though he could communicate this—if he so willed—to someone else, increasing and intensifying joys and delights in such a great measure. If it were so, he would be right in preventing angels and anyone else from seeing him; he would be right in being ashamed to be seen and recognised, since he would have such a great lack of benevolence.

Let it not be so! Let us always abstain from thinking that the supreme majesty has something that it cannot boast and for which it cannot receive praise! Where would fullness of glory be, otherwise? No fullness can be absent in God, as we have demonstrated before. What is there more glorious, rather, what is more magnificent than the desire to allow others to participate in everything that one possesses? It is thus evident that there can neither be a tight stinginess nor a disorderly generosity in that highest goodness and in that supremely wise reason.

There, we have clarified, as you can see, that the very fullness of glory in the supreme majesty requires someone with whom to share this glory.

V

Therefore, regarding the plurality of the divine persons, we have provided such clear arguments that, if someone wanted to reject such evident proofs, he would appear to be a victim of folly. Actually, who, if not a foolish person, could claim that supreme goodness does not have that which is more perfect and better than anything else? Who, I say, if not someone who lacks brains, could deny that supreme happiness has *per se* that which is above every joy and every sweet thing? Who, I repeat, if not someone who has lost his mind, could say that fullness of glory could be without that which is at the topmost point of glory and magnificence? Well, there is certainly nothing better, nothing more joyful, absolutely nothing more splendid than true, genuine, and highest charity-love, which—on the other hand—could not even exist without a multiplicity of persons.

Thus, the affirmation [of the existence] of this multiplicity is confirmed by a three-fold testimony. In fact, that which the highest goodness and the supreme happiness indicate in one accord in this regard, is also loudly confirmed—and cleverly underlined—by the fullness of glory. Hence, on this article of our faith, we have three testimonies, which are sublime on the supreme realities, divine on the divine things, solemn on the profound truths, very clear on the mysteries. And we know that *every word* is confirmed *by the evidence of two or three witnesses*.[5] This is the three-stranded rope that is hard to break and with which we will be able to tie firmly any foolish opponent of our faith, by virtue of God's wisdom.[6]

VI

As we are obviously to conclude from our previous considerations, [that the] perfection of a single person requires association with another one. We have noticed that there is nothing more glorious, nothing more splendid than being unwilling to possess a single thing that one should not want to share [also with others]. Then, the supremely good person did not want to be deprived of another one participating in his greatness; and that which he willed to happen, had to take place necessarily, as his will was omnipotent. Yet, he [must have] always willed that which he has once willed, since his will was immutable. Thus, it was necessary to the eternal person to have [another] co-eternal [person], and it was impossible for any of them to precede or follow the other [in time]. [In

5. Deut 19:15, as quoted in Matt 18:16.
6. Eccl 4:12.

fact], nothing can grow old and disappear in the eternal, immutable divinity, just like no new thing can develop either. As a consequence, it is absolutely impossible for the divine persons not to be coeternal.

Actually, there is also complete happiness where true divinity is found, where supreme goodness resides. And supreme goodness—as it has been observed—is not able to subsist without perfect charity-love, and perfect charity-love cannot be produced without a plurality of persons. After all, complete happiness cannot be realised without a true immutability, and true immutability cannot be without eternity.

True charity-love requires multiplicity of persons. A true immutability requires eternity of persons.

VII

We must closely observe that just as genuine charity-love presupposes plurality of persons, supreme charity-love requires also equality of [these same] persons. However, we have demonstrated that even when real love is already present, charity-love is not supreme where one does not love at the highest level. Yet, when one loves someone who should not be supremely loved, love is not well regulated; on the other hand, in the supremely wise goodness, the flame of love does not burn in a different fashion or in a higher measure than that which is required by the supreme wisdom. Thus, he who should be loved to the highest degree according to the highest richness of charity-love must be supremely loved also according to the supreme law of discretion. Besides, the very nature of love persuades us that he who loves supremely is not satisfied if the other one, who is supremely loved, does not respond [to this love] with a supreme love.

Thus, in reciprocal love, fullness of charity requires that each of the two [persons] be loved by the other at a supreme level, and that—by consequence—both be worthy to be supremely loved, according to the abovementioned law of discretion. But if either of the two is equally worthy to be loved, both of them have to be equally perfect. Therefore, it is necessary that both of them be equally powerful, equally wise, equally good, and equally happy. So, in those who reciprocally love each other, supreme fullness of love presupposes supreme equality in perfection.

To conclude, just as in divinity itself charity-love requires a plurality of persons (by its own nature), in an authentic plurality perfection of the same charity-love requires [the] supreme equality of persons. However, in order for these [persons] to be equal in everything they need to be completely similar. In fact, it is possible to have similarity even without equality, but equality without reciprocal similarity can never take place. In fact, how can those, who do not have any similarity in wisdom, be equal in it? Anything that I affirm regarding wisdom, I also say regarding power. And we could reach the same conclusion with respect to all the other [attributes] if we analysed them one by one.

VIII

In our research, we discovered that if a supreme love has to rightly occur between the two [persons] who love—and have to love—each other reciprocally, it is necessary that both highest perfection and fullness of every perfection have to dwell in each one of them. In the one and in the other, thus, fullness of power, fullness of wisdom, fullness of goodness, [and] fullness of divinity will be present.

Thus, here we find again that which we have mentioned much earlier, although, [there], we did not formulate any definition: divinity—which, as we have observed there, cannot be shared by multiple substances—here, is common to multiple persons. Yet, if every perfection is shared by those who love each other reciprocally, as we have said, it is clear and certain that if one of them is omnipotent, the other one is omnipotent as well; if one is immense, the other one is immense as well; if one is God, the other one is God as well. However, as we have demonstrated with sufficient evidence in [our] previous [considerations], there can only be one omnipotent, there can only be one immense, [there] can only [be] one God. Then, what? It is certain and unquestionable that both of them will be omnipotent, but in such a way to be—together—one, single omnipotent one. They will both be immense, but in such a way to be—together—one, single immense one. Both of them will be God, certainly, but in such a way to be—together—one, single and only God. *Who can understand these things?*[7] Now, if divinity itself—as we have said—is certainly shared by both of them, both of them will

7. 2 Cor 2:16.

definitely share also the divine substance, which coincides with divinity itself—as we have already demonstrated. We deduce, then, that both of them share one, single and same substance, or—if one prefers—both of them together constitute one, single and same substance. What reason is there to marvel if the two together are not but one, single omnipotent; one, single eternal; one, single immense; one, single God and Lord; if both of them together constitute one, single substance?

Observe, then, the extraordinary way in which unity of substance resides in that plurality of persons, and plurality of persons [resides] in a real unity of substance, in such a way that properties are preserved in the persons, oneness [is preserved] in the substance, and equality [is preserved] in majesty.

IX

When reading or listening to this, one can be surprised. One is surprised, I repeat, for the way in which more than one person can be found where there is only one substance. But, can one be surprised—I repeat: can one be surprised—by the fact that he, who is extraordinary in many of his works, is extraordinary most of all in himself? One is amazed at the fact that in the divine nature more than one person is present, whilst there is not more than only one substance. Yet, one is not equally astonished at the fact that we have more than one substance in the human nature, whilst there is only one person. As we know, in fact, the human being is constituted by soul and body, and these two [elements] together constitute a single person. Thus, the human can see and recognise in himself, by means of antithesis, that which he has to retain about his own God.[8]

Let us compare—if we can—that which reason perceives with its arguments in the divine nature with that which experience verifies in the human nature. There is unity in both of them, and in both of them there is plurality. In the first one, we have a unity of substances, in the second one we have a unity of person. If in the [first one] we have multiplicity of persons and unity of substance, in the second one—on the other hand—we have plurality of substances in unity of person. In this

8. In God we find one substance with multiple persons; in man there is only one person but with multiple substances.

way, the human and divine natures seem to look towards each other, as from two opposite positions; in fact, each of them corresponds—so to say—to the other's antithesis. In the same way, created and uncreated nature, temporal and eternal one, corruptible and incorruptible, mutable and immutable, infinitesimal and immense, limited and infinite, must look to each other and correspond reciprocally [to each other].

X

Let us add that there is perfect similarity and supreme equality in the plurality of [divine] persons. We record a noticeable dissimilarity and a great inequality, on the contrary, in the [human] plurality.

Actually, in the plurality of the [divine] persons, one is incorruptible and the other one is incorruptible as well; one is immutable and the other one is immutable as well; one is infinite and the other one is infinite as well. Both of them are equally powerful, equally wise, equally good, and equally blessed. On the other hand, in the multiplicity of substances by which the human person is made up, one is corporal [while] the other one is incorporeal; one is visible, the other one is invisible; one is mortal, the other one is immortal; one is divisible, the other one is indivisible; one is perishable, the other one imperishable. In spite of this, though, with regard to the person, [these substances] are linked as one with each other in such a way that separating them or even distinguishing them, both in common suffering and joy, is impossible.

So, you have been able to observe the great diversity of substances in the human nature. On the other hand, you have been able to understand the similarity and equality of the persons in the divine nature. Explain to me, please, how it can be possible for personal unity to be present among substances so dissimilar and diverse from each other. On my part, I will show you the way in which substantial unity can be found in such a great similarity and equality of persons.[9]

"I do not understand it"—you may reply—"I am not able to grasp it." But, that which intelligence may not comprehend, experience however can clarify to me. Very well, good! But if experience teaches you that there is something transcending your intelligence in the human

---

9. Perhaps it is possible to detect here an echo of James' argumentative technique. See Jas 2:18.

nature, should [the same experience] not have taught you that in the divine nature [too] there is something above your intelligence?

Consequently, the human being has the possibility to deduce from itself—as by antithesis—that which it should believe regarding the faith-based teachings in its God. All this has been expounded to benefit those striving to measure and determine the depth of the divine mysteries according to their own ability, and not according to the tradition of the holy Fathers, who clearly learnt and taught by virtue of the Holy Spirit.

XI

Yet, now, let us continue developing our reasoning according to the criterion by which we have started. It is now plain that a plurality of divine persons exists; however, we cannot yet formulate the same affirmation about the Trinity, since there can be plurality even without the presence of any Trinity. In fact, even duality in itself is plurality. In order to assert the Trinity, then, let us interrogate the same witnesses, whom we have summoned earlier to affirm plurality. And before anything else, if possible, let us ask supreme charity-love what it can testify on this specific topic.

Well, supreme charity-love has to be absolutely perfect; in order to be supremely perfect, it must be so great that it could not be greater and at the same time, it must be of such a [high] quality that it could not be better. In fact, just as supreme charity-love cannot lack the highest greatness, similarly, it cannot lack the greatest excellence. And in authentic charity-love the greatest excellence seems to be this: to will that someone else be loved just as we are. Actually, nothing is more precious and more admirable in reciprocal, burning love than one's desire for someone else to be loved in the same fashion by him who is supremely loved, and by whom one is supremely loved. Therefore, the witness of perfect charity-love consists in desiring to share [with someone else] that love of which one is the object.

Truly, the greatest joy, for him who loves supremely and seeks to be supremely loved, is generally found in the realisation of his desire, i.e., in obtaining the love he hoped for. Consequently, if one is still not able to enjoy communicating his greatest joy, he demonstrates that he does not to possess perfect charity-love.

Not being able to tolerate this sharing of love is the symptom of great weakness. Being able to accept it, instead, is the sign of great perfection. If the ability of accepting this [sharing] is a great thing, happiness in accepting it will be an even greater merit. Finally, the greatest thing of all will be to seek this [kind of sharing of love] specifically. To summarise, the first condition is great, the second is better, the third is the best. Then, let us associate the supreme being with that which is excellent; [let us associate] him who is the greatest with that which is best!

The arguments expounded up to this point demonstrated that if those two reciprocally loving beings are absolutely perfect, both of them—for the same reason—must necessarily will that another being be [also] associated [with them] to share the love of which each of them is the object. In fact, if [one of them] does not will that which is required by perfect goodness, where will the fullness of goodness be? And if he wills that which cannot happen, where will the fullness of power be?

Therefore, from this, we can clearly deduce that the highest degree of charity-love and—together with this—the fullness of goodness cannot be present if a lack of will or power prevents someone [else] from being associated with this love and [prevents] communication of the greatest joy. Thus, it is necessary that those who are—and are worthy to be—supremely loved seek with the same desire someone else to be included in their love and [seek] to possess [him] in absolute concord, according to [that very] desire [of theirs].

As we can perceive, then, perfection of charity-love requires a Trinity of persons. In fact, without this, [charity-love] cannot subsist in the fullness of its totality. In summary, when everything that is universally perfect is present, neither absolute charity-love nor the very Trinity can be absent. Therefore, in true unity is found not just a generic plurality, but a true Trinity, and a true unity [is found] in the true Trinity.

XII

What kind of good reason—I wonder—could be found in the affirmation of someone, saying that in the true divinity only those two who reciprocally love each other—and whose existence has already been demonstrated previously—are found? Will none of them—I wonder—

have anyone else to associate with their supreme joy? Perhaps both of them did not will it so? Or perhaps only one [of them] did not? But if only one willed it so and the other did not, where is that which is customarily present amongst perfect friends and which should never be absent? Where is that characteristic prerogative of profound love: i.e., unanimity of spirits and intimate agreement? Certainly, if we claim that one [of them] wills [it so] and the other one does not, we will admit that one [of them] cannot prevail with his own will and we will deny that he is supremely powerful. If we say that neither of the two can desire to communicate the love they have towards themselves, how can we excuse them for this lack of love, that we have already recognised previously?

Furthermore, we know that nothing can remain hidden to those who are matchlessly wise. If each of [these persons] truly loves the other profoundly, how can one see the defect in the other without suffering? In fact, if one of the two sees the other's shortcoming and is not saddened by it, where will the fullness of love be? If he sees it and is saddened by it, where will the fullness of happiness be? After all, it is clear [that] in a situation where a cause of sorrow will always be present, fullness of happiness will never be possible.

Therefore, from this we certainly conclude that fullness of happiness cannot admit any lack of charity-love. On its part, perfection of [charity-love]—as it has been said—requires a Trinity of persons and does not tolerate its absence.

Therefore, highest good and supreme happiness testify the Trinity unanimously, confirming [its existence] with a two-fold affirmation.

XIII

Without a doubt charity-love that cannot permit a community of love is deeply lacking. Who could ignore or hide it?

Thus, if this omission were to be often present in those who love each other—whom we have already mentioned—each of the two would not simply suffer because of that which [each would see] in the other, but also would be ashamed of that which [each would see] in himself. In fact, like the sincere and devout friend cannot notice a defect in someone he loves without truly grieving, likewise, doubtlessly, he would be embarrassed of one of his faults before a friend. Now, if the plurality of [divine] persons had good reason to be embarrassed, where—I wonder—would the fullness of glory be, which the very divinity cannot lack in any way? Therefore, just like supreme happiness cannot have [any] source of sufferance, the fullness of supreme glory cannot have [any] reason for shame. After all, none could ignore how foolish it is to envision—even from afar—that the supremely blessed majesty ever had within itself something capable of obscuring the splendor of this great a glory—even only slightly.

Therefore, fullness of divine goodness, fullness of happiness and glory concur to testify to the same truth, and indicate with clarity that which one should think regarding the fullness of divine charity-love in the plurality of the [divine] persons. They push away in equal measure the suspect of any kind of deficiency in that supreme charity-love and univocally proclaim [the presence of] fullness of perfection in it. Then, in order to be authentic, charity-love needs a plurality of beings; equally, in order to be perfect, it requires a Trinity of persons.

XIV

So, after the exposition of these many arguments we admit that we have no right to doubt. We recognize that in the very divinity each person is so good that he does not to want to possess any richness [or] any joy without being willing to share them. [We recognize that that each person is] so powerful that nothing is impossible to him, and [he is] so happy that nothing is unpleasant to him. If [we admit all of this], the consequence is: we need to admit that there must be a Trinity of divine persons.

Nonetheless, in order for this to be clearer, let us summarise together that which we have expounded for a lengthy while.

One thing is certain: if there was only one and single person in the divinity, this [person] would have no one to whom he could communicate the abundance of his greatness. Besides, and on the contrary, he would never enjoy the delights and sweetness that he could have gained by being the object of a profound love. Yet, the fullness of goodness does not allow him, who is supremely good, to keep with greediness those [delights above]. Similarly, fullness of beatitude [does not allow] the supremely blessed being to lack them. Conversely, the excellence of his glory requires him not only to enjoy them abundantly, but also to boast in the enjoyment of them. All this shows how impossible it is for each person in the divinity to be deprived of participation in a communitarian life.

However, if [the divine person] had only one, single [person] associated with himself, on one hand he would not lack someone to whom he could transmit the richness of his greatness, but on the other he would have absolutely no one to whom he could communicate the delights of charity-love. Nothing more pleasant can be found than the sweetness of love. [There is nothing else] that the soul could enjoy more [than this]. If one has no friend to involve in the love he has for himself, he enjoys alone the pleasures of such a sweet thing. Thus, communication of love cannot happen at all with less than three persons. Besides, as we have said, there is nothing more glorious, nothing more splendid than sharing [with others] every fine and beautiful thing which one possesses. Indeed, highest wisdom cannot ignore this, and supreme goodness cannot but enjoy this. Consequently, just like the happiness of him who is supremely powerful, or the power of him who is supremely happy cannot take place without [this person's] consent, it is likewise impossible for the two persons of the divinity not to be associated with a third one.

XV

It must be rightly underlined that in the divine persons the perfection of one [of them] requires the addition of the other. And consequently, between the two [persons], perfection of both requires the association of a third one. Regarding the two persons, in fact—as we have already observed elsewhere—if we want each of them to be supremely loved by the other with good reason, it is necessary for both of them to be supremely perfect. Thus, as in both of them we find one single wisdom and one single power, similarly we will certainly have to recognise one single, supreme goodness in each of them. Now, that which distinguishes supreme and totally perfect goodness consists of sharing in all the abundance of their own fullness. Thus, since in both [divine] persons an equal goodness subsists, both of them—with the same desire and by a similar motivation—will necessarily have to require someone to participate in the supreme joy, with the same desire and by a similar motivation.

Actually, when two reciprocally loving [persons] hug each other with the greatest desire and enjoy their mutual love very much, the supreme happiness of one consists of the intimate love of the other and, conversely, the prime joy of the latter, resides in the love of the former.

Until one is the sole person being loved by another, he alone enjoys the delights of such an extraordinary sweetness. Similarly, even the other cannot communicate the greatest joy until he has someone to participate in his love.

If we want both of them to be able to communicate delights as such, they necessarily have to have another one to be loved in the same manner. Consequently, as we have said, if the two [persons] who love each other are so generous to be willing to communicate every perfection of theirs, it is necessary that both of them require with equal desire and for the same reason a third [person] to be loved in the same fashion. [It is also necessary that they] possess him, according to their desire, in the fullness of their power.

XVI

Amongst the delights of charity and of wisdom, the prime difference usually consists of this: while the delights of wisdom can be received—and this is that which happens most of the time—from one's heart, the profound delights of charity-love can be received from someone else's heart. In fact, one who loves profoundly and seeks to be profoundly loved is not happy—but rather he is tormented—when he does not receive the sweetness of love he so vehemently desires from his loved one's heart. The delights of wisdom, instead, give more joy when they come from one's own heart.

Thus, nothing contrary to nature is affirmed if we say that fullness of wisdom can subsist [even] in one, single person. In fact, even if one, single person was to be found in the divinity, he could still have fullness of wisdom.

However, there cannot be fullness of wisdom without fullness of power, just as fullness of power [cannot subsist] without fullness of wisdom. In fact, there is no doubt that if one ignored the way in which [he could] obtain the portion of omnipotence he lacked, he would not possess fullness of wisdom. Conversely, he, who could tolerate—in spite of himself—some lack of wisdom, would certainly lack fullness of power [as well]. For this reason, there cannot be fullness of one without the fullness of the other.

So, we should also say of power that which we have said about wisdom. In fact, if it is true that omnipotence cannot be absent where there is fullness of wisdom, it is absolutely clear that fullness of both power and wisdom can be possessed by one single person.

XVII

On the other hand, perfection of true and supreme happiness cannot possibly take place without a duality of persons. This already appears to be as clear as the sun, on the basis of that which we have previously said. In fact, if there was only one, single person in the divinity itself, this [person] would certainly have no one towards whom to address his supreme love, and nobody would love [this person] in return with supreme love. Then, where would [this person] get, in such abundance, those very sweet delights, which—as we have said—are received normally by someone else's heart and not by one's own? As we have already observed, in fact, nothing is sweeter than these delights; nothing is more pleasant; nothing is more beneficial, noble, and joyful than this sweet pleasure. Then, how could divine happiness have obtained the abundance of total fullness, if it had always lacked sweetest pleasure and greatest joy? Consequently, as it has been said, happiness—in order to subsist in its entire fullness—requires duality of beings.

XVIII

None should be troubled, none should be upset, if we talk in a human manner when we want to offer a more complete understanding of divine and transcendent realities. After all, in our modesty, we have decided to use more comfortably this sort of language, as we have often encountered it in the Holy Scriptures.

The highest level of goodness is evidently shown when a supreme love is transmitted without receiving anything in return for the fullness of our happiness. Yet, this degree of supreme perfection cannot be found between only two mutually loving [persons], as it evidently appears from that which has been said before. In fact, in this case, each of the two loved ones manifests love, and thus [each of them] certainly enjoys the sweetness of love, which he could not enjoy if he were alone and lived in a solitary fashion. Thus, a communion based on offered and received love causes in each of those [two] a great and increasing amount of joy and happiness. Thus, from this we clearly conclude that the highest level of goodness cannot have a place in the divinity, if a third person were absent in that plurality of persons. In fact, it is obvious that in a certain duality of persons there would be no one to whom each of the two could transmit the greatest delights of his joy.

Because of this, one can understand that perfection of true and supreme goodness could not subsist without the achievement of a Trinity.

XIX

The claims that various rational arguments have suggested in favour of the Trinity can be confirmed by a rather brief but very enlightening reflection.

Let us carefully observe the value and property of *co-love*[10] and we will soon find that for which we are searching. When one feels love for someone else and he is alone in loving another, single one, he certainly has love but he has no *co-love*. If two people mutually love each other and reciprocally demonstrate a very intense desire, this affection—going from the first one to the second, and from the second to the first one—is dispersed and, so to say, turns in various directions; there is love on both sides, but there is no *co-love*. On the other hand, we rightly speak of *co-love* when a third [person] is loved by the two, in harmony and with a communitarian spirit. [We rightly speak of *co-love*] when the two [persons'] affects are fused so to become only one, because of

---

10. The original, Latin word *condilectio* has been rendered as "co-love." The idea of co-love is ultimately the central theme of Richard's argumentation. Co-love is neither self-addressed love, nor reciprocal love, but it is ultimately what makes plurality harmoniously coexist in unity. It is love in harmony between the first and the second person that cannot but be directed also at a third person.

the third flame of love. From this, it is clear that not even divinity would have *co-love* if only two persons were present and a third one was missing. In fact, we are not dealing here with just any type of [*co-love*], but we are talking about supreme *co-love,* of such a nature that no creature will ever be able to deserve from the Creator or ever be worthy of it.

Who, I wonder, could adequately explain how great is the excellence of the supreme and totally perfect goodness? Who, again, could conceive in an appropriate way the quality or the quantity of the value of intimate and supreme concord? If in these two virtues—each of them considered separately—excellence is so great, what value, I wonder, [and] which merit, will they have when each of the two is built on the other one; when one is exalted by the other, and the latter one is perfected by the former? What else is the intimate and supreme *co-love* if not the joining together of the most profound goodness and the highest concord?

In summary, just like it is impossible not to find a quality of such a value and extraordinary excellence in the highest and universally perfect good, likewise, it is impossible for it to subsist without a Trinity of persons.

XX

Consider now, the way in which the association of the third person gives rise everywhere to affection based on concord and determines a communitarian love amongst all [the persons] and in each [of them].

If you examine any of the three persons, you will see that the other two love him in full harmony. If you observe a second [person], even here you will notice that the other two love him with the same love and in harmony. Consider, lastly, the third [person] amongst them: you will certainly perceive that the affection of the other two is directed towards him with the same concord.

If we analyse [this] concord, [we notice] that the bond of love is multiplied three-fold in it, so that where the suspicion of a lack of love could have risen more easily, certainty [of love] is confirmed by a more profound union. Then, in this way, because of the addition of the third person of the Trinity, it happens that charity-love is in agreement, and that love is communitarian everywhere and never exclusive.

So, the witness we receive from everywhere, effectively confirming the Trinity, appears to be so valid and full of truth that if someone were not convinced by such a certain demonstration, he would certainly look like a madman.

XXI

That which has been said before regarding the two [persons] can also be applied to [all] three, by the same reason: each of [these persons] is worthy to be supremely loved by the others, and [actually] each is supremely loved, as he is supremely perfect. Fullness of highest happiness requires fullness of highest joy. Fullness of highest joy requires fullness of highest charity-love. Fullness of highest charity-love demands fullness of absolute perfection.

Then, since all [three persons] need to be equally perfect, all of them need to be harmonized in a supreme equality. Thus, all of them will have equal wisdom, equal power, glory with no disparity, equivalent goodness, [and] eternal happiness. That which [our] profession [of faith] declares every day, according to the Christian doctrine, is true: all three [persons] possess in equal measure one, single divinity, identical glory, and co-eternal majesty. Here, none [of them] is greater than the other, none is lesser than the other, none precedes, and none follows. Consequently, it is evident that in the Trinity all persons are at the same time equal to each other and co-eternal. If they were not co-eternal, in fact, by the same reason, they would also not be equal to each other.

XXII

In that supreme and absolutely perfect equality, these persons possess the highest and supremely simple being in common. Then, regarding all [three persons], their being corresponds precisely to their living, their living to their understanding, their understanding to their power. Therefore, in the Trinity, wisdom coincides with power, power is identical to essence, and so on, and so forth. So, you can see how each of the [three] persons has everything in equal measure in itself.

However, if we find supreme perfection in this equality and supreme equality in this perfection, supreme fullness of wisdom will be in each and every [person], [and] supreme fullness of power will be in each and every [person as well]. But what is highest and fullest power if not omnipotence? Besides, we know that omnipotence is named as such because it can do everything. If omnipotence really consists of being able to do everything, it will have had no difficulty to [act] so that no other power could have done anything. Thus, this demonstrates that omnipotence can only be one. After all, we have proved earlier that omnipotence is absolutely the same thing as divine essence. Therefore, if possessing omnipotence—or rather, [if] being [the omnipotence]—is common to all persons together, since in the Trinity *having* corresponds with *being,* the reality of being one and the same essence will also be common to all [of them]. In fact, the divine essence—just as omnipotence—can only be one. Thus, not only is each of the persons neither more nor less than that which the whole is, but any [of these persons] is exactly identical to that which any other is [as well].

In summary, in each [person] we have supreme simplicity, and in all [of them] together we have highest unity. Everywhere, then—if you think well—there is amazing identity.

XXIII

We can understand that which we have affirmed regarding the equality of persons either in a right way or in a wrong way. Actually, before such a great simplicity and unity of persons, it would seem more appropriate to speak of identity rather than of equality. Let us imagine three golden statues of the same carat, with the same weight, looking alike in every aspect. In this case we are able to affirm—as we do—that they are identical. Yet, such equality has little in common with that in the divine persons' Trinity. Actually, even if those statues are identical, the gold mass of one is not the gold mass of the other, and thus, one does not coincide with the other. We must believe nothing of this sort about the true and highest Trinity, as if in it we had [persons] at the same time different and equal to each other. In fact, as has been already demonstrated, that which is found in each one person is also entirely and identically present in each of the others. Let us think of three rational spirits: we rightly define them as equal if they have the same power, the same wisdom, and the same purity and goodness. It is clear, however, that just as there are three persons in this trinity of spirits, similarly, there are also three substances. On the contrary, the supreme Trinity is founded upon a unity of substance. This is the reason why we notice diversity together with equality in the first trinity [we have considered]. But such equality has no relationship with the divine Trinity. In the supreme Trinity, we claim the persons to be equal in the sense that the highest and supremely simple being, which belongs to one person in [its] full perfection, [also] belongs in fullness and perfection to any other of those persons.

XXIV

This is certain: one single and same substance is neither a greater nor a lesser entity, neither better nor worse than itself. Thus, each person in the Trinity will not be anything greater or better than each of the others, as one, identical substance is truly present in each of them. Furthermore, this [substance] is the same for each of them [taken] singly and for all of them together. Thus, any two [of these persons] will not constitute a greater or better entity than only one [of them]; and three [of them] together will not be [greater or better] than any two [of them] or only one, whichever this one might be, considered *in se* and *per se*. Conversely, when there are multiple substances in a trinity of persons, one, single [person] is less than two, and all three together will constitute a greater entity than [only] two, whichever they may be.

Consider, now, how incomprehensible this absolute and total equality in greatness is in the supreme Trinity, where unity is not compromised by plurality and plurality does not transcend unity.

XXV

However, in order for you to be able to better admire this equality of divine persons, observe also that which [takes place] in all of the other persons. In fact, in one same person—whichever this might be—singularity is not cleaved from plurality, and unity is not cleaved from inequality. I will not discuss the fact that this [person] may grow or diminish, becoming different from itself; I will not talk about the fact that its power is one thing, its wisdom is another, and its justice is another, so to be able to be greater or lesser—according to its own various aspects—better or worse. Even if we consider its power alone—or its wisdom alone—this is different from itself, unequal to itself. The same happens with all the other attributes: consider its power and you will see that something is easy for it, something else difficult, something else impossible, thus it proves to be also different and uneven within itself. Similarly, also with respect to wisdom, one thing is comprehensible, another one—in contrast—is incomprehensible. In fact, neither human nor angelic intelligence will ever be able to understand the very immensity of the divinity, not to mention everything else. Consequently, in the moment when one, single and same nature is at times more effective [and] at other times less effective, it is also less important in one case and greater in another, showing itself to be different and uneven to itself. Thus, we can conclude that where there is no true simplicity, there is also no true equality.

Contrarily, in the Trinity no [person] is in any way different from himself, or unequal to any other. It is clear that where there is true eternity there can be no before or after. Similarly, when there is an immutable immensity, there can be no thing greater or smaller. Then, those who possess the same condition of immensity and eternity, can absolutely not have reciprocal differences or mutations, as with them *there is no variation or shadow due to change;*[11] there is no before and no after; there is neither a greater nor a smaller, but all three persons are coeternal with respect to one another and equal to each other.

Thus, with clear and numerous arguments, we have demonstrated the truth of that which [our] faith offers to us, that is, to venerate one, single God in the Trinity and the Trinity in unity.

11. Jas 1:17.

Synopsis of the Topics of the Fourth Book

I. How incomprehensible it is to human intelligence that a plurality of persons be found in a unity of substance.

II. How numerous the things are that intelligence does not comprehend and yet, that its experience requires it to recognize.

III. How there are numerous incomprehensible things, which are nonetheless determined by an evident reason, even though they escape experience.

IV. In order to make the doctrinal teaching clear, we must define the meaning of "person," and according to that definition, explain the unity of the Trinity.

V. Before us, some have looked for the reason why the three components of the Trinity are called "persons." The true meaning of this term must be recognized.

VI. That which "substance" means is very different from that which "person" means.

VII. With the word "substance" we do not really indicate *someone* but *something*; the term "person," conversely, defines *someone* rather than *something*.

VIII. Every time that more than one person is present, it is not necessary to refer also to multiple substances.

IX. We do not fall into contradiction when we say that our God is one, with respect to his substance, and triune, with respect to his persons.

X. In the human nature, plurality of substances does not destroy the unity of person. In the divine nature, plurality of persons does not disrupt the unity of substance.

XI. Regarding the persons' distinction, we require a twofold consideration: it is necessary to know that which [a person] is and from whence it derives its being.

XII. The term "existence" can suggest both [of the following] considerations: that which is connected to existence or that which is connected to the way in which to obtain it.

XIII. On the general level, we distinguish three varieties of existences:

XIV. The way in which personal existences are distinguished in the human nature, and the way they are distinguished in the angelic one.

XV. The difference between divine existences is to be sought only with respect to their origin.

XVI. Divine nature possesses an existence that is common to many, and [at the same time, it possesses] an absolutely incommunicable existence.

XVII. The way in which existences can be incommunicable in the divinity. [In the divinity, existences] correspond in number to the persons.

XVIII. With respect to God, the person is nothing more than the incommunicable existence.

XIX. Where we have a unity of substance, there can be multiple existences and, thus, multiple persons.

XX. The way in which the different formulations are to be put together and understood: three substances and one essence; or: three subsistences and one substance; or: three persons and one substance or essence.

XXI. How "person" is to be defined with reference to the created person, and not just to any person.

XXII. How "person" is to be defined with reference to the uncreated person, and not just to any person.

Book Four

I

At the beginning of this work, we have shown the tenets of our faith regarding the unity of the divine substance by such a clear demonstration and so transparent [a set of] arguments that—if one reflects with attention—one can [now] have no doubt left [in him] to trigger the slightest perplexity. Similarly, when the moment arrived, we explained the content of our faith regarding the plurality of persons, with such a valid argument and [we] confirmed [it] with so many reasons that, if one is not convinced by such a blatant testimony he appears to have lost his mind. And actually, if those considerations and affirmations are analysed one by one, nothing appears to be more credible, nothing truer.

But if we confront them with one another and we study the way in which they can co-exist and be in harmony, everything that has been demonstrated by any sort of reasoning loses its certainty immediately, in the event in which our faith starts to shake. Understanding how there can be more than one person where there is no more than one substance is not easy for the human intellect.

This is the cause of the infidels' countless mistakes and the schismatics' various heresies. This is the reason why some disrupt the unity of the divine substance and others fail to distinguish the plurality of persons. This is the reason why the Arian and Sabellian sects oppose one another, and this is also the reason why some, more recent [theologians] assign a multiplicity of significances to the term "person," rendering the understanding of such a profound truth even more uncertain, rather than explaining it as they should have. Indeed, if we want to interpret the word "person" both according to its common meaning and in a technical way, we cannot conceive how a multiplicity of persons—understood commonly—can subsist in a unity of substance.

II

But I wonder: is this claimed Trinity of unity and unity of Trinity not possible, since it cannot be understood? Who could declare this, unless he is crazy? Who would dare assert it? The things human intelligence cannot understand are so many! And yet, a quantity of experiences forces human intellect to recognize how true [these things] are! Please, explain to me, if you can, this phenomenon, which we cannot doubt in any way: how is it that the corporeal eye cannot see [the place] where it is, although it [can] see [well], and it sees where it is not with its visual ability? In heaven, where it is not, it sees whether there is a star; if the eye's lid shuts it, though, it cannot see the very eyelid hiding it. All the other senses of our body feel and distinguish only the objects with which they are in contact; only our sense of seeing is powerless with that which it is in contact, [while] it is unfailing with those things in the distance and further away. Will you deny that this is true only because you do not understand how this may happen? Explain to me, if you can, [another fact] that you would not dare to deny: how is it that soul and body, although very different indeed in their nature, constitute in yourself one single and same person? And [if you are able to answer these questions,] then you can also ask me how it is possible that the Trinity of persons is one, single and same substance in one supremely simple nature, common [to all these persons]. But if the production of these things—which human nature knows—by experience is incomprehensible, that which no human experience can reach [will] be even more incomprehensible.

III

However, if you declare not to be able to doubt those data provided by experience, even though they transcend the limits of human ability, I [will] add that no one [can] doubt the existence of certain incomprehensible things, even though they can not be experienced. Evident reasons, in fact, require us to recognize many realities, even though the human mind is not able to explain them. Can you perhaps comprehend God's eternity? And yet you have no doubts about his eternity. Perhaps, do you have any doubt about God's immensity, even though you are not able to comprehend it? Perhaps, are all those who preach about God's omnipotence—and believe it—able to understand it? If you ask the theologians, one right after the other, all of them would answer that in God power is identified with wisdom, and that goodness coincides with both of these. [Lastly,] if you asked of what these three [qualities] consist, [you could only answer by saying that they are] the divine substance. Evident reasons demonstrate all of this, and force us to admit it. Certainly, all theologians agree in this regard, with no exception, all [of them] hold this view.

Now, which one is the most comprehensible and most understandable amongst these affirmations? [Is it] that one, single substance corresponds to three persons or [is it] that three persons constitute a single substance? Both [of these affirmations] are incomprehensible, but neither of the two is incredible.

Nonetheless—in my opinion—this incomprehensibility allows [confusion]. Some believe that the meaning of "person" has multiple significances every time. In fact, some claim that the term "person" sometimes indicates the persons' substance, sometimes [it refers to] their subsistences and some other times [it refers to] their attributes. And according to them, [the term "person"] is always singular when it refers to the substance and it is never plural. Otherwise, whoever proclaims three persons would also seem to proclaim three substances. In order to prove that "persons" are [actually] "personal properties," they advocate Jerome's authority, who claims as follows: "Opposing Sabellius' heresy, we distinguish three persons, each with its own attributes. In fact, we do not only proclaim names, but also those attributes the[ir very] names signify, that is the persons or—as the Greeks say—the hypostases, i.e., subsistences."[1] In my opinion, however, with these words Jerome is not

---

1. Although mediaeval scholars believed this passage to be authentic, Richard's quote is found in an epistle, which most commentators of our time consider an apocryphal composition of a different author. As Salet determines in his research, "[The text] is part of the 'Epistle XVI' . . . listed among the apocryphal writings of St. Jerome . . . In reality, this is a profession of faith stated by Pelagius, which is mentioned in St. Augustine's *De gratia Christi* . . . This text is abundantly quoted in the Middle Age." ("[Le texte] fait partie de l' 'Epistola XVI' . . . signalée parmi les apocryphes de S. Jerome . . . Il s'agit, en réalité, d'une profession de foi de Pélage, mentionnée dans le

saying that the persons coincide with their personal attributes, but with the names' attributes; that is, with those realities properly indicated by the persons' names.[2]

IV

Let us leave out the name "hypostasis," which—according to Jerome—perhaps hides poison in itself.[3] That is, let us leave out the Greek term, since we are not Greek. However, we cannot tacitly ignore the word "subsistence." Some explain that "persons" are subsistences, affirming—more than demonstrating—that there are three subsistences and one substance in the single divinity. And all of this is [generally] described promptly and with no explanations, [almost as] if it is blatant to every reader that three subsistences can be present where there is one, single substance. Now, I do not despise this notion of theirs; I neither criticize it nor say it is false. Nonetheless, I cannot give up telling the truth, i.e., that this theory of theirs does not convince me in my simplicity.

If you want to persuade people like me, you need, first of all, to specify with care the meaning of both "substance" and "subsistence" and, on the basis of such a specification, demonstrate the way in which you can find more than one subsistence where there is only one substance. Otherwise, I wonder, what sort of advantage may there be in demonstrating to me something obscure by an [even] more obscure argument? The term "person" is on everybody's lips, even the unlearned. Instead, the word "subsistence" is not even known to all the learned ones. For this reason, I will point out: how can the less educated, who ignore the proper meaning of ["subsistence"], conclude that three exact subsistences—that is, three persons—can exist in the unity of sub-

---

De gratia Christi de S. Augustin . . . Ce texte est abondamment cité au Moyen Age.") Salet, *La Trinité,* 235.

2. By saying that what identifies a person is the name's attribute, Richard is stating that the substance "divinity" is common and identical to all three persons, but each person is distinct, in a typically Augustinian fashion, as its name's attribute is distinct (i.e., the Father is Father because he is Father of the Son).

3. As Jerome writes, "But believe me, poison hides underneath the honey; the angel of Satan transfigured himself into an angel of light." ("Sed mihi credite, venenum sub melle latet; transfiguravit se angelus Satanae in angelum lucis.") Jerome, *Epistola 15,* 357.

stance? How can such a doctrine, which solves a problem with another problem, be satisfactory?

Therefore, since my intention in this work is to facilitate the simple ones rather than "teaching Minerva," so to say, explaining the meaning of "person," and not just that of subsistence, will be my prime concern, in the measure the Lord allows me. Afterwards, on the basis of this explanation, I will try to demonstrate in which way plurality of persons can be reconciled with the unity of substance.

V

I will say this: I will say that which I think and that which I believe with no doubt. In this so sublime and important mystery of the Trinity, the term "person" has in no way been adopted with no divine inspiration, without the Holy Spirit's authority.

Let us think of how the same Spirit has predicted by the prophets so many mysteries of our faith, our redemption, our sanctification, and glorification. [Let us think how the Spirit] has spoken these [mysteries] by the evangelists and has illustrated them by the doctors' mouths. Whoever ponders over this will not be able to claim in any way that [the Holy Spirit] has left the supreme article of our faith to human discretion, rather than having regulated it by his own inspiration. [He will not be able to argue that the Holy Spirit has not regulated] the holiest and most secret mystery of the Trinity, that name that he wanted as the object of every soul's faith and every mouth's confession.

Certainly, let us also admit that whoever has applied the term "person" to the divine reality for the first time has done so by necessity. [He has done so] in order to give some answer to those asking how the three in the Trinity were three. It could not have been answered, in fact, that we were dealing with three gods. Yet, the Holy Spirit, who was guiding their hearts, knew well the manner and the meaning in which he wanted them to employ [the term].

Now, we are honestly convinced of this, let us try to know carefully the meaning with which [this word] has been given by the Spirit of truth to those who used it, and the reason why it has entered the universal usage of the Latin church. [Let us not linger on knowing] by which meaning [this word] was initially used by humans or the reason why later on it has been applied to the divine reality.

Indeed, no judgment is more certain than one formulated on a common concept of the spirit. I will try, then, to derive our affirmations from the simple and common idea, which each spirit conceives regarding the word "person."

VI

First of all, let us repeat that which others have said, i.e., that [the word] "person" is used pertaining to the substance and apparently indicates a substance. Nonetheless, there is a great difference between the meaning of each one of them. Yet, in order to make more intelligible that which we are affirming, let us explain more clearly this very point. Who could deny or who could doubt that [the term] "animal" indicates a substance? And yet, the meaning of the first [word] is very different from that of the second one. The word "animal," in fact, indicates an animated and sensible substance. "Animal," then, means a substance, but at the same time it means also something else. In fact, with the word "animal" we indicate a substance, but with a specific difference added to it. In the same way, the term "human" clearly means "animal" and—because of this—[it means] substance. What is a human, in fact, if not a rational animal subjected to death? Thus, we have a prime significance of this term and a secondary one, at the same time. For this reason, "animal" indicates a sensible substance, not just of any kind; "human," on the other hand, does not [indicate] any sensible [substance], but a rational one. Yet, we never speak of "person" if not in relation to a rational substance. And when we say "person" we do not intend anything else other than a single and individual substance.

Thus, with the concept of substance, under the name "animal" we mean a property common to all animals; [instead,] under the name "human" we mean a certain property that is pertinent to only one, although without the determination given by a proper name. Thus, at times, a generic property is implied, at other times [we imply] a particular property. Regarding the word "person," finally, [we imply with it] an individual, singular, incommunicable property.

From all of this—I think—you can easily deduce that the meaning of "substance" and the meaning of "person" are very different from one another.

VII

If you pay good attention and observe carefully, [you realize that] the word "substance" does not indicate *someone* but *something*. On the other hand, the term "person" does not indicate *something* but *someone*.

When something is so distant from us as not to be distinguishable, we ask what it [might] be, and generally the answer we receive is that it is an animal, a man, a horse, etc. However, if [this *something*] has come closer so as to enable us to see that it is a man, we do not ask "*what* is that?" any longer, but rather "*who* is that?" The answer we receive is that he is Matthew, or Bartholomew, or someone's father or son. You see well that to the question "*what is it?*" we answer with a generic or specific word, with a definition or with something of that sort. On the contrary, the answer to the question "*who?*" is a proper name or something equivalent. Thus, with "*what?*" we enquire about a common property; with "*who?*" we enquire about an individual property.[4]

We must observe, then, that if one asked another "*who is this?*" before an angelic vision, and if he were answered that this is an angel of the Lord, very well, such an answer would not correspond to the logic of language but to the mood of the one who asked. [It would be] as if he had been answered more clearly: "This is not a man as you think, but an angel of the Lord." Actually, if [the enquirer] knew that that was an angel, he would not ask such a question and would not receive such an answer, because this thing would make no sense. Consequently, just as we said, with "*what?*" we enquire about a common property; with "*who?*" we enquire about an individual property. With "*what?*" we ask to know the characteristics of a substance; with "*who?*" we ask to be informed of a person's attributes.

---

4. Here and elsewhere, Richard's *singularis proprietas* has been translated with "particular property" or "individual property," since Richard's use of the adjective implies the notion of a property that is "isolated," "set apart," "alone," "individual," which would not be readily conveyed by a mechanical translation, employing the word "singular."

And we must underline that we generally answer the question "who is this person?" or "who is this man?" with the same answer, [that is,] with a proper name or in an equivalent manner.

On the basis of all of this, I believe it can be understood that with the word "substance" we do not really refer to someone but to something, while the term "person" does not really indicate something but someone. Furthermore, with the word "person" we always indicate someone who is unique, distinct from all the others by a particular property.

VIII

Now, what do we mean when we speak about three persons if not three "someones"? The meaning of "person" remains absolutely identical, both when the [term] is used in the singular form and when it is used in the plural. The only difference is this: it is clear that in one instance we are dealing with more than one [person], [and] in another instance [we are dealing] with one, single [person]. When we say "one person," we are certainly talking about someone who is only one, and yet who is a rational substance. When we are talking about three persons, we are doubtlessly referring to three "someones," each of them being a substance of a rational nature. But [the fact] that more than one [person]— or even all [of them]—constitute one, single and same substance has no importance with regard to the person's proper nature and its reality.

Yet, people are more ready to formulate their judgments on the basis of that which experience demonstrates than according to the need of reasoning. We see human beings, obviously; we are not able to see the divine ones, though. In the human nature the substances are as many as the number of persons, and our everyday experience pushes us to think in the same way regarding the divine realities. Actually, the carnal spirit is so content with that which experience has suggested to it, that it can hardly accept something that does not look somehow alike to that which he already knew because of experience. Yet, at least, let whoever sleeps in the faith be awakened by a blatant rational argument! Well, as we have already demonstrated with a plain rational argument, it is not necessary to think that where there are multiple persons, multiple substances must be [found] as well.

IX

One thing is certain: it is absolutely necessary that, wherever we have three persons, the [first] should be someone, the [second] should be someone else, and the third should be even someone else. [It is necessary] that each of them has an individual existence *per se* and is distinct from the other two on the basis of his own singularity and of his particular identity. Similarly, there is no doubt that where we have three substances, the first one must be something, the second [must be] something else, and the third one—with regard to the first two—[must be] even something else. In fact, if [the substances] did not show any difference between each other, they could not be more than one, because there can be no plurality where there are no differences.

Now, we have previously noticed that in the supreme Trinity all [the persons] have the highest and supremely simple being in common, and that none [of them] is something different from any of the others. And for this reason, we say that there are not three substances in the Trinity. In [our] rational nature, [any] distinction between one thing and another is pertinent to the diversity of substances, whilst [any] distinction between one [person] and another is pertinent to the "otherness" of the persons. Yet, since in the divine and supremely wise nature we noticed this otherness but [we did] not [notice] the abovementioned diversity, we assert for this reason that there are multiple persons in God and we deny that there are multiple substances.

Here we have demonstrated, with that which we believe to be a clear and brief argument, that affirming that our God is one in substance and triune in persons is no contradiction at all.

X

We must carefully observe and ponder the following comparison: just like the plurality of substances in one being does not suppress the person's unity, similarly, the persons' otherness never destroys the substance's unity. In fact, in the human nature, the body is a substance and the soul is a different substance: yet, there is but one single person. In the divine nature, on the other hand, one person is someone and another person is another someone; yet, they are but one, single and same substance.

Then again, just as we know and we have previously demonstrated, there is extreme similarity and extreme equality in the multiplicity of the divine persons. Conversely, a great dissimilarity and a noticeable inequality reigns among the plurality of substances, [which make up] the human nature. Then, what is so incredible about the fact that a true, substantial unity subsists in such a great personal equality? [After all,] in such an evident difference of qualities we observe the person's unity and identity. Indeed, in the human nature, one, single and same person is both corporeal, on one hand, and incorporeal, on the other. It is visible under a certain aspect, and [it is] invisible under a certain other. From one viewpoint it is mortal, from another one it is immortal. And yet, in spite of such a diversity of substances, the person's unity remains. Therefore, plurality of substances does not produce multiple persons in [one, same] human nature. Plurality of persons does not determine multiple substances in the divine nature. Furthermore, we add that which follows as a consequence: the substance's plurality does not compromise the person's unity in the first instance, and the person's multiplicity does not erase the substance's unity in the second instance.

XI

In this way, we realized that it is not impossible for more than one person to be in a substantial unity. It is logical, now, that we investigate how a persons' otherness may exist without a substance's otherness. Indeed, a twofold consideration is necessary—I think—to distinguish [each] person: we must know that which [a person] is and from where he derives his existence. The first of these enquiries aims to discern the object's nature; the second aims to discover its origin. The task of the first is to investigate carefully that which a person possesses, with whom he shares [these possessions], that which is [to be considered] as generic, specific or proper to the considered nature. The [objective of] the second is to carefully examine [the source] from which everything that exists has its origin, that is, whether from itself or from another one. And in the case of an origin outside itself, [this enquiry will have to investigate] whether [that which exists possesses its being] in a certain way or in another, or [even] in any other [possible] form of existence. On one hand, then, we will search for a definition of the object itself, some sort of description, some sort of identification of its particular nature; on the other hand, [we will investigate] the nature's order, the object's origin, and any other distinction of such kind. The first analysis has to do with the mode of being, the second revolves around the means to obtain [being]. One [of them] seeks [to understand] the existence's nature, the other—so to say—seeks the nature of obtaining [essence].

In order not to talk about the rest of the terms, I realize that "obtaining" is not a helpful expression when referring to divine realities. However, let no one be scandalized if I explain that which I think regarding the divine realities with the words I can find. After all, if whatever truth I say, in an improper or inappropriate form, is expounded by anyone else with more appropriate and more correct words, I [will] be thankful [for this] and consider [it] as a great gift. Here, by [the word] "obtaining," I mean the manner in which one obtains that which he substantially is or [that which] he possesses by nature. In fact, in each case, the way to obtain is very different, both when one receives and when one does not receive. Similarly, the way of giving and receiving is also different.

XII

Now, with the term "existence" we can refer to both [of these] considerations: one concerning the essence's nature and another concerning the nature of obtaining [it]. I mean, [we can refer to] both [the consideration] in which [every being] seeks that which it is in itself and [the consideration] in which every being tries to know from where it derives its being. The word "existence" comes from the [Latin] verb *existere*. We observe that the term *sistere* refers to the first consideration. Equally, we can notice that by adding the preposition *ex* [the word] refers [in meaning] to the second consideration. When we say that something exists—(in the meaning of *sistere*)—those realities, which do not derive their being from themselves but have it from someone [else], are immediately excluded. [These realities] do not really "*ex*-ist"—so to speak—but they rather "*in*-sist,"[5] that is, they are joined to some [other]

5. I.e., "they exist *in* something," according to an etymological reading of the word

subject. The term *sistere*, however, seems to be appropriate to both of them: both to that which subsists in some way, [and] to that which cannot subsist in any way; both to that which is necessarily subordinated and to that which cannot be [subordinated] in any way. In effect, the first condition is proper to the created nature, the second to the uncreated nature, since that which is not created subsists in itself in such a way that nothing in it can be found, as [if it were its own operating] subject. For this reason, the word *sistere* can refer to both the created and uncreated nature.

The term *ex-sistere*, on its part, not only expresses the possession of being, but also the [being's] coming from outside. [It expresses] the fact that one possesses its being because of someone [else]. Indeed, this is shown in the compounded verb, by the preposition that is added to it. What does *exsistere* mean, in fact, if not *sistere* "from" (= *ex*) someone? That is, [what does it mean if not] receiving one's own substantial being from someone [else]?

Consequently, with this single verb *exsistere*—or with the single noun "existence"—we can intend both that which has to do with the object's nature and that which refers to its own origin.

XIII

As we can deduce from that which has been said before, existence can generally appear in three different forms. In fact, it can vary only according to the object's nature or only according to its origin, or according to both aspects at the same time.

Existence undergoes variations only with regards to the object's nature when more than one person has an absolutely single and same origin, while each of them possesses a unique and separate substance. A multiplicity of substances, in fact, cannot subsist at all without a qualitative difference. Thus, this is the variety of existence only according to nature, without having any difference from the point of view of their origin.

---

used. Notice that the entire passage is set up as a play on the Latin word *existere* and its meanings, the imaginative etymology Richard associates with the analysis of this term, and the word's linguistic interaction with selected prepositions. Richard employs rhetorical force, creativity of grammar, and sheer ingenuity of wit to corroborate the case in favor of his position.

There is diversity of existence with regards to the sole origin when, even though more than one person possesses the single and same being with no distinctions, they are distinct from each other with regards to their origin. And they differ in origin when one [of them] has an origin and another one does not, or if—amongst those who have an origin—they have a different origin from one another. Therefore, such an existence presents diversities only with respect to their origin, not according to some sort of natural difference.

Finally, we have different existences, both according to the object's nature and according to its origin, when each person has a singular and separate substance and a different origin. Therefore, just as we have already said, the variety of existences—in general—appears in three ways: either only according to the nature of the existing, or only according to its origin or according to an alteration in both [the nature of existing and its origin].

XIV

In the human nature, which we know from experience, we notice that the persons' existence certainly differs both in the person's quality and in their origin. One thing is certain: each human person possesses a particular and specific identity, thanks to which—no doubt—it is different from any other. Similarly, each of them has a specific origin, different from all the others and distinguished from an exclusive property of its own. In fact, one person has one ancestor and another person has a different one, because one has a father and the other one has another father. And when more than one person has the same father, one of them has originated from a [certain] element of the father's substance, while another is derived from another element of the [same] father's substance. Thus, we see—as we have said—that specific existences in the human persons are differentiated both according to the quality of each of them and according to their very individual origin.

Conversely, in the angelic nature, there is no transmission [of life], but only simple creation. Then, each one and all [of the angels] have one, single, common principle, as all of them have as their beginning the only Creator, and each one and all of them derive only from creation. In the angelic nature, however, there are as many substances as the number of persons: as a consequence, it is necessary for them to differ according to quality. If they were not qualitatively different, there would absolutely not be a plurality of substances. Existences, in the angelic nature, are distinct [from one another] only according to quality [whilst] in the human—as we have already observed—both [they are distinct] according to quality and to origin.

XV

Amongst the divine persons—as has been demonstrated—there is absolutely no dissimilarity and no inequality: just as one person is, the other one is also, and so—in every way—the third one as well. Thus, since all of them are similar and equal to one another, [the divine persons] cannot differ according to quality. In fact, since they possess an entirely single, identical, and supremely simple being—as a clear argument demonstrated—it is not possible for them to differ from one another according to any qualitative distinction. Now, if we have no difference, we cannot have any plurality; thus, plurality of persons requires—in the Trinity—the presence of distinctive properties and a difference between [such] properties. However, since the identity of the substance completely excludes any difference of quality, different persons' properties will have to be sought with regards to the sole origin.

Finally, to summarise briefly that which we have explained at some length, it is evident that in the divine nature plurality of existences can be distinguished only with regards to the origin; in the angelic nature, on the other hand, only according to quality; in the human nature, lastly, both according to quality and according to the origin.

We have thus found that which we have previously set out to investigate, i.e., how there can be otherness of persons without any otherness of substances. In fact, we have noticed that although the multiple divine persons possess a single, identical, and absolutely undifferentiated being—as it is for the identity of substance—they can be distinguished from each other on the basis of their original cause, as one exists by virtue of itself, the other two originate from outside themselves. Furthermore, these last ones differ from each other in the way in which they obtained their being. Now, if one factor influences the persons' specific character by modifying it, it likewise doubtlessly alters the existences' own nature. In fact, in the divine nature, we must seek both the persons' and the existences' distinction only in their origin.

XVI

With the word "existence," as it is clear after that which we have previously considered, we mean that which owns substantial being, because of this or that property. To own substantial being only for propagation [of life] is proper to animals. To own substantial being for propagation and also for procreation is proper to humans. This is due to the fact that the flesh is transmitted and the soul is created. To own substantial being only for creation is proper to angels. To have the super-substantial being, yet with no creation or beginning, is proper to the divine nature.

On one hand, existence is common to a multiplicity [of beings]; on the other hand, however, it is totally incommunicable. In fact, without considering those [beings] which cannot be called persons, the divine, the angelic, and the human nature possess rational being in common. However, not being able to exist by itself but by someone else's activity is proper to both the angelic and human [nature]. Being from itself and not out of another being's activity is [a feature] only of the divine nature.

The incommunicable existence, then, is that which cannot but belong to a single person.

Yet, even if we omit the rest, we have no doubt that in the divine nature reside both the existence common to a multiplicity and the existence that is absolutely incommunicable. It has been previously demonstrated that "existence" corresponds to "substance," yet not so simply put, but with reference to some kind of property in which we reflect its original cause. Yet, to take the original cause into consideration does not only mean to search and to find that there is an origin—when there is one—but also to seek and discover that this [origin] is absent—when there is not any. Then, to own substantial being—or rather the super-substantial one—with no creation or beginning is proper to the divine existence. To possess a composite being, exposed to accidents, is typical of every substance whose name truly expresses its reality. Contrarily, only the divine substance possesses a simple, non-composite being, which [cannot] be subjected to any accident, since it transcends the substance's nature. And it is for this reason that we affirm that God possesses super-substantial being rather than substantial [being].

However, we need to know that existence indicates a substantial being, existing by the action of a property both common and incommunicable. We speak of common existence when we refer to him who possesses being because of a common property. On the other hand, [we speak of] incommunicable [existence] when we refer to the one who has his being because of an incommunicable property. Actually, being from itself—and not by the action of any substance—is proper to the divine substance. Likewise, not being from another is proper to a person with no origin. In one instance, we are dealing with a common property, in the other, [we are dealing] with an incommunicable property. And all of the divine persons have [this] in common: being that substance which is not derived from some other substance but is from itself. Consequently, the divine substance—which we say and believe to be from itself—coincides with the common existence.

All this relates to the common existence. Let us spend some time, now, on the incommunicable existence.

XVII

To say it properly, an incommunicable thing is that which is not common and certainly can never be so. It must be examined, then, whether—and in what manner—there might be an incommunicable existence in the divinity.

Yet, with no doubt, in that Trinity we must have as many personal properties as the number of persons. Now, certainly, the personal property is incommunicable. The personal property is that which gives to each [person] that which he is. We define "personal property" as the thing by which each one is unique, distinct from everyone else. Actually, we speak of "person" only when we refer to someone, distinct from everyone else by an individual property. Therefore, if you affirm that a personal property is communicable, it is as though you affirm that one, single person can be two [persons]. However, if we say that one, single [person] is two [persons] and that two are one, we can easily deduce that none of the two is a person, as none of the two is distinct from the other with regards to an individual property. From this, then, we clearly conclude that—as we have already claimed before—a personal property is absolutely incommunicable.

Without a doubt, it is necessary that there be personal—i.e., incommunicable—properties in the Trinity of persons. Yet, as has been demonstrated, the same difference, which is found between the existences, occurs among the persons. Thus, if persons are distinguished by incommunicable properties, existences too will certainly be distinguished by incommunicable [properties]. Then, one who has an incommunicable difference needs to have also an incommunicable existence. As a consequence, in the divinity, the [number of] persons is equal to the [number of] the incommunicable existences.

XVIII

If we ponder this more carefully, concerning the divine realities, one person in God is nothing else but an incommunicable existence. As demonstrated above, all personal properties are absolutely incommunicable. Similarly, difference among persons in God corresponds to the difference among the existences. Therefore, what will the "incommunicable existence" be in God if not someone possessing the super-substantial being by virtue of a personal property? And what is the divine person if not someone possessing the divine being by virtue of an incommunicable property? Yet, what is the divine being if not the super-substantial being? Actually, whether you call this [subject] divine, or super-substantial, or supremely simple, or omnipotent, or any other definition of this sort, we always refer to the same [subject]. Then, both the divine person and the divine existence possess divine being. Both of them have substantial being. Both of them possess the personal property and both of them possess the incommunicable one. You can see that that which we can say about one [of them] can also be said about the other.

Finally, as it has been said regarding the divine realities, a "divine person" is nothing else than an "incommunicable existence."

XIX

We are persuaded by that which we have previously affirmed that there may be multiple existences in the divinity. Now we need to verify whether these [existences] may subsist without altering the substance's unity. If [the language] allowed, just as we say that "*essence*" derives from "*esse*" (= "being"), we could say that "*sistence*" comes from "*existence*." Maybe you are laughing whilst reading or listening to these things, but I would much prefer you to laugh than to misunderstand or even carelessly tease what I would like to say. Actually, if it were possible to speak of "*sistence*" just as [we speak] of "*essence*," [such a word] would simply indicate the object's being. Now, in the word "existence" we should infer something more. In fact, just as we rightly define "subsistence" as that something which sustains someone,[6] similarly we can rightly speak of "existence" regarding that which possesses being by someone [else's] action.[7] "Existence" therefore, signifies an object's being, and that this [being exists] *from* a certain property. After all, who would not notice that a being, who is omnipotent by a certain property, and another being, omnipotent by another property, constitute two different existences? Indeed, even though both of them have a single mode of being, they do not actually possess one, single mode of existing. Who, I wonder, could think as impossible or even absurd that two or three are said to be equally powerful and equally wise? Or why would you label as impossible or even incredible the claim that the very being they share is possessed by one [of them] according to a determined property and by another one [of them] according to a different [property]?

Thus, it does not appear as impossible or incredible that there are multiple existences in the divinity, and consequently multiple persons. And since we define these [persons] as equal in power, which we have proved by clear reasoning, we must also admit that if one of them has omnipotence, the other has omnipotence too. After all, all theologians know with absolute certainty that the *being* is absolutely simple in the true divinity. It will be necessary, therefore, that *being* omnipotence and *having* omnipotence are the same thing in God, and that omnipotence is nothing other than the divine substance. Yet, as we have proved else-

6. In Latin "*sub-sistere*" = to be underneath.
7. In Latin "*ex-sistere*" = to be from.

where, omnipotence cannot be but only one; consequently, the divine substance must be one as well.

Thus, on the basis of that which is plausible to everybody and necessary to the theologians, we reach the conclusion that we are seeking: multiple existences can be found [even] where we have only one substance.

Then, to add something even more subtle—in order to benefit the more subtle minds—[we observe that] in the natural and created things, [we find a] distinct[ion between] "*being*" and "*the thing which is.*" In the uncreated realities, however, "*being*" and "*the thing which is*" coincide perfectly. As a consequence, it is evident that divine substance is nothing else than substantial—or better, super-substantial—being. [It is] substantial because it is a reality subsisting in itself; [it is] super-substantial, because this reality is not subordinated to anything.

Those *who fear where there is no reason for fear*[8] would rightly fear to speak of "persons" according to the substance if "person" just meant substantial being, rather than something else. Instead, [this term] indicates one who possesses substantial being by virtue of a particular property. For this reason, we do not hesitate to claim that in the divinity we talk about "persons" with reference to the substance and to indicate the substance, and that in God there are multiple persons but not multiple substances, since [in God] many possess the single and undifferentiated being,[9] although according to different characteristics. As a consequence, in God we have unity with regards to the essence, plurality with regards to the existence. [We have] unity of essence because there is a single and undifferentiated being, [whilst we have] plurality of persons because we have a plurality of existences.

I believe this to be sufficient for those who search with the right intentions. After all, no one in this life must ask or expect to be entirely satisfied when he deals with topics as profound as those above.

Now we should observe the relationship between persons and existence, since that which appears to be uncertain regarding one of the two [notions], if taken separately, is proven by the other. For example, the fact that there must necessarily be multiple persons in the divinity is proven more easily using the notion of person. On the other hand,

---

8. Ps 13:5, according to the order in the *Vulgata*.
9. I.e., the substance.

the fact that a plurality may be found in the substance's unity is deduced more easily from the consideration of existence.

XX

Someone, maybe, expects me to clarify how we must interpret and bring together the fact that someone talks about "three substances and one essence," others [speak of] "three subsistences and one substance," [and] others [speak of] "three persons and one substance or essence."

[We], the Latins, affirm that in God we have only one substance, while the Greeks [claim] that [in God] there are three [substances]. Apparently, there is noticeable disagreement and total contradiction. Yet, let us not think of their beliefs as contradictory and either [of us] to be wrong in the faith! Indeed, we need to detect a single truth in this variety of words, even though in different [authors, the very] interpretation of terms is different.

Although persons are defined as "substances" by some and as "subsistences" by others, the meaning—as it seems—does not change. It is certain that when we speak of substances or subsistences, we refer to that which is generally pertinent to them, i.e., that which they seem to sustain. Now, we know that everywhere in the world Christ's church sings that the property resides in the persons and the unity in the essence.[10] Because of such properties, which seem to be inherent to the divine persons and distinguish them from one another—according to a certain similarity with that which is really the object of inherence— these persons can be called (even if this is not appropriate) "substances" or "subsistences." Indeed, the three elements of the Trinity—whether they are called persons, substances, or subsistences—are not to be intended in any other way than "those who possess substantial being under a distinctive and particular property." For this reason, then, if we consider the words [above], I said "*under*" and not "*through*" so that you would understand the reason why the elements of the Trinity are defined as "substances" or "subsistences" (although improperly). In truth, we say that properties are pertinent to the persons, and yet—if we ponder well—this pertinence does not allow them to subsist but to

---

10. See Augustine, *Trinity*, V.8.10.

exist. And it is for this reason that persons must be more rightly defined as "existences" than "substances" or "subsistences."

Those who concentrate their attention only on divine realities do not detect any property by which the divine essence could be distinguished from another divine [essence]. In the divinity, in fact, there is only a single essence, contrary to that which happens with properties which make the divine persons different from one another. Consequently, from this point of view, they do not see how one could define the [divine] unity as substance, and thus they call it simply—and rather appropriately—"essence." Regarding the plurality of persons—to which properties are pertinent—they call these "substances," although less appropriately.

In the uncreated essence there is no property that makes it different from another uncreated [essence], since—as we have said—there is only one uncreated [essence]. Nonetheless, we certainly find [in it] a property by which it is distinct from any other created essence. Looking at this, some do not simply call it "essence" but also "substance." Equally, they alter the proper meaning of subsistence and use it to indicate the persons.

Now, in order to be able to distinguish briefly between substance and subsistence, according to the interpretation of these [theologians], by [the word] "substance" you should understand that which I have previously called "common existence." By [the word] "subsistence" [you should understand] that which I have called "incommunicable existence." Thus, if someone has understood how multiple existences may be found in the unity of substance—from that which I have previously said—he [must] have also understood how multiple subsistences may reside [in that substantial unity]. I do realize that these arguments might be discussed with a more subtle reasoning, but I am convinced that that which we have said is enough for the simple people and to those I intend to serve.

After all, we must observe and firmly believe that the three components of the Trinity—in any way in which they are named (be they substances, subsistences, or persons)—are to be understood with regards to the substance. In fact, all these terms, according to objective truth, do not indicate anything else but three [entities] possessing rational being, [each one] according to a different and personal property. It is known that where we have no rational substances, there can be no beings provided with reason. In actual fact, each person must possess this "being provided with reason" by effect of an incommunicable property. I am not referring to the Greeks because, as Augustine writes, they interpret "substance" in a different way than us.[11] As it is for the Latins, though, I think that it is not possible to find any word that can be applied to the divine plurality better than the term "person." Besides, to a faithful soul, nothing must be more authoritative than that which is on everyone's lips and is confirmed by the catholic authority.

XXI

In the measure in which we have been able, we have accomplished the task that we had previously set. [We have clarified] the manner by which the meaning of substance is different from the meaning of person, and the way in which multiple persons can exist in the unity of substance. Thus, now—if you please—let us verify whether that famous definition of person formulated by Boethius may be appropriate [to indicate] only the person and each [person]. In fact, it will not be necessary to look for another definition if [this] is satisfactory and has universal value. Now, in order to be perfect, a definition must take entirely and exclusively into consideration the reality of the object that is to be defined. Indeed, in order to deserve its name, [such a definition] needs to reach the limits of the defined [reality] without breaching them. It must be appropriate to all [the defined reality] and only to it, and it must be an adaptable [proposition].

Boethius' definition of a person is as follows: *an individual substance of rational nature.*[12] In order for [this definition] to be universal and perfect, it is necessary that each individual substance of rational nature be a person, and conversely, that each person be an individual substance of rational nature.

Thus, with regards to the divine substance—I wonder—since [such substance] is absolutely one and single—again, I wonder—is it perhaps individual? Actually, we do not hesitate to believe that such a substance is a Trinity of persons, and—as proven above—we deduce it from evident arguments. Thus, if the divine substance must be defined as individual, then an individual substance of rational nature will be

---

11. See Augustine, *Trinity*, V.8.10.

12. Boethius, *Liber de Personas et duabus Naturis*, 3 (*PL* 64, 1343).

something different to a person. The Trinity, in fact, is not a person and cannot properly be defined as person. From this perspective, then, such a definition of "person" does not appear to be convenient only to "person." Conversely, if that substance is not to be defined as individual, it seems certain that there is a person who is not an individual substance, because he is divine. Therefore, this definition of "person" cannot be appropriate to each person. Therefore, whether you say that the divine substance is individual or not, the aforementioned definition seems not to be universal.

XXII

It is certain that the infinite cannot be the object of an adequate definition. Yet, perhaps we might record some sort of progress in the knowledge of God if we tried to delineate a definition of the divine person, in the measure the Lord will allow. According to that meaning of "existence," which we have previously expounded, without inconvenience we could perhaps affirm that a divine person is an incommunicable existence of the divine nature. With the term "existence," as it is to be understood by the previous considerations, we indicate that which a substantial being is and from where it comes. These definitions are appropriate to each substance.

There is a generic existence that is common to all substances and [there is another] generic [existence], that is only common to all the rational [substances]; lastly, [there is] a specific [existence], common only to the angelic substances or only to the human ones. However, all existences of this kind are excluded in the case of God, since [in him] the meaning of existence is specified and determined by reference to divine nature. If we think carefully, we will be able to discover in the divine nature both a common existence to a plurality and a convenient existence to one, single person and—for this very reason—incommunicable. Is [the existence] common to a multiplicity not excluded, perhaps, from the term "incommunicable"? As a consequence we can affirm—not without foundations, we believe—that a divine person is an incommunicable existence of the divine nature.[13]

---

13. The divine substance has three incommunicable existences, each one distinct from the other.

XXIII

We define as "divisible" that which can be split both into multiple persons and into multiple substances, and that which can be shared by a plurality and entirely possessed by each of them. Conversely, we name "indivisible" that which can be appropriate only to one. Now, if we accept this definition of "divisible" and "indivisible," we will perhaps be able to affirm that any created person is an individual substance of rational nature, and that any person is an individual existence of rational nature.

Yet, in order to make more clear that which we have said, let us analyze it with greater accuracy. We have said that the term "existence" indicates substantial being. Without doubt, in line with the discussion above, this does not indicate the [etymological] origin of the word "substance," but that which is primary to it and which is appropriate to each substance. Thus, that which is primary to the substance is not the fact that it sustains and is subject to pertinence, but rather [the fact] that it is that which it is, that it subsists in itself and that it is not inherent to any subject. This condition is common to every human, angelic, and divine substance, and it is right to consider it as the most worthy and important characteristic in the created substance, since because of this it comes much closer to the divine similarity. Actually, in the measure in which it is subjected to accidents, it seems to move away from divine similarity. Thus, with reference to that which is primary to each substance, we can more appropriately speak of "essence" rather than "substance."

Besides, as we have said, with the word "existence" we indicate both that which possesses being in itself and that which obtains it from someone else. These conditions are common to each substance, since each being exists either because of itself or because of someone else's action. All the remaining things concerning this description of [person] are quite clear from our previous considerations, and do not require a new study. There is no need to explain why we call "person" only the individual and incommunicable [existence] rather than any existence.

XXIV

Maybe it will be made clear and intelligible if we say this: "person" is one who exists *only per se* according to a certain, singular mode of rational existence.

In our previous explanations we have clarified sufficiently the way in which the words "*one who exists*" should be interpreted. If we add "*only per se,*" it is because we properly talk about person only with respect to one, single being, distinct from the others by a particular property. Existing only *per se*, however, is a common condition to all individuals, both the animate and the inanimate ones. However, we never speak of person if not referring to a rational substance. It is because of this that to the first part—"one who exists only for himself"—we add: "according to a certain, singular mode of rational existence." Amongst the modes of rational existence, however, one is common to multiple natures, another is common to more than one substance of the same nature, and another one [is common] to multiple persons of the same substance. Yet, the personal property postulates a singular mode of rational existence without which the person cannot subsist. As a consequence, in order for "one existing only for himself" to be a person, he will necessarily have to possess a certain singular mode of rational existence.

The meaning we should associate with each of these [terms] seems quite clear from the above considerations; thus, there is no reason to linger and give explanations in this regard.

Therefore, we have expounded these arguments—within the limits of our ability—regarding the meaning, mutations, and description of person. At this point, if someone interprets the terms "individual," "person," or "existence" in a different way than that suggested by us and with a meaning which is not ours, rather his own, he will develop his argument and will bring his reasoning to an unacceptable conclusion. Let him know that he is not damaging me in any way, and if he is convinced that [he is doing] so, he will ridicule himself without even noticing.

XXV

To imply a plurality of persons in a unity of substance is typical of the divine nature. On the contrary, involving a plurality of substance in the person's unity is typical of the human nature.

Now then, if at some time the human person presents himself in one, single substance, this is not dependent on the nature's own condition but on its own degradation. From this we can easily perceive how the divine and human properties are opposite to each other. Thus, while these two [natures] look at each other from two antithetical positions and respond—so to say—in an opposite way, the angelic condition is to be put in an intermediate space. It comes close to both of these [two] because it is similar to both the first and the second [nature]. With the divine nature, it shares the fact that it never implies a plurality of substances in the unity of person, whilst with the human [nature] it shares the fact that it never involves a plurality of persons in the unity of substance. Behold, [this is] how the angelic dimension, by being intermediate, links [those two] opposite factors, as if by a sort of proportional criterion, and joins into one single harmony the dissonance of those contrasting [natures].

By saying so, I do realize that there is someone who thinks otherwise concerning the angels. In fact, even today there are people who think they have a body. Yet, if they searched with more effort, if they considered it more accurately, they would quickly discover—I believe— the correctness of my observations.

Who, if he is sane in his mind, will dare to deny that the rational nature's condition is so much more sublime and more noble the more it comes closer to the non-composite and supremely simple nature? Who could deny that an incorporeal creature, who is not subjected to each corporeal mass, by the effect of this property of its own, is closer to divine simplicity? [Who could deny that it is] more intimately united to [divine simplicity] than the nature composed by a corporeal and an incorporeal substance, in which the simplicity of one, single person is derived from the union of two essences? There is no doubt that the creature of higher quality is that subsisting in single and simple purity of a spiritual nature.

Now, let us imagine a human work in which we represent a human body with no head. The divine work—that is, the universal creation—would appear as such if there was no creature of higher level.

Let us add to this the arguments contained in the previous study about the attributes of the angelic nature. Which one seems to you—I wonder—[to be] the more worthy and more convenient order to the design of him who is supremely wise? [What about the fact] that in the trinity of natures—the divine, the angelic, and the human one—the characteristics of two [of them] be radically opposed to the third one, without any intermediary of any kind between them? [What about the fact] that a third [nature] is interposed between the two extreme [ones], united to both by a similarity and able to harmonise the abovementioned contrast?

Yet, if someone continues not to trust this argument that we are demonstrating, let him look at the Gospel's testimony and let him be persuaded by it. Indeed, does the Gospel not inform us that the Lord expelled a legion of demons from one, single man?[14] Now, a legion is made up of 6666 persons. If so many [demons] were cast out of a single man, they were in him before the expulsion. If we admit that demons have a body, I ask: where were they in that man? Were they in his spirit or in his body? We know that all bodies have a length, a width, a height; they have spatial dimensions and they can subsist only in a space containing them. The spirit, on the other hand, is not like that at all. Therefore, [the demons] were not in the spirit, but in [that man's] body. But in which way and in which part of [that] man could these many bodies find a place? Maybe you will observe that the angelic spirits—both the good and the evil ones—possess subtle bodies, but as subtle as they may be, two bodies—especially if of the same quantity—cannot occupy a single and same place. How small—I wonder—do you think the angelic body is, if you think the sole skin wrapping a man's body is capable to contain such a great number of angelic bodies? In making this digression we have gone too far from our argument. In the end, I am convinced that that which has been said about the set question is sufficient for a devout and simple spirit. There is nothing irrational in the commandment we receive to venerate one, single God in the Trinity and the Trinity in the unity.

14. Mark 5:9–13; Luke 8:30–33.

Synopsis of the Topics of the Fifth Book

I. Since we have established the unity of the divine substance, the plurality of persons, and the condition or reciprocal agreement between unity and plurality, the study of the properties of the persons remains.

II. In the supreme happiness there must necessarily be a fraternity full of joy amongst the persons, just as a state of absolute harmony amongst the properties cannot be missing from the supreme beauty.

III. The nature of things implies that there is a person who is from himself rather than from someone else.

IV. There can only be one person who exists only from himself.

V. In the divinity two persons possess being from an origin outside themselves, according to that mode of being which is eternal but not from itself.

VI. The procession of a person from another one can only be either mediated or non-mediated, or [it can be] mediated and non-mediated at the same time.

VII. On the procession that is only non-mediated. In the divinity, there must be a person who comes from only one.

VIII. On the procession that is both mediated and non-mediated. In the divinity, there must necessarily be a person that comes from two.

IX. In the divine nature, there is no room for a personal procession, which is only mediated.

X. In the divinity there can only be one, single [person] proceeding only from one, just as there only be one, single [person] receiving being from two.

XI. In the divinity there must necessarily be a person from whom no other is derived, and yet [this person] also does not come from himself.

XII. In the divinity, there can only be one person from whom no other is derived.

XIII. In the divinity there must necessarily be a person proceeding from another and from whom another one proceeds.

XIV. In the divine nature there can only exist a single person who proceeds from another and from whom another proceeds.

XV. In the divine nature there cannot be a fourth person.

XVI. The fullness of true love and the distinction of properties are considered in relation to this love.

XVII. The person of the Trinity in whom the possession of only gratuitous love in its fullness is appropriate.

XVIII. The person of the Trinity in whom the possession of only due love in its fullness is appropriate.

XIX. The person of the Trinity who possesses the exclusive attribute of obtaining fullness of both gratuitous and due love.

XX. Clear, rational demonstration of the fact that in the divinity there can be no room for a fourth person.

XXI. The numerous conclusions that can be derived from the reasoning formulated above.

XXII. The fact that fullness of gratuitous love consists of giving and fullness of due love consists only of receiving should not be interpreted as a work of grace but, rather, as an activity of nature.

XXIII. Concerning the substance of affection, there is supreme and single love in all persons, although in each of them it is distinct because of the difference of property.

XXIV. With regards to integrity and perfection, there are no differences in love and dignity [within the Trinity].

XXV. [On] that which is common to the persons and [on] that which is proper to each one. Further enquiries that are still to be made.

Book Five

I

As we have already said on previous occasions, each person necessarily possesses rational being according to an incommunicable property. However, in order for a person to be suitably defined divine, more than just this is necessary. Indeed, the requirement of a divine person is to have divine being. The divine being coincides with the super-substantial one, which is identical to the supremely simple being. In the supremely simple being the very *being* is identified with wisdom. In truth, only the divine substance possesses this being, and for this reason it is rightly defined super-substantial essence. Since in the divine nature we have only one supremely simple being, with no distinctions [within itself], it is for this reason that we claim—when referring to this [nature]—the unity of substance. Just as the unity of substance is certain, likewise the plurality of person [is certain as well]. After all, there cannot be plurality where there is no otherness, just as there cannot be otherness if there is no distinction of any sort.

How can plurality be in harmony with an undifferentiated being? Yet, where there is no differentiated being, differences and distinctions can take place in existence. In fact, if a plurality possesses a being which has no distinctions [yet has] different origins, [this plurality] will indeed present a unity of substance, but on the other hand, will not exclude multiple existences. Just as we have previously demonstrated, the divine person is nothing else but an incommunicable existence.

Hence, we must observe that any divine existence convincingly reveals itself to be a person by this feature [alone], i.e., as long as it has even just one incommunicable attribute. In fact, even if it may have more than one incommunicable attribute, just one is sufficient to prove that we are dealing with a person. In this way, it seems clear that this [person] is someone individually distinct from all the others by that property. We have touched on these topics again with this brief summary—even though they have already been discussed—so that we will approach the themes we still need to examine both in a quicker and more equipped way.

Now, since we have proven the divine substance's unity, the persons' plurality, and the reciprocally agreeing relationship between unity and plurality, we will enquire about the property of the single persons and we will detect that which distinguishes each of them [from the others]. We now know that the three components of the Trinity (whether they are defined "persons," "existences," or any other way), again, these three components are distinguished according to certain properties. We know that they are to be sought only in relation to the diversity of [their] original cause. Yet, we still have not discovered, in [the] light of reason, which attributes are proper to each of them.

Thus, let us now carry out these enquiries in the same manner as those that we have already made, so that we may be allowed to prove by reason that which we believe by faith, and so to confirm this by the witness of a certainty, grounded in rational demonstration.

II

In the first instance, let us affirm that which we all universally recognise by natural instinct—so to say—and that which we see confirmed by the continual life practice and daily experiences. It is evident that the more multiple persons are closely related, the more they are united, and the more they are united, the happier they are.

Who would dare to affirm or be so presumptuous to claim that that which is recognized as the happiest thing may lack that fullness of supreme happiness? [Who would dare to say] that he would find [in it] that which is undoubtedly considered as less happy? Thus, if you claim that each person possesses being by his own activity, the plurality constituted by such persons would neither result in being united by any affinity nor bonded by any link of reciprocal relationship. Truly, who could think or dare to affirm that the supreme unity's plurality is [at the same time] united on one hand but distant on the other, and, in fact, almost extraneous to itself? [Who could think] that there is a total lack of distinction in the [persons'] unity and that there is no kind of union in their plurality?

Which plurality do you consider to be more beautiful? Which is preferred in your opinion? Is it, perhaps, the [plurality] in which distinction comes from different properties in absolute order, and [whose] union is the result of beautifully arranged relationships of proportions? Or is it the [plurality] in which we neither have reciprocal ties of agreement in distinction nor [reciprocal ties] of distinction in agreement, and in which there is no harmonic order of different realities? I think that no one believes that that which is more beautiful may be absent in the supreme beauty, and that conversely one could find [in it] that which is less beautiful.

Thus, we must be convinced that, on one hand, the happiest kinship amongst persons cannot be absent in the supreme happiness, and that, on the other hand, highest beauty necessarily requires multiple attributes, arranged together in perfect harmony.

In any case, in order to avoid this expounded reason appearing to someone as perhaps plausible but not necessary, it will be opportune to analyse these very affirmations with a deeper reasoning.

III

That which has been observed about the "substance" at the beginning of this work can now be applied without hesitation to the "person." In fact, in both instances the same arguments come to mind and, if applied to similar realities, they lead to conclusions that resemble each other.

Let us repeat now with regards to the person [that which] we have already said concerning the substance: i.e., one [person] must necessarily exist who has his being by his own action and not by someone else's [activity]. Otherwise, without doubt, there would be an infinite number of persons in the single divinity. Actually, if one [person] originated from another one, and this other one from a third, and if according to this manner of progression any person existed by the effect of another one, a chain such as this—no doubt—would continue indefinitely and such a process would never end. In this way, it would happen that the series of beings and their succession—which absolutely must have a beginning—would not have any. I refer not to a temporal principle, but rather to a [principle] of origin or, at least, of cause.

Yet, in these considerations—and in others of the same kind—truth is *per se* so evident and [my] argument so clear that it does not require any confirmation at all. It appears evident to anyone who has intelligence and uses his reason that no one does that which he cannot do. [It is evident] that no one can give that which he does not have. [It is evident] that there was a time when all things that started being did not exist; that all things that did not exist at a time started being in time; that no composition can be without anyone composing it; that no division can be without anyone dividing it. [It is evident] that there is someone of whom nothing is higher; that there is someone of whom nothing is better. Whoever listens to these [affirmations], and to [others] of the same sort, will immediately agree and will have no reason to doubt, as long as he understands the meaning of the words.

Consequently, if we want to go against our good common sense multiplying infinitely the number of divine persons, we must admit with confidence that one person possesses his being from himself, without originating in any way from elsewhere.

Now, since we have established that there is a person [originating] from himself and not from someone else, we must verify whether [such] an existence is communicable or incommunicable, i.e., whether possessing being from himself belongs to only one person or if this same [property] may be shared by a plurality [of persons].

IV

Since this subject necessitates a more attentive consideration and invites us to a more sublime understanding, it is necessary that, like builders, we dig deeper, so to say, and base our reasoning on the solid ground of certainty. In fact, it is our duty to construct our building as high as the intelligence of the most sublime mysteries. We must start, then, from that which no one can doubt.

It is clear that every existing thing possesses either a composite or a simple being. Likewise, it is clear that everything that [a being] possesses is possessed either by participation or in fullness. It is one thing to compose something single on the basis of multiple and distinct elements, [it is] another thing to divide between a plurality that which is single and share it amongst many, as one prefers. Yet, as we have observed, there is no composition without anyone composing it, and there is no division without someone dividing it.

Therefore, let us verify whether that which really possesses being from itself can have a composite being. It is obvious that any composition requires someone to compose it. Then, if something is not capable of existing without the help of him who composes it, it obviously does not possess *that which it is*, by its own [ability]. Therefore, it is clear that that which exists because of itself cannot have a composite being. Consequently, that which has no origin or source necessarily possesses the absolutely simple being.

In addition, in him who has the absolutely simple being, *being* is necessarily identified with *being able*, just as wisdom coincides with power. Thus, we know that which we need to know concerning *being*; now, let us enquire concerning *being able*. Then, let us examine his *ability*:[1] whether he has it in fullness or by participation. But, where there is participation there is also partition, as there is neither participation without partition nor partition without anyone to divide it. Thus, whoever can only have a participated power doubtlessly needs the intervention of one who divides. Consequently, it is clear that he who exists because of himself, has this *ability* of his by someone else's action, if he has received a participated power. But if his *ability* is derived from someone else's action, his *being* too [will] certainly [have the same origin], as *being* and *being able* are not different realities in him (as it has been demonstrated). To summarise, either he has both of them from himself, or he has neither of the two from himself.

---

1. It is rather unfortunate that throughout the entire chapter the tight and effective force of the Latin can hardly be maintained in translation. The rhetorical force of the construction is clearly built around Richard's use of *posse* as a nominal infinitive in parallel with *esse*. In addition, a further challenge to any English translation is given by the subtle technical vein of the term *posse* as Richard appears to use in this instance. In this chapter, Richard's *posse* has been translated as both *being able* and *ability* (clearly implying an active meaning!), leaving the most common rendering of *power* for the following chapters. In fact, it is important to understand immediately here that that which Richard is interested in highlighting is not really the infinite strength of the absolutely simple being, which operates wonders, but rather its omnipotence as the actualized capability of doing anything, as that coincides with its very being and it is a consequence of it.

From this, then, we deduce that he who exists from himself cannot have *ability* from a participation in power. Then, he possesses in fullness that which he cannot have by participation. But fullness of power means *being able* to do everything. Thus, if one person—in whom being and *being able* are identified—possesses his being from himself, he also possesses his *ability* out of himself. Yet, his *being able* [really] means *being able* [to do] everything: therefore, all *ability* comes from him [i.e., this very person]. If all *ability* comes from him, every *being* and every existence come from him as well. Thus, everything that exists comes from him: every essence, every existence, every person. I mean: every human, angelic, and divine person.

Therefore, if all persons have their being by this person's action, it is absolutely certain that only [this person] has no beginning. It is also equally clear that no other [person] can exist if not because of this one, since it is from him that all *ability* comes.

You can see that such an existence is absolutely incommunicable and cannot be shared by a plurality.

V

We are now certain of the fact that to be a person that originates from himself constitutes a totally incommunicable existence. Therefore, we can obviously conclude from this that to be a person with an origin outside of himself does not constitute an incommunicable existence. Otherwise, there would not be—and there could not even be—more than two persons in the divinity. Thus, to exist from himself is specific and proper to only one person, while it is a common characteristic to the other [persons] not to be from themselves. You can perceive, then, how the incommunicable existence produces a communicable one—or rather a common one—which proceeds and has its origin from the first one.

Thus, with irrefutable arguments, we have come to that mode of existence of which we have spoken at the beginning of this work, when we brought forth reasons [that seemed] more plausible than compelling. In fact, as we anticipated there, we have a three-fold mode of existence: one by which we have an eternal, self-originated existence; another one, by which existence is neither self-originated nor eternal; a third [mode], which is intermediate between the two above, which implies an eternal existence but not self-origination. In fact, as demonstrated before, all the persons are equal amongst themselves and co-eternal. Thus, just as that existence which finds in itself its own origin exists from eternity, similarly even that one which proceeds from it has its being from eternity. Conversely, the mode of existence which distinguishes between two persons implies an eternal being, yet not a self-originated one.

You can see, then, how different—actually, completely opposite—the properties of the other two modes of existence are. With regards to the third mode of existence, it unites these opposite properties according to a sort of proportional relationship and, with its mediation, favours a mutual agreement between the two extremes, sharing with one the fact that it exists from eternity, and with the other the fact that it is not self-originated.

At this point we know the specific property of a single person. We also know that which the other [two] have in common. However, we have not yet discovered by reasoning what the attributes are of each of these [two].

VI

Those realities which we know by experience indicate to us that which we are to look for regarding the non-experienced, divine realities, since *the invisible realities which concern God are contemplated by the intellect through created objects.*[2] When we want to climb we generally use a ladder, because we are humans and we cannot fly. Let us use, then, the resemblance [offered by] the visible realities as our ladder. In this way, from such an observation point, we will be able to discern as in a mirror that which we are not able to perceive *in se* as it is.

In the human reality we observe that a person proceeds from another [one]. And such a procession[3] can evidently happen in three ways. A person proceeds from another [person] sometimes only in a

---

2. Rom 1:20.

3. In this case the term *processio* is not used as a technical term, as it is when applied to the Holy Spirit, but as a term of general applicability. The reader must always pay attention, as Richard sometimes uses the same term with different significances, generating the possibility of confusion.

non-mediated way, some other [times] only in a mediated way, [lastly,] at other times both in a mediated and a non-mediated way. Both Jacob and Isaac proceeded from Abraham's substance: the procession of the first [of them], however, was only mediated, while that of the second [of them] was only non-mediated. In fact, Jacob came forth from Abraham's flesh, but through Isaac. Eve, Seth, and Enoch proceeded from Adam's substance, but while the first of these processions was only non-mediated, the second one was at the same time mediated and non-mediated. Actually, Seth proceeded from Adam's substance in a non-mediated way as he was derived from his seed, but [also] in a mediated way, as he was generated through Eve. In the human nature the persons' procession happens in three different forms. Even if this [nature] appears to be very distant from that single and supremely excellent one, we still can find a certain resemblance, since the [human] was created according to the image of the [divine one].[4] It is necessary, thus, to go up from this nature to that observatory of contemplation, and to enquire with extreme care about that which we [can claim] to be [found in the divine nature and that which we] cannot, on the basis of a similarity/dissimilarity relationship. However, if we claim that in God there are three genres of existence, which we have previously identified, besides that [existence] that originates from itself, we seem to introduce in that nature a four-fold number of persons. Consequently, we need to carefully examine which of these properties are really found in God, since it is impossible for all of them to be there together.

VII

Now, it is absolutely certain and indubitable that from that existence which precedes everything, must necessarily proceed [another one] in a non-mediated way, otherwise that one will be destined to remain alone. Indeed, it is clear that there cannot be any other existence that does not proceed from that [existence] in a non-mediated or mediated way.[5] Now, if there is no non-mediated procession, there cannot be any mediated one, and there cannot be that [procession] which is

---

4. Gen 1:27.

5. I.e., Every existing thing must have been either immediately originated or originated through a mediation of the first, who caused himself.

both mediated and non-mediated at the same time. On the other hand, nothing prevents a non-mediated procession from taking place, even if it were the case that a mediated one would not happen. Whilst the non-mediated procession takes place between two persons, the mediated one always requires a trinity of persons. In fact, it is necessary that in the non-mediated procession there be a person who produces another one, and another person who proceeds from the first. Furthermore, this mediated procession demands a third [person] in which the mediation is realized, besides the [two] persons in which [this procession] begins and ends.

According to nature, duality precedes trinity, as the first one can subsist without the second, but the second one can never subsist without the first. With regards to nature, then, even that procession which can take place in a duality of persons has priority over that which can only be realized in a trinity of persons. However, in the plurality of divine persons and in true eternity, nothing precedes and nothing follows, and there is neither a before nor an after from a temporal viewpoint. In spite of this, that which cannot be "former" on a temporal plane, can precede under a causative profile, and—for this reason—a natural [profile].

Actually, as we have affirmed much earlier, perfection of a single person necessarily postulates coexistence with another one. It happens, then, that one is the other one's cause. Indeed, where there is fullness of divinity, there is also fullness of goodness and—consequently—fullness of charity-love. Fullness of charity-love, for its part, wants each [person] to love the other as [each person] loves himself.[6] In the opposite instance, one's love could still increase. It is necessary, though, for [this person] to have someone who is worthy of him, in order to rightly love him as [he loves] himself. Then, if it is true that the first person is supremely good, he will be completely unable not to want that which highest charity-love implies. And if it is really true that this [person] is omnipotent, everything that he wants will happen. In summary, according to charity's necessity, [this person] will want to possess someone equal to himself in dignity and, by the work of his own power, he will possess him whom he wants to possess. This corresponds to that which we have already said, i.e., that the perfection of a single person is the cause of a second [person's] existence. This [second person] clearly

6. Matt 22:39.

has his existence from him who is the very cause of his existence.[7] After all, as we have already observed, [this second person] could only have existed because of him, from whom all *ability* comes.

Thus, one reason confirms another reason with its witness, and that which the first demonstrates is confirmed by the second. As you can notice, a person comes from [another] person; an existence from [another] existence; one, single [person] from [another] single [person]; that which can proceed from that which cannot proceed; that which can be born from that which cannot be born. To be brief: one, single [person], united with no mediations to [another] person, as one, single [person] proceeds immediately from another one. We have recognized, [in a manner in which] no doubts can remain, how such an existence is proper to the divine nature. But we have not yet concluded by firm reason whether this [existence] is communicable or incommunicable.

VIII

Since in the Trinity it is certain that the third person has an origin outside of himself, he necessarily receives his being from one of the [other persons] or from both at the same time. Then, we are left to examine how things really are and the way in which we can demonstrate them.

It has been previously demonstrated with an indisputable argument that a supremely worthy person requires someone equal to himself in dignity. Yet, in order to be worthy at the same level as an omnipotent person, it was necessary for him to receive omnipotence from [such an] omnipotent [person], so to possess an equal—or rather, the very same—omnipotence. In fact, as we have often said, omnipotence can only be one. But if this [other person] has received the same power, he has certainly received it from him who possesses power, being, and existence in an absolute way. [That is,] from him who—as it has been argued before—confers being to every essence and every existence. Thus, if both of them hold the same power in common, it follows that the third person of the Trinity has received his being and possesses his existence because of both [of them].

Yet, facing these affirmations, someone may object: if the same power, held by him who cannot be born, has been received and is pos-

---

7. I.e., the person who caused it.

sessed by the person who is born, it must mean that this [last person] has received and possesses the power to be from himself, which is only proper to the person who cannot be born. Whoever formulates this objection, however, seems to me not to realize that which he is saying. Yet, in order to better clarify that which we are affirming, let us perform a deeper analysis of this particular argument. You observe that if he who cannot be born has communicated fullness of his power only to that [person] who proceeds from him in a non-mediated fashion, he has also given this [person]—because of this—the ability to exist by his own activity, since [he who cannot be born] is omnipotent and holds every power.

To this I answer by saying that [this person] exists by his own activity only if it is possible for him to exist by his own activity. Indeed, the divine nature is absolutely unchangeable. Thus, if [this person] exists because of himself, it is certain that he is that which he is without anyone being his cause. However, if this power has been given to him by him who cannot be born, this means he has received it as a gift from someone else. Then what? Does he possess because of himself that which he possesses by effect of someone else's gift, if the other [person] has not donated it to him? You see very well—I believe—how contradictory such an affirmation is. In fact, it is absolutely contradictory that one and the same thing be possessed because another one has donated it without this other one having donated it. [In such a case], only one being [would] be something and at the same time he [would] not. Is there anything more impossible?

Thus, as we have previously said, [the supremely worthy person] has transmitted to the existence that proceeds from him in a non-mediated fashion all that could have really been transmitted by him who is omnipotent. [And] the supremely worthy person [did this, so that he might] have another [person] worthy of him, according to that which fullness of goodness required. [Both] these [persons], then, share that power from which both everyone's being and power derives. So, every essence, every person, every existence is derived from this twofold existence: even that [existence] who is the third person of the Trinity.

Without a doubt, this affirmation is confirmed by the conclusion of the above reasoning in our investigation of the Trinity. It is proven, there, with a clear argument—or better, it is repeatedly demonstrated—that just as perfection of the sole [first person] is the second [person's] cause, likewise, perfection of both [persons] certainly causes the third person of the Trinity. Just as one, single [person's] perfection demands another one with his same dignity, similarly—without a doubt—both [persons'] perfection requires another [one], to be loved in the same way. But, since we have already accurately expounded these arguments, it does not seem appropriate to waste time here again on the same themes: if one pleases, one will be able to go back to that section.

With regards to the third person, that which must come out as absolutely certain—and of which we must be strongly convinced—is that he receives existence from those very [persons] who are the cause of his existing. Thus, in the light of reason, we can affirm, at this point, that the third person of the Trinity has his being from the other two. Well, we know that he originates from [these other] two. However, we have not yet demonstrated in a rational way whether such an existence is communicable or incommunicable.

IX

We have now discovered for the greatest part that which we previously set out to investigate. We have discovered that by necessity there is one, single existence united only in a non-mediated way with the one who cannot be born. We have also discovered another existence linked to the same existence with both a mediated and non-mediated bond of kinship. We are left to discover, then, whether there is—or there can be—another one, united to it only in a mediated way.

There is a thing that no one in his right mind, I believe, could think, i.e., that in the divinity there is a person who is not able or willing to see him who cannot be born without mediation—so to say, face to face.[8] What else can *"to see"* mean in this case if not *"to know by seeing and to see by knowing"*? Yet, of what does knowledge of him who cannot be born consist, if not of possessing fullness of wisdom? In God, knowing and being are identical. As a consequence, whoever communicates knowing communicates existing as well. Thus, he from whom one obtains wisdom is the same as the one from whom one obtains existence. If [a person] immediately receives wisdom from another one, he will also receive existing from the same one. If we say that [this person] does

8. Gen 32:30; Exod 33:4; Deut 5:4; 1 Cor 13:12.

not see [the other] immediately, we must logically recognize that this [person] does not have an entire contemplation of truth. Therefore, he does not posses—in this aspect—entire fullness and, consequently, he does not have true divinity.

Someone could counter [that which I have said] with the following: just as every person sees the one proceeding from him, similarly, every proceeding [person] sees the one who produces him. Why could the same reasoning, demonstrating that the latter proceeds from the former, not demonstrate that the former proceeds from the latter? To this, then, I briefly answer by saying that when every divine person contemplates another [divine person] he receives fullness of wisdom and—for this reason—divine being, unless he obtains it from another source. In fact, if he does not obtain it from another source, he must necessarily receive it in the way in which we have said. But if he obtains it from another source it is not necessary for him to receive it also in that way. This can be made clearer by an example. Let us consider a truth written [in a book]. Someone knows it from another source. Some other does not know it from another source. Both of them, anyway, can read and understand: from such a reading, though, only he who has not learned from a different source achieves the knowledge of the truth written in the book.

Thus, since all the divine persons reciprocally and with no mediation contemplate one another, they diffuse the ray of supreme light onto each other or receive [it] from each other. And since they see with no mediation, they are united with no mediations. Then, it is impossible that in the divine nature there is a person united to another only through a mediated kinship, and this reasoning confirms that which has previously been said on the third person's procession. Actually, who could deny that this [person] knows the other persons by seeing them and sees them by knowing them? Now, both these persons constitute one, single, and same wisdom. Thus, since he does not possess anything from himself, as it is known, it must follow that he receives knowledge from contemplation of wisdom, and because of this [he receives] his being, since being and knowing coincide in God.

At this point, our reflection has allowed us to find that which we had set out to seek. We have learnt that in the divine nature we have a procession which is only non-mediated and another which is at the same time both mediated and non-mediated. There is absolutely no procession [that is] only mediated—and there could not be any.

X

From these solid affirmations of ours, we can certainly and indubitably deduce that if there could have been also a fourth person in the divinity, he would have had his origin—without a doubt—from the other three. If it were not so, he would be united to one of them only through a mediated bond of kinship, and he would contemplate him only in a mediated way. If there could have been also a fifth [person] in God, for the same reason, this would proceed with no mediations from the other four. By this type of reasoning, we will always reach the same conclusion, no matter how we want to prolong with our thought the series of these progressions.

After all, this assertion is confirmed by that which we have already said. Actually, just as the two persons share that power from which the third [person] originates, likewise the three [persons] would certainly share that power from which the fourth would necessarily originate, if there were room for a fourth [person] in the divinity. In the opposite instance, the two persons would be so stingy to keep for themselves that which they could give to a third one, without compromising their respective properties. That which we are saying concerning these [persons] could also be considered valid with regards to other [persons] who would follow. As much as you can continue on this line, in fact, you will always see the same arrangement.

We must underline that properties are differentiated only on the basis of the number of persons who communicate being. In fact, the first one of them has his being from no one else; the second one receives it only from one; the third one receives it from the [other] two. And if the number were greater, we would find for all, the same kind of progression. This is how this order of differences is born and how it is developed, in the same manner as the succession of numbers.

It must also be observed that on the grounds of each of these differences [in the way of procession] there can be no more than one person. [The person] proceeding from another person can only be one. Similarly, from two [persons] only one [person] can proceed.

Otherwise, if two [other persons] proceeded from only one [person], certainly none of these two would be bound to the other without mediations, and we have already demonstrated with clear arguments how this is impossible. That which has been said regarding only one difference [in the way of procession] can also be affirmed concerning any other.

In this way, we have solved two problems, which we had previously left unsolved. In fact, since from one person only one, single existence can proceed, and from two [persons] only one, single [existence] can proceed, it is certain that both these existences are incommunicable. As a consequence, just as in the divinity there is only one person who is from himself, likewise, there can be only one person originating from one, single [person]. And [there can be] only one [person] possessing his being from two [persons].

XI

We have previously detected the differences between the personal properties. [We have discovered] how [the persons] are united with one another and proceed according to the series and succession of numbers.

But if there were as many divine persons as the possible number of such differences, they would certainly be countless. Then, one must investigate more deeply the persons' properties so that no troublesome doubt may be raised regarding their number.

Earlier we demonstrated that in the divine persons' plurality, necessarily there must be one, single person, who originates from himself. However, just as there must be a person who is not derived, similarly, there must be another one from whom no other person is derived. In fact, reason requires [us to affirm it so], in both instances, and [our] demonstration proves it. Actually, if in the true divinity there was no person from whom no other [person] derived, but each person proceeded from another and produced another [person], the prolongation of such a succession would continue indefinitely and this series would not find an end to its own multiplicity. No thought can conceive this, and every reasoning dismisses [this option] neatly. In the plurality of divine persons, then, it is necessary that there should exist one [person] from whom no other originates. It is necessary that this very person obtain the principle of his existence from another [person]. Likewise, the [person] who does not exist by some other [person's] activity must be another [person's] cause of existence. Both of these affirmations have the same rational motivation and a parallel argument [can be made]. Since rational evidence demonstrates that only one, single person can be from himself, if [this person] did not have another [person] originating from him, he would eternally remain alone. However, as we have demonstrated, a multiplicity of arguments proves that true divinity and solitude are incompatible, and it declares plurality of persons. It is necessary then that in God there be [one, single person] who does not receive the principle of existence from any other source, but who [is able] to communicate it. It is necessary also that there be [another person] receiving from others that which he is, but who does not communicate this to any other [person].

XII

It must be considered certain that in the divinity there is a person from whom no other [person] proceeds, as we have already said. Someone, however, could still have this question in mind: is such a characteristic proper to only one person or, rather, can it be shared among multiple [persons]?

If the persons sharing this characteristic were two, then certainly none of these two would proceed from the other. If none of these two proceeded from the other, they would not be united with each other in a non-mediated fashion. However, if they were not reciprocally united in a non-mediated way, they would be linked to one another only through a mediated relationship bond. The above demonstration shows with clear reasoning that [this] is utterly impossible. As a consequence, it is the exclusive property of only one, single person to have absolutely [no other] that proceeds from him.

Just as in the divinity there is only one person who does not proceed from another, likewise—without a doubt—there is only one, single [person] from whom no other is derived. In both instances, we will have an incommunicable existence which cannot possibly be shared by multiple persons. In such a plurality of person, in fact, there is only one that receives and has his being from another, without communicating it to another.

We have now analysed with clarity the attributes of two persons of the Trinity. At this point, we are not allowed to doubt that any longer.

XIII

With this twofold property of persons in mind we can deduce with confidence that which our understanding must be regarding the attributes of that intermediate [person] between the two considered. Since in God there can only be one [person][9] derived from no other, it follows that the [person] that we are going to analyse now does not exist from himself. Likewise, if it is true that in God only one person[10] has no one proceeding from him, it is necessary that this [person] of whom we are speaking [now] gives origin to another person. In summary, this person proceeds from one, yet allows another person to proceed from him.[11] Thus—as we have said—we know with certainty that which we must believe regarding this person's properties. Without a doubt, this affirmation agrees with that which we have previously claimed on the basis of our reflections. In fact, this [intermediate] person, proceeding in a non-mediated fashion only from the [person] who did not originate from another, seems to have—or even, he actually has—both characteristics [of the other two persons]. In fact, he communicates to another—integrally and with no diminishment—[that very] being which he possesses from the fullness received from him who did not proceed from any other person. In the divinity, in fact, the third person proceeds both from him who is generated and from him who is not generated.

Here the [various] reasons agree with one another and the [various] evidences refer to each other. Therefore, it appears to be clearer than light that we have detected three distinct properties in the three

9. I.e., the first one.

10. I.e., the last one of the divine series of persons.

11. That is, this person—which is now the object of Richard's analysis—both proceeds and continues the procession chain. He is, therefore, an intermediate person in the sequence, distinct from the one that starts the procession series (as he has his origin in some other person outside of himself) and from the one who concludes this chain (as he continues the procession sequence).

[persons]. One is characterized [by the fact] that he does not proceed from any other [person] but he has another one proceeding from him. The second [person] is characterised [by the fact] that he proceeds from another [person] and that at the same time he has another [person] proceeding from him. The third [person] is characterised by [the fact that] he proceeds from someone else without having any other [person] proceeding from him. Furthermore, we already know that two of these properties are incommunicable. That which should be thought regarding the third,[12] is still to be determined on a rational basis.

XIV

Since by rational proof we are already know that two of the aforementioned properties are incommunicable, by the same reason we are keen to believe the same regarding the third. In any way, in order to avoid [the possibility] of letting this persuasion appear plausible rather than necessary, we will go deeper in our investigation on this point.

First of all, we must observe and carefully consider how the two persons' respective properties are in a relationship of opposition with one another and correspond reciprocally in an opposite sense, so to say. Indeed, transmitting fullness—and not receiving it—is proper to one [of them]; receiving [fullness]—without communicating it—[is proper] to the other one. No perfection can be absent, however, where we have supreme beauty. The consequence is evident and it is such that no balanced intellect can doubt it. Plurality of divine persons necessarily requires union in the most harmonious beauty and distinction in the most orderly balanced otherness. It is necessary, then, that in the divine plurality of persons—[which is] supremely good and most orderly balanced—a harmony in distinction and a difference in harmony may reign in [these] reciprocal relationships. Therefore, between the [person] having the property of communicating fullness without receiving it, and that [person] having the characteristic of receiving [fullness] without communicating it, it seems necessary to have an intermediate [person], having both the property of transmitting and receiving [fullness]. In this way, [this person], situated in an intermediate position

---

12. I.e., the intermediate person, which will turn out to be the *second* person in the Trinity.

[between the other two], is united on one hand to the first of them and on the other to the second one. In giving, [this intermediate person] will be in accord with the [other] giving [person]; in receiving, [he will be in accord] with the [other] receiving [person]. Conversely, in giving, he will be different from the non-giving [person] and in receiving [he will differ] from the non-receiving [person]. Therefore, as we have said before, with regards to both the [other persons], there will be a harmony in distinction, and a difference in harmony.

Conversely, let us see that which problems we must face if we claim two intermediate persons to be between the two extreme ones. Evidently, the first [person] will not be derived from anyone else; the second [person] will be derived only from one; the third [person] from two; the fourth [person] from three, as we have thoroughly explained above. Such a disposition, as it is laid out, seems to have something of an arithmetical balance.

Yet, let us see how that sort of geometrical proportion, shown above in the Trinity of persons, would be compromised by this insertion of a "quaternity" on the basis of a different reasoning. The property of the first person, in the causative order, will certainly be only that of conferring fullness. [The property of the two intermediate ones] will be that of both communicating it and receiving it. [The property] of the fourth one will only be that of receiving it without transmitting it on. As a consequence, the first of these persons is in harmony with the second one in only one respect. The second, is in harmony with the third one in two respects and not only in one. As for the third [person], it is not in harmony with the fourth in two respects, but only in one. You can clearly see how duplication and communication of one, same property not only does not establish proportion but also disrupts it and diminishes the beauty of the order rather than increasing it. But who can assert that in that sovereign beauty there is, or there could ever be, something capable of diminishing beauty and disrupting order? On the other hand, in the disposition of properties—as it has been identified before—the arithmetical proportion that results from one consideration, the geometrical proportion that results from another consideration, and the harmonic proportion that results from the linkage between Trinity and unity, [all] converge in an evident fashion and superbly refer back to each other.

It is proven that both giving and receiving fullness constitute the specific property of one, single person, and that such property—just as the other two—is incommunicable.

XV

It has been demonstrated without a doubt that all the divine persons share possession of fullness in its entirety. The distinction among the properties consists of two things: that of giving and that of receiving. Actually, as is clear from that which has already been said, giving-only is the property of only one person;[13] receiving-only [is the property] of only another person;[14] while the intermediate [person][15] between these two [has] both [the property] of giving and of receiving. Maybe, someone will object to this: if one property consists only of communicating, another one only of receiving, and the intermediate one between the two [consists of] communicating and receiving at the same time, why could there not be a fourth [person consisting] only of possessing, without giving and without receiving? Welcoming this hypothesis is like admitting the "quaternity" of the divine persons.

However, the clear argument made before loosens so well the knot of this question so that an attentive reader, although illiterate, cannot hold the slightest doubt in this regard. As it has already been demonstrated, in fact, evident reasons encourage us to conclude that in the divinity there is only one, single person, who exists because of himself. If this [person], who does not receive being and power from anyone else, does not transmit to anyone that which he possesses—as it has been said elsewhere—no doubt, he would eternally remain alone.

Therefore, we must conclude that in the divinity there is no room for a fourth property. Thus, even only as a hypothesis, "quaternity" is completely excluded. Thus, it is absolutely impossible that a fourth person could exist in the divine nature.

---

13. I.e., the first person of the Trinity.
14. I.e., the third person of the Trinity.
15. I.e., the second person of the Trinity.

XVI

We can confirm with an even higher and more evident reason that which has just been argued to exclude the hypothesis of "quaternity" from the divine nature. If we ponder over the fullness of true love and if we analyse with care the distinction of properties, we will probably discover more quickly that which we are seeking.

Fullness of true love resides only in the supreme and universally perfect love. But what really deserves the title of supreme love? Only so great a love than which none greater could exist! Similarly, [only] a love of such nature, than which nothing better could exist. From this we can deduce that fullness of authentic love cannot be possessed by a person who is not God. Contrarily, if even someone else—besides God—had been able to possess fullness of true love, this would mean than a person distinct from God could be equal to God in charity and—for this reason—in goodness. But who could say so, or could even be so presumptuous to think this?

Furthermore, we know that true love can either be only gratuitous, or only due, or of [a kind, combining] both these types together, i.e., gratuitous on one hand, and due on the other. When do we have gratuitous love? When someone gives gratuitously to someone else, from whom he has received no benefit. When is love due? When someone returns love to someone else, from whom he has received it gratuitously. And what about [the kind of] love combining both of these types together? It is that [love] by which one receives and gives gratuitously in a reciprocal love-relationship. Fullness of gratuitous love, fullness of due love, just like fullness of combined, perfect love, cannot be possessed in any way by a person who is not God. This is quite clear from that which has been said so we do not need to add anything else.

XVII

It has been clarified by now that in the Trinity there is one, single person who has everything by his own activity. This [person] does not receive anything from anyone else and possesses nothing coming from someone else's gift. Then, due love—such as we have described earlier—does not seem likely to be possessed by him, who has not received anything from anyone else—according to that which we have concluded—and who could neither be obliged nor indebted to anybody at all.

Conversely, [this person] is demonstrated to possess gratuitous love, as he gives abundance of his own fullness to those proceeding from him, with much generosity, with much liberality and gratuitously. Actually, what can the persons proceeding from him demand as due? What, I repeat, [can they demand], since they receive from him as a gift even [that] due love, with which they repay his gratuitous love? If this were not the case, they would possess something that they have not received from him; but our previous considerations demonstrate how this is impossible.

Hence, he has gratuitous—and only gratuitous!—love. I repeat: he possesses gratuitous love, and more importantly, [he possesses] fullness of gratuitous love. He is demonstrated to have fullness of gratuitous love because he does not keep this fullness for himself alone but he communicates it entirely. If he possessed all fullness but did not want to communicate it—although he could—he would not have fullness of gratuitous love. Our conclusion, then, is that he possesses fullness of gratuitous love, since he lacks no will and no power, with regard to actualizing generosity as a whole.

XVIII

[Let us now consider that] person who has the property to proceed without having any other [person] proceeding from himself. Since he receives from others everything he possesses, it is necessary for him to have fullness of due love. In the opposite instance, had he not re-paid those who supremely love him with a supreme love he would not be worthy of supreme love. He is loved by those very [persons] from whom he has received the whole of his fullness, as we know, precisely with a supreme love. Thus, what sort of undue love could he give in return to those who have communicated to him the whole of fullness? Since it is his own property—as we have said—not to have anyone pro-ceeding from him, there is no one in the divinity to whom he can direct fullness of gratuitous love. He can have gratuitous love with regards to a created person, but he cannot have fullness of gratuitous love for a creature, as he cannot conceive a disorderly love. Indeed, his love would be disorderly if he loved with supreme love him who does not deserve to be supremely loved. In fact, he who is not supremely good does not deserve supreme love. A person who is not God cannot be supremely good, because he cannot be equal to God.

As a consequence, for the above reason, such a [divine] person can possess—and actually does possess—fullness of due love. Conversely, he does not have—and absolutely cannot have—fullness of gratuitous love. Thus, it is necessary that the person who has no other [person] proceeding from him possesses fullness of only due love.

XIX

These considerations that we have formulated regarding these two persons shed light on that which we are to think about the remaining one. In fact, since his specific property is both to proceed from one [person] and to have [another person] proceeding from him, he must necessarily be full of both gratuitous and due love. He must address the fullness of both [types of love to the other two persons]: the first [type] to one and the second [type] to the other. Specifically, the supreme love, by which he loves that [person] from whom he receives everything without giving him anything in return, is due [love]. Conversely [the love] by which he supremely loves that [person] from whom he receives nothing [in return], but to whom he gives everything, is gratuitous [love].

At this point, now, we clearly know how to distinguish the single [persons'] properties—according to these thoughts. In fact, we have proven that in only one of the three we find supreme and solely gratuitous love. In another one [of them], we have supreme love but only of the due kind. In the remaining one, lastly, we find a supreme love, which is due, on one hand, and totally gratuitous, on the other. This is the threefold distinction of properties in supreme love. Nonetheless, in all [of the persons] there is one and the same love, the love [which is] supreme and truly eternal.

Now, on the basis of this consideration concerning true and supreme love, we can finally examine whether in the plurality of the divine persons there is room for a fourth person.

XX

The argument expounded up to this point proves with sufficient certainty that in the divinity there can only be one person existing from himself. From this, the scrupulous seeker of truth can conclude—with indubitable reason—that in that reciprocal charity-love among persons there can be only gratuitous love, due [love], and love that is [a combination] of both at the same time. On the other hand, regarding these three [persons], we know that fullness of gratuitous love is found only in one [of them], fullness of due love only in another one [of them] and fullness of gratuitous and due love [combined] is found only in the last one. What can we say about this? Does perhaps each of these three [persons] constitute a different reality from their [particular] love? Is, perhaps, [their] being different from [their] loving and [their] loving from [their] being, for each of them? Of what does that authentic and highest simplicity consist which we have already sought, found, and demonstrated with a rich witness of arguments?

It is necessary, then, without a doubt, that in sovereign simplicity being and loving coincide with each other. Therefore, in each of the [three, divine persons] the [single] person is identified with his [respective type of] love. As a consequence, the fact that there are multiple persons in one, single divinity means precisely this: that a plurality possesses one single and same affection, [i.e.,] the supreme affection. Or even—to say it better—a plurality *is* this affection, according to different properties. In God, the first person is nothing other than supreme love, distinguished by such a property; the second person is nothing other than supreme love, distinguished by another property; the third person is nothing other than supreme love, distinguished by a third property. The number of persons, then, will correspond to [the number] of properties. Since each person—as we have said—is identical to his own love and [the persons'] particular distinctions reside only in the three aforementioned [properties], we will not be able to find in God a fourth property and thus a fourth person.

No one must misinterpret us and reproach us for the way we spoke of "gratuitous" and "due." We know very well that these [words] do not always convey the same meaning. For example, we say than one person must love another because [this second one] deserves it. We also say that one has the duty to love another because through a gift or a benefit he has become his debtor. Likewise, even "gratuitous" can be used in both situations with different meanings. Thus, in order to avoid giving reason to critiques, with the formulated explanation we have specified the sense in which we want both terms to be understood. Then, let no one be surprised, let no one get annoyed if we use the words we possess to express that which we think of such a profound mystery.

Thus, in light of these explanations of ours, an evident argument concurs to confirm that which we have previously demonstrated, i.e., that in the divinity there can be no room for a fourth person.

XXI

If someone with a well-exercised intellect in matters such as these wants to meditate carefully on this last consideration he will be able to reach certain conclusions and solid arguments by this road alone on many questions already dealt with and proven by different demonstrations.

If one understands deeply that God is one, he will also understand by obvious reason that [God] is supremely good and supremely happy. However, if [this thinker] is not convinced about the plurality of persons, he will be able to climb up from that which he already believes to that which he does not yet understand in this perspective. Starting from this consideration only, I believe, he will be able to clearly see the persons' plurality—or rather, the whole Trinity—face to face, and to affirm it with solid arguments.

This consideration—as we have already demonstrated on the rational level—excludes the hypothesis of "quaternity," while it validates the persons' plurality, and—at the same time—it demonstrates also the substance's unity to those who believe and sincerely confess the true divinity.

By the effect of this consideration, the characteristics proper to each person appear clearly and are manifested. In fact, if accurately evaluated, it testifies—with clear arguments—that in the divinity there is one person who does not have his being from anyone else, a second [person] who exists by only one [person's] activity, and a third one who derives his origin out of two persons.

Let the reader understand the importance and profit of being able to give account of all these truths to whomsoever may ask.[16] In any case, since the considerations formulated up to this point have granted us the possibility of opening up an approachable way to this kind of research, let us leave a further study on this subject to the more zealous researchers.

XXII

We have claimed that one person possesses—or rather is—fullness of gratuitous love, while another one [possesses—or rather is—]fullness of due love. However, let nobody interpret this by saying that one [person] has some sort of superiority to the other, or that one [person] possesses—or rather is—a better or more perfect reality.

In God there are neither differences in levels nor hierarchical grades. It is known that one [person's] property consists of communicating fullness without having received it, while the other one's [property consists of] having received it without communicating it. Now, does this require that one be superior to the other? [Does this require] that one be more gifted than the other? Let us avoid [this]! Let us absolutely avoid such a hypothesis! Many have fallen into this and have got lost in a number of mistakes. He who possesses everything without having received it from another does not possess in any way any greater thing, any better thing, than he who received everything he possesses from others. Every perfection, every goodness, every blessedness are possessed by both him who has the particular property of giving, and—in the same fullness—by he who is characterized by the fact that he has received everything.

When we say that fullness of gratuitous love resides only in giving and fullness of due [love resides] only in receiving, no one must think that [this fact] is a work of grace rather than the effect of nature in that absolute equality.

The depth of such a great mystery is profound and a human will hardly ever—or even, never—be able to explain it with an adequate language. Let no one be surprised, let no one be critical if I wrap [truth] with poor clothes—such as my words—as the Virgin Mother [wrapped]

16. Allusion to 1 Pet 3:15.

the conceived Truth, when she gave birth to him. In fact, I am not able to use that which I know I do not have, that is the silk of a sophisticated prose. In any case, the truth of [my] thought has been demonstrated. It is up to the attentive and careful reader to express true concepts with opportune terms. As it concerns me, I will be profoundly grateful to him.

XXIII

Sincere and profound love has this effect: even in persons who differ in their being, [love] works in such a way that the same will and the same unwillingness may reign. The identity of will that we will find in those persons will be even greater, as in them their being coincides with their will! Consequently, there is only one being as such, with one, single will! In the Trinity, all have one, single truth, one, single charity, and one, single goodness, with no differences.

Thus, concerning the substance of affection, we will find one and the same love in all of the persons. Since this love in all [of them] is only one and supreme, it cannot be under any aspect greater in one than in the other, or better in one than in another. There is no doubt [about this], since in all [of the persons] there is absolutely the same will, and each one [of them] loves the other as himself and just as much as himself. If each of them loves the other as himself, he wants all that in God is communicable for any other [just as he wants it] for himself. If he loves [the other] as much as himself, he does not desire more ardently for himself as [he desires it] for the other—or more tepidly for the other as for himself—everything that in God is communicable.

Therefore, such a love will be of such a quality that a better one could not exist; it will be of such an intensity that a greater one could not exist. So, as we have said regarding the substance of affection, there will be one, single, and same love in all persons. However, [this love] will be beautifully distinct in each of them, on the basis of the different properties. In fact, in the meaning we have given to [these words] before, one will only have gratuitous love with respect to the other; this last one [will] only [have] due [love] with respect to the first one; in the third, [love] will be due towards one [of them] and gratuitous towards the other one. According to the human language, in fact, we rightly call gratuitous, that love which gives everything without asking for anything; [we define as] due [love], instead, that [love] which gives nothing to him from whom he receives everything.

Finally, we can say that this wave of divinity, this fullness of supreme love, only pours out without expanding in one [person], in another [person] it pours out and expands, in the third [person] only expands without pouring out. [This happens] even though we are dealing with one, single and same [wave] in all [three persons], and with one, single truth for all of them, although expressed in a many-fold way.

XXIV

At this point, perhaps, someone [may] consider that person who possesses everything he has by his own activity as superior in dignity and more excellent than the other [persons], if he considers the divine persons with a human mindset. Let us not claim that a hierarchy of any sort in dignity may be found there where supreme equality reigns without a doubt. He who is still not capable of understanding this by intellect will have the possibility to correct his thinking, through another consideration.

We must know—as I have previously said—that each person desires every communicable thing in God for another [person] as much as for himself. Conversely, [each person] desires every incommunicable thing which is proper to himself more for himself than for the other [persons]. Each person, actually, is the same substance with the others by that which is common to all of them, and is a unique person, distinct from the others, by his incommunicable property. Therefore, if each [person] desired that which is proper to himself more for another [person] than for himself, and desired that which is proper to another more for himself than for the other, what would [such a situation] mean? Should we not think that [this person] does not want to be the person he really is and he wants to be the person he is actually not? But I think no one would be so foolish to dare to believe this, or [to be able to] remain calm while listening to it.

The fact is that the person to whom a particular property belongs—which you believe to be an honorable peculiarity—desires it, no doubt, more for himself than for the others. The other [persons]—with no contradiction at all—prefer this [peculiarity] more for the former [person] than for themselves. So what? Should we, perhaps, judge as more generous those [persons] who prefer to see in another person more than in themselves that which you consider to be a trait of superiority? Or rather [should we, perhaps, judge as more generous] the [person] who prefers it more for himself than for another person? However, if we are right in considering [the two persons above] as more generous, why should they not also be judged as superior for the same reason?

You could add that possessing and donating fullness is much more glorious than being limited to having it without communicating it to anyone. Here, again, if one judges with a human mindset, one finds a superior glory in two persons. I claim again, though, that the third person of the Trinity prefers the [condition] you think of as superior, for the above reasons, more in the others than in himself, while the others prefer it for themselves more than for that one. Should we conclude, perhaps, that [the third person] is more generous than the others and for this reason more glorious?

Here, then, if we continue on the basis of human judgements, we reach the understanding that each divine person would be more or less generous and more or less worthy that the other: this [is] a false conception and blatantly in contradiction with itself! We must eradicate from our heart fantasies as such and we must accept in every aspect as faith truth that which we are still not able to perceive by intellect. It is certainly unquestionable that according to total perfection there is no difference of love or worth in the Trinity.

XXV

At this point, if you please, let us briefly summarise the results of our considerations brought forth in this book.

All the divine persons share together possession of the whole fullness. Only two persons share [the ability] of communicating the whole fullness. Only two share [the peculiarity] of receiving fullness. Only two share the fact that they do not possess both properties together. Indeed, only one has the property of transmitting only; only another one has the property to receive only; only a third one has the property of both receiving and transmitting. Only two persons share the fact that they have only one person proceeding from them. Only two of them share their origin from outside. Only two [of them] share the characteristic of not having both properties. In fact, one has only the property of having another person proceeding from him; another has only the property of proceeding; another one has the property both of proceeding from another and having [another person] proceeding from him. It is proper to one, single person not to proceed from any other. It is proper only to another [person] to proceed from one, single person. It is proper only to a third [person] to proceed from two [persons]. Finally, there is only one [person] who gives origin to no other, just as there is only one [person] at the origin of only one, and just as there is only one who is the [causative] principle of two.

Therefore, we have established that two persons share the property of not existing from their own activity, but proceed from elsewhere. At this point, we are left to analyze—with the highest care—how the processions of the first and the second [person] differ from one another. Once the differences distinguishing their reciprocal relationships are detected, on the basis of analogies, it is necessary to determine their proper names.

Truly, I had set forth to make my thought known on these topics. However, before their extraordinary depth, I will prefer to leave the task of delving even deeper into them to better-gifted minds. As it concerns appreciations or critiques that I may deserve for that which I have expounded up to this point, it will be better to trust in the judgment of others.

Synopsis of the Topics of the Sixth Book

I. In the true divinity nothing is given by generosity of grace, but everything is a product of the [divine] nature's own richness.

II. The relationship bond between Father and Son seems to be fully realized between the person who cannot be born and the prime person proceeding from him.

III. The ways in which progeny is produced vary between different natures.

IV. The legitimacy of the custom that has prevailed to indicate one of the two [elements] in the Trinity as Father and the other one as Son.

V. If we call one Father and the other one his Son, the reason is clear and evident.

VI. Since the other two [persons] both proceed from the Father, what is the difference between the procession of one and that of the other?

VII. The person who cannot be born has different bonds of relationship with one [person] than with the other.

VIII. It is right that he who proceeds from the Father and the Son is not said to be their Son.

IX. For what reason has he who proceeds from the Father and the Son been named Spirit of God?

X. By what reason has "he who proceeds from both" been defined [as] Holy Spirit?

XI. For what reason has only the Son of God been called the Father's image?

XII. Why has only the Son of God been indicated as the Word?

XIII. The definition of Word is appropriate because it has its origin in the way in which only the Son glorifies his Father.

XIV. Why is the Holy Spirit called God's Gift? For what reason and in what way can he be sent or donated?

XV. For what reason is power attributed particularly to the unbegotten one, wisdom to the begotten one, and goodness to the Holy Spirit?

XVI. Why is the Father defined as unbegotten, the Son as begotten, and the Holy Spirit neither as begotten nor unbegotten?

XVII. What does it mean to [affirm] that the Father begets and that the Son is born of the Father? What does it mean to proceed by generation and to proceed without generation?[1]

XVIII. Another way to explain the Son's generation by the Father.

XIX. The Holy Spirit is not the image of the only-begotten, and must not be defined as his son.

XX. The Father's image is to be sought in a reciprocal resemblance, which does not exclude some differences, and in a difference that goes together with a reciprocal similarity.

XXI. The criterion by which God's only-begotten is indicated as the image of his substance.

XXII. Concerning unbegotten substance and the begotten one, we must believe that which the holy Fathers have passed unto us, according to the catholic faith, even though—as it is now—our intelligence cannot fully comprehend how true this is.

---

1. Richard demonstrates a very technical use of *"gigno"* and the words associated with it (like *"generatio"* and *"genitum"*), basing his enquiry on the technical meaning which this family of words assumes in the Nicean Creed. The most common, English equivalent with the same technical meaning is *"to beget."* However, given the limited family of words pertaining to this verb in standard English, the wealth of Richard's language requires a greater linguistic flexibility. For the purpose of this work, therefore, it has been chosen to translate the extensive family of words of *"gigno"* with both the verbs *"to beget"* and *"to generate"* and their respective derived words.

Book Six

I

It is certain that, as we have said, only two persons share the characteristic of not being from themselves but proceeding from elsewhere. Now, it seems that we are left to verify whether the manner of proceeding is the same in both of them, or rather whether there is a different manner for each of them. We are dealing with a rather limited topic, which requires a very deep and careful analysis. After all, I think that that which has been said up to this point clearly illuminates [certain principles] that can contribute effectively towards a solution to this matter. According to the apostle, *that which in God is invisible is made known to the intellect through created objects.*[2] For this reason, when we are investigating something deep regarding the divine realities it is right to look up to that nature in which the image of God is portrayed by God's own work. After all, it is known that the human being has been made in the image of God.[3] Even though the aspect of dissimilarity is incomparably more apparent than that of resemblance, there still is some—or even quite a noticeable—resemblance between the human and the divine nature. As a consequence, I believe that by a judgment based on reason we can observe—or better, we can discern—in this mirror of the divine image that which must be attributed to God (due to our resemblance) and that which must be rejected (considering our dissimilarity).

Indeed, we may notice how the production of a person by another is not everywhere uniform amongst the human persons. In fact, if we go back to the beginnings of our propagation, we notice that even with regards to the first man, the production of his wife and that of his chil-

2. Rom 1:20.
3. Gen 1:26–27.

dren were very different to each another: the [first was] supernatural, the [second was] natural. The first one was solely due to the work of creative grace, the second [was due] to nature's action. On the other hand, in the divine nature nothing exists or could exist by the work of grace, since that which is derived solely from a work of grace may [either] exist or may not exist, according to the author's pleasure. Now, it is not possible to find something such as this in the divinity also, since if this were true it would be subject to mutation and would not possess true eternity. Consequently, in God there is nothing that is a gift given by grace: everything is due to necessity proper to the [divine] nature. In fact, just as it is natural for him who cannot be born not to proceed from another, it is likewise natural for him to have someone proceeding from him.

II

Thus, we must carefully examine the natural order of procession amongst men and investigate with great attention that which is similar to this in God. Once this is discovered and understood, we will have to transfer the terms defining properties, from the human dimension to the divine one, according to the method used by theological science, which is based upon the principle of analogy.

In human nature, as we have said before, we observe that the production or procession of a person from another can be either solely non-mediated, or solely mediated or at the same time both mediated and non-mediated. The non-mediated procession is that of a son proceeding from two parents, without another intermediary person's intervention. We can observe a mediated procession only when we [see] someone's grandson: this procession, in fact, requires the son's mediation. We have a mediated and non-mediated procession only when one and same man is both someone's son and [someone's] grandson at the same time.

Whilst the mediated procession is multi-faceted in the human nature, the same is utterly impossible in the divine nature. In the human nature, the different procession orders and various affinity types differentiate and multiply the degrees and names of relationships. For example, the relationship bond that a man has with his son is different from that which he has with his grandson, and the same considerations are valid for the remaining situations. Yet, amongst the many relationship types, the prime relationship is that occurring between the father and the son. Indeed, if such a bond were not present at the beginning in the human nature, absolutely no other [bond] could have [ever] been possible. Conversely, even if [there was no other relationship bond], the relationship bond between father and son could have still existed.

Then, if a man has many sons, all of them are said to be his sons for the same reason. If only one, single man happens to be both son and grandson of the same person, he is [generated] both [in a mediated and non-mediated way], even if not for the same reason, but for a different one.

We must take note that Eve has been non-mediatedly produced by Adam's substance, but not according to nature's work. It is for this reason that she is not defined as Adam's daughter, and [Adam is not defined] as her father. Conversely, when one person is produced from another's substance—I mean, produced according to the prime procession type and nature's work—we use the term "father" for one of these persons and "son" for the other.

Therefore, since we are used to applying to God terms defining human relationship, according to that principle of analogy that we find in divine Scriptures, we can rightly affirm that the same relationship occurring between father and son occurs between the person who cannot be born and the prime person proceeding from him. Such a procession of a person from another [person] is absolutely non-mediated, and it happens according to the prime order of procession and by the effect of [the divine] nature's work. All this is quite clear from our previous considerations and does not require further explanations.

III

I suppose no one can have doubts about the fact that the way of generation is different according to nature's differences. If we want to know the manner of production, which is distinctive of the super-eminent and most excellent nature of the divinity, we must look into the goodness of the ungenerated—his wisdom and his power. Perhaps it will not take long to discover that which we are looking for. It is certain that he who possesses a supremely wise goodness cannot want anything at all—especially regarding the divine realities—if [he is] not [motivated] by a reason, which I would call intimate and sublime. After all, if he truly is omnipotent, all that he has wanted will be realized according to his pleasure. Indeed, how could we define him as omnipotent, I wonder, if he is not able to obtain that which he has wanted with his sole will? Thus, the production from himself of a consubstantial and similar [person] will correspond to his immutable will by the effect of a reason that necessarily demands [such a production]. Without a doubt, the generation of a son will mean to him finding in this very son enjoyment under every aspect.[4]

IV

We must observe that there are two [different] sexes in the human nature, and for this reason, the terms defining relationship are different according to the difference of sexes. We call one who is a parent either "father" or "mother" [according to their] sex. In case of progeny, [we say] in one case "sons" and in another "daughters." In the divine nature, instead, as we all know, there is absolutely no sex. It was convenient, then, to associate the terms referring to the more worthy sex—as it is recognized—to the most worthy being in the universe. This is the reason why the custom of indicating one as Father and one as Son in the Trinity has suitably come into habit. However, in order not to leave anything unexamined, which would disorientate the weaker reader, let us pause and ponder more accurately that which we have said regarding the transposition of the [above] terms. Perhaps, someone may consider it strange that certain terms are applied to the divine realities by a criterion of similarity rather than in light of a concordance of modes of being, even partial, as compared to one another. Actually, in the human nature the son does not naturally proceed only from the father.

---

4. A literal reading of the sentence would refer "*in eo ipso*" to the act of generation in itself, suggesting that the Father is "well pleased" by his enacted ability of production of a Son. As Salet cleverly suggested, on the basis of Richard's understanding of the Father's "enjoyment" in the Son, whom he generated, one should prefer an *ad sensum* translation which implies an allusion to the text in Matt 3:17; 17:5. In this case, "*in eo ipso*" should be read as "*in eo ipso Filio*," as also Spinelli implies in his version of the passage.

In humans, there has been only one man who proceeded only from his mother, without any carnal father, but yet with nature's intervention. It is not convenient to apply to divine realities [those] terms connected to [human] relationships, only on the basis of the criterion of analogy. Then, [if that is so], how will such a transposition be acceptable when beings do not demonstrate any concordance of proportions?

Now, let us underline that which follows: if it is right to call "Son" he who proceeds only from one [person] in the divinity; if it is right to define as "Father" him who is [the Son's] sole and only origin, then these words indicate to us that in God this prime relationship [must] certainly exist, even though [this is] in such a way in which it is absolutely impossible in our nature. These words compel our carnal spirit not to think anything carnal of anything connected to divine generation, but to elevate ourselves with our heart to a higher understanding, avoiding the judgement of such a deep mystery with a human mind.

V

In any case, if we go back to that which we have concluded before with a solid argument, we will be able to elicit enough elements to solve this problem. With our considerations, we have discovered that to him who is ungenerated, the production of a person from himself means wanting it by a necessary reason. There is no doubting the fact that if the first man Adam had by nature the possibility of producing at will and only from himself a consubstantial being totally similar to him, the two of them would have been bound together by a prime type of relationship. They would rightly be called by the very terms used [to describe such a] relationship: one [would be called] "father" and the other "son." Indeed, if they were similar in everything, they would not be different in sexual gender either.

Therefore, from such a consideration you can conclude that it is right for one of the two [persons] in the Trinity to be called "Father" of the other, and the other [person] to be called "Son" of the same and only Father, by effect of a blatant and manifest reason.

In this way, in the depth of such a great mystery, the mirror of our resemblance with God and the consideration of our weakness clarify a dissimilarity (which is never separated from resemblance) and a resemblance (which is never separated from dissimilarity). Without a doubt there is dissimilarity, since a son cannot proceed only from the father in our nature. However, there is no lack of similarity either, because if a situation of this sort had been possible and had happened, then the very terms of relationship would be adapted to both [persons] to designate an analogous relationship. Therefore, I believe that we now understand—thanks to certain and transparent arguments—the reason why we call one "Father" and the other "his Son." "Father" [is] he who is not derived from anyone else; "Son" is [he] who comes only from the first.

VI

We know, by now, the type of relationship that occurs between the first and the second person. We are left to analyze that which we must believe regarding the relationship between the [first] two [persons] and the third one. Perhaps, some will think that we could define he who proceeds non-mediatedly from both [the first two persons] as son of both of them. But if this [person] is the Son's son, will the ungenerated [person] at the same time be both his father and his grandfather? Will he be both son and grandson of the ungenerated [person], at the same time? In the development of our considerations, the more complex and far from solution [these problems are], the more deeply they need to be investigated.

Now, this fact is most certain: the remaining two persons share the [property] of proceeding from the ungenerated person. First of all, then, we will have to see what the difference is between the two processions, with regards to the intentions of he who produces them. Actually, although both proceed from the Father's will, it is still possible that the causes of [these] two processions are different. However, if we recall the previous conclusions of our reasoning, perhaps we will not need a long and painful effort on this topic.

Actually, a clear and plain reasoning has demonstrated that the ungenerated [person] has wanted—and according to such will, it was necessary for him to have—another [person] worthy of him, so to love him with a supreme love and to be loved by him in return with a supreme love. He not only wanted another one worthy of him, but

[he] also [wanted] someone else to be the object of their common love and—by the action of such will—he necessarily had to have it. [He did this] in order to have him share that love and in order not to keep for himself alone that which could have been shared. In summary, he wanted to have one [person] equal [to himself] in dignity [to whom] he could communicate the richness of his greatness, and another [person] to be loved by both [of them], in order to give him the delights of charity. The communication of greatness has been—so to say—the cause of the first [procession]. The communication of love appears to be somehow the original cause of the second [procession]. Finally, even though the production of both persons proceeds from the Father's will, as we have said, there are different reasons and different motives behind this twofold production or procession.

VII

There is a noticeable difference in every aspect between wanting to possess one of equal dignity and possessing one who is the object of common love. Thus, let us verify which one of these [desires] is the first and which one is the second, as we intend "first" and "second" not from the perspective of a chronological succession, but according to an order of [the divine] nature. After all, what does it mean to have one of equal dignity? [Certainly, it means] to want someone to intimately love and who demands and deserves this love by reason of his equal dignity.

On the other hand, what does it mean to want to have someone as the object of common love? [Certainly, it means] to want someone who is loved in the same measure as he is loved himself by the second one and who enjoys with himself the [same] delights of love which the two lovers exhibit for one another. The first [desire] can be realized only in the duality of persons. The second one cannot be brought into effect by any means without a trinity of persons. In the natural order, then, duality precedes trinity. In fact, while a trinity presupposes necessarily a duality, a duality can exist even in the eventual absence of a trinity. Naturally, it is clear that he who is loved precedes the [second one] who is loved with him. Then, in the order of nature, the procession which comes first is that one whose cause [also] comes first. We know that the order of relationship corresponds, without a doubt, to the order of procession. Certainly, in the human nature we find first that relationship a man has with his son; secondly, [we find] that one that a man has with his grandson. Thirdly, we find [that relationship] that a man has with his great-grandson, and so on, and so forth. In this nature of ours, what constitute these different degrees of relationship if not the different ways of procession in the various cases? In fact, if there is no diversity of procession amongst multiple individuals there will not be any difference in relationship either. If one man has more than one son, by considering the identical form of procession, he has the same relationship with all of them. In summary, according to the type of procession (i.e., whether it is similar or dissimilar) the kind of relationship changes as well.

At this point it seems clearer than light that both [divine persons] proceed from the Father. Nonetheless, each of them has a certain, distinct way of proceeding. Consequently, he who is ungenerated has necessarily a certain relationship with the first, and a different one with the second.

VIII

Now, in the way nature works, the prime procession is that of him who proceeds only from the ungenerated [element]. Where we have a prime procession, though, we also have a prime relationship. Yet, the prime relationship is that of a father with his son. Rightly, then, as we have said before, he who proceeds in a prime manner from the ungenerated one is called his Son. But if the ungenerated has a determined relationship with this one [person] and a different relationship with the other [person]—since one is rightly called his Son—the other cannot rightly be defined in the same way. In fact, what does it mean when one is defined as son of another? [Certainly, it means] that he is bound to the other by the prime relationship bond. He who is the third person in the Trinity is not united to the ungenerated—as we have proven—with a prime relationship bond. Therefore, there is no reason why he should be called his Son.

Yet, as we have sufficiently demonstrated, we know that he who is third in the Trinity proceeds from the other two. If he is not the Son of one [of them] he is not the Son of the other one either, since he proceeds in one, single fashion both from the Father and from the Son. In both cases the reason [for the procession] is one and identical under every aspect. Again, this appears to be quite clear from our previous considerations. It is not necessary to insist on the same arguments.

However, if he is not the Son's son, the Son's Father will not be his grandfather, and he will not be his grandson. Yet, in the human nature, there are no intermediate relationships between the *father-son* type and the *grandfather-grandson* type. Then, I ask, which kind of relationship will the Father and the Son have with that third person in the Trinity?

Certainly, in the human nature, each personal procession which is non-mediated is also prime. Conversely, in the divine nature things are different, as it is now clear. Actually, we find there [both] a procession that is non-mediated and prime, and another one that is non-mediated yet *not* prime. As a consequence, since in the human nature there is absolutely [no procession] which is non-mediated without being prime, we cannot transpose any word from the human to the divine dimension to define such a relationship. You can understand that in order to define the Father and Son's relationship with the person proceeding from both of them, our ordinary language is totally inadequate.

IX

Even though we have not been able to apply [to the third person] a relationship term suitable to our use, it is not without any criterion of analogy that in the divine Scriptures [this person] is presented as the "Breath of God" and as the "Holy Spirit." The breath is by definition that which comes out of a human, and without which the human being cannot survive. Yet, if this is the only similarity that allows us to call the [person] about whom we are talking "the Spirit of God," this description might appear too loose when referred to him. It is evident, in fact, that the breath proceeding from a human is not consubstantial to the human being, while the Spirit of God is certainly consubstantial and equal in all aspects to him from whom he proceeds. Yet, none disapproves if, by analogy, he who is referred to as the "Finger of God" in the divine Scriptures, is called "Spirit of the Father and the Son." With the expression "Finger of God," we do not introduce any inequality [in him], but we refer to a resemblance with one of his characteristics.

When do we point our finger? When we want to direct someone's gaze to a determined place. Then, when by the illumination of his Spirit, God reveals to someone the mysteries and secrets of his wisdom, what else does he do if not point with his finger to that which he wants us to see? The Father and the Son—one and same God under every aspect—teach us everything through the inspiration of their Spirit. Did the Teacher of truth not teach with a sort of simile, that the Holy Spirit is a divine "breath," when he appeared to the disciples and breathed [on them], saying: "*Receive the Holy Spirit?*"[5] Just as we have said before, the breath proceeds from man and without it man cannot live at all. Therefore, in defining the Holy Spirit as the Breath of God, we highlight the fact that his procession from him who is eternal is eternal in itself. Indeed, from the very fact that his procession from God is eternal—yes, I say again, from this very fact—we can understand that [the Spirit] is consubstantial to God, since whoever is not God can neither proceed from God nor possess eternity. Yet, we will explain in the following considerations the way in which [the words] "Breath," "Breathing," or "Spirit" of God express a characteristic that is exclusively proper to [the third person].

X

The fact that he who proceeds from two is called Holy Spirit is profoundly mysterious and invites us to a deeper understanding. In fact, as we read in the Gospel, the Father is spirit and the Son is [also] spirit. *God is spirit.*[6] In the same way, the Father is holy and the Son is certainly also holy: both terms can be applied with no fault to either of them. Then, if this name [i.e., holy spirit] is appropriate to both of these two, how is it that it has been attributed only to the [third one] as a proper name? The fact is that the appropriation of such a name is not unjustified at all to express one of [his] properties. In fact, if the breath coming out of the human body as corporeal presents a certain resemblance with the divine property, should the breath coming out of the human spirit as being spiritual not present an even greater resemblance? After all, what is the breath coming out of the human heart—in a weaker fashion in some, in a stronger manner in others; in a more tepid way in some

5. John 20:23.
6. John 4:24.

people, in a more ardent way in others—if not an intimate motion of the soul and a sprint of the inflamed heart? It is because of this that we say that those who have the same sentiments, the same aspirations, and the same desires have the same spirit, act in the same spirit, possess one, single design, and an identical goal. But, when is it that this spiritual breath is truly holy? When is it that with good reason it can be called holy? When it is moved by piety and operates according to truth! No spirit is holy if this spirit is absent: neither the human nor the angelic; as the human spirit starts being truly holy when it loves that which is pious and hates and despises that which is impious. This very sentiment of piety—this very spirit—renders a multitude of hearts a single heart and a single soul, when he breaths.[7]

Then, we define Holy Spirit as that [person] who, in the Trinity of persons, emanates from two, because he resembles this spirit proceeding and breathing out of the hearts of many. Actually, who could doubt that the same sentiment of piety and the same and single love reside in the Father and in the Son, unless one is totally a prisoner of folly? Then, this love—which both of them share—has been called Holy Spirit and he is the one who is inspired in the saints' hearts by the Father and the Son. He is the one who sanctifies [these hearts] so that they may deserve to be holy. Just as the human spirit is life to our bodies, this divine Breath is the spirits' life. The [bodily] one is the life transmitted by the sensible world, the [spiritual] one is the life communicated by holiness. It is because of this that not without reason he is called "Holy Spirit." Without him, in fact, there is no spirit who becomes holy. In summary, his name comes from reality. He is named so because of an analogy.

XI

This name "Holy Spirit" is attributed to only one—as his own proper name—even though, from the point of view of the substance, it seems to belong to everybody in common.

We must observe that certain definitions of properties may be applied to only one person. It is because of this that only one has been defined as Father, only one has been called Son, as we have already demonstrated enough. It is because of this that only the Son of God is

---

7. Acts 4:32.

said to be the Father's image, just like only he is presented as the Word of God. The catholic faith declares—and a multiplicity of arguments confirms it—that "That which the Father is, the Son is and the Holy Spirit is."[8] There is no doubt that both of them are similar to the Father and that both of them are equal to the Father in everything. If you think of wisdom or power, if you ponder over goodness or beatitude, it is absolutely certain that you will neither see any greater thing in one, nor any lesser thing in the other.

Given that things are such, since the Son of God has been rightly defined "image of the Father" as he expresses in himself the resemblance [with the Father], why should the Holy Spirit not also be presented as the image of the Father, since he is similar and equal to both of them?

Yet, we will immediately untie the knot of this problem if we pause to consider the properties [of the persons]. Possession of the whole fullness is common to all—as we have said before. The Father and the Son share both having and giving. The Holy Spirit has the property to possess without giving to anybody. As a consequence, only the Son expresses in himself resemblance with the Father and possesses [his] image. In fact, just like fullness of divinity springs from one [of them], likewise, the same effusion of fullness is diffused from the other one. The Holy Spirit does not receive anything less or in a different fashion from either of the two. However, no [other] person receives in any way fullness of divinity from the Holy Spirit. Thus, he does not express in himself the image of the Father. Now you can see the reason why only the Son—and not also the Holy Spirit—is defined as "image of the Father."

Yet, in the simplest [readers'] interest, let us formulate in a more clear way—or, so to speak, in a less precise way—the concepts that we have expressed. Human beings are used to speaking of "image" when referring to an exterior resemblance rather than an interior one. For example, we say a statue to be the image of a man and this is clearly due only to an exterior resemblance. In fact, inside a statue we would find dissimilarity rather than resemblance. Yet, in order to speak of the Trinity of persons in a human manner that which is internal to each [of them] is that which [each person] is in itself, while that which is external is [each person's] relationship with another. As we know, the Father has the same relationship with the Holy Spirit and with the Son—I repeat:

8. See the Athanasian Creed.

the same. Thus, since the Son seems to manifest his relationship with the Father in the communication of his fullness, it is right for him alone to be called "image of the Father." The Holy Spirit is defined neither as the image of the Father nor of the Son because from the point of view we have considered, he does not resemble any of the two. So, in the face of such deep mysteries, where we are not able to see clearly, we fumble[9] when we use similes.

However, we must not omit to observe the following, at this point. If the Holy Spirit is named rightly in this way, it is to avoid a wrong conception, i.e., that someone may undervalue his goodness because of his property mentioned above.

XII

If we wonder why only the Son of God is defined as Word, the [answer] can also only be derived, as it seems, from reflecting on the properties. First of all, we say that the word that one utters usually expresses the sentiments and wisdom of him who utters it. For this reason it is proper to call him who manifests the knowledge of the Father, who is the fountain of wisdom, Word.[10]

To these arguments you may reply by observing that the Father's name is not revealed only by the Son[11] but also by the Holy Spirit, as the Holy Spirit is that *anointing* which instructs us in everything;[12] [he is] the one who teaches and suggests to us everything, introducing us to all truth.[13] If it is for this reason that the Son is presented as the Word, why should the Holy Spirit also not be called Word?

It is opportune to remark, then, that the word comes directly out of the heart and thus it manifests the thoughts of him who utters it. It is right that the only Son of the only Father is called Word, since he manifests him who is primordial wisdom. Consequently, because of this, the name "Word" seems convenient only to the Son, by reason of analogy.

9. Isa 59:10; Acts 17:27.
10. Sir 1:5.
11. John 17:1–6.
12. 1 John 2:20.
13. John 14:26.

Yet, you may still contend that the word of the heart seems something quite different from the word of the mouth: one is born out of the heart, while the second one is uttered by the mouth. The first one is hidden inside, the second generally expresses the heart's thought. None of the two possesses both these properties, but—as it seems—one [of them] has one [property] and the other [one] has the other.

But I will answer: if you think more carefully, you will see that both that which is conceived by [one's] heart and that which is uttered by [one's] voice is the same word. Actually, what is a vocal emission if not a word's vehicle, or if you prefer, the word's clothing? [Consider] a person in his clothes and the same person naked: are they perhaps two different persons? You could have not spoken out the word you utter with your lips, I suppose, if you had not first conceived it in your heart with your thought. Once the uttered word has been received by a listener, [then] this same word that used to be in your heart before starts existing [from that moment] in the [listener's] heart. Actually, if the heart's word could be perceived like the mouth's word, there would be no reason to communicate with [your listener] through an exterior language. These arguments, I believe, demonstrate clearly that the word existing on [one's] lips is the same as that in [one's] heart: it has no voice in the heart while on the lips it is pronounced by the voice. Without a doubt, the truth conceived by [one's] heart, expressed by [his] word and perceived through listening is one, single, and same [truth]. The word exists by the heart's activity only. Listening, instead, depends on both the heart and the word.

Therefore, since the word proceeds only from the heart—and the heart's wisdom is manifested by it—it is right that by analogy the Son of God be defined as the Father's Word, for through him the fatherly splendor is revealed. In the Father, all truth is conceived; in the Son, all truth is formulated; in the Holy Spirit all truth is listened to, according to that which we read about him in the Gospel: *he will not speak of his own, but will speak whatever he hears.*[14] Thus, we can define as "Word" neither the Father (because he does not proceed from anyone) nor the Holy Spirit (because he does not proceed from only one). [We can define as "Word"] only the Son, who proceeds from one only and who is the origin of the manifestation of all truth. The Psalm refers to this

14. John 16:13.

Word: *From my heart a good word came out.*[15] The Father speaks to the Holy Spirit in this Word. Through him, he communicates to the created spirit, both angelic and human. As has already been said, the word can be interior, on one hand, and exterior, on the other. It is interior when it is understood only by the Holy Spirit; it is exterior if it is perceived [also] by the created spirit. Just as the interior word is formulated in us without the intervention of human breath, and conversely, the exterior one is not articulated at all if this intervention is missing, similarly, for certain, in the super-eminent nature the interior word has only the Father as its author, as only the Father speaks and only the Holy Spirit listens. Conversely, the exterior word is produced also by the activity of the divine Breath, i.e., the Holy Spirit. This is also the reason why the same Spirit is said to be at times, "Breath," at [other] times "Breathing," at [other] times "Spirit of God." By his work, the Word of God inspired the angelic and human spirits.

As you can see, we have answered the question that we have asked before, i.e., the reason why in the Trinity only one is called "Spirit of God." At this point, you can also understand the reason why only the Son is defined "Word of God."

XIII

While we are trying to solve one problem we find another one immediately. We have said that the Son of God is called Word, as he displays the Father's glory and manifests through himself its nature and how great it is. Now, then, since the Son glorifies his Father, so too the Father glorifies his Son in revealing him; as the Son says to Peter, "*Blessed are you Simon son of Jonah, because neither flesh nor blood has revealed this but my Father in Heaven.*"[16] Observe, however, that the Son has a certain way to glorify his Father, which his Father does not have to glorify his Son. The Son, in fact, proceeds from the Father, while the Father does not proceed from the Son. Thus, it is evident in the Son how great the glory distinguishing the Father is—[the Father] who wanted and could have such a Son, equal to him in everything. How much goodness, how much sweetness, how much benevolence is found in the fact that

15. Ps 44:2 (45:1).
16. Matt 16:17.

[the Father] did not want to keep exclusively for himself any part of his glory's richness, and that he did not want to possess anything without communicating it to him! This is the very particular way in which the Son glorifies his Father.

Yet, perhaps you may disagree and say that the Father is glorified in the same way by the Holy Spirit as well. Indeed, just as the Father wanted his Son to co-exist with him so to have someone to whom he could transmit the richness of his greatness, he also desired the Holy Spirit to be united with him so that there would be someone to whom he could communicate the delights of his charity. Both of them, then, express the Father's glory. Both of them manifest the character distinguishing the Father. You must observe, though, that such a glorification of the fatherly identity—which the Father obtains in the Son—is not shared by him with anyone else, since the Son is derived only from the Father. Conversely, the glorification shining in the Holy Spirit is not a manifestation of the fatherhood and, as such, it does not belong only to the Father, as he shares [this glorification] with the Son. The Holy Spirit, in fact, does not proceed only from the Father, but absolutely in the same way from the Father and the Son.

In summary, it is correct to define the Son as "Word," that is "Tongue of the Father," as only in him is the Father's glory manifested in the way that we have described.

XIV

I believe the reason why the Holy Spirit is called "Gift of God" deserves careful consideration. As we have previously demonstrated with clear arguments, the fullness of gratuitous love resides in the Father, the fullness of due love [resides] in the Holy Spirit, the fullness of both gratuitous and due love [resides] in the Son. I have explained quite accurately on that occasion the manner in which to interpret all these expressions. Now, in the divine and supremely simple nature where no composition is admitted, it is certain that the Holy Spirit and his love do not constitute two different realities. Then, what is the Holy Spirit's gift or mission if not that of infusing due love? The Holy Spirit, then, is given by God to man when due love residing in the divinity is inspired into the human soul. In fact, when this Spirit enters the rational soul, he inflames its sentiments with divine ardor and transforms it by communicating to it a character similar to his own, in order [to enable] it to express back to its own Creator the love it owes him.

Actually, what is the Holy Spirit if not a divine fire? After all, every love is a fire, though a spiritual fire. That which material fire does with iron, this fire of which we are talking does with a sordid, icy, and hard heart. In fact, as soon as this fire enters, the human soul gradually puts away every darkness, every coolness, every hardness, and it becomes similar in every way to him by whom it is inflamed. By the effect of the flame of divine fire, [the human soul] burns up everything, blazes and is melted in God's love, according to the apostle's words: *God's charity has been infused in our hearts by the Holy Spirit's work who has been given to us.*[17]

But why do we say "by the Holy Spirit's work" rather than "by the Father and Son's work?" The fact is that we know that the Father has no origin and no donor, so he is only capable of possessing gratuitous love. On the contrary, as it has been said before, the Son possesses both gratuitous and due love. In divine love, then, we can neither conform to the character distinguishing the Son nor to that [character] proper to the Father, since we can neither have both loves towards God, nor an exclusively gratuitous love. In fact, I wonder, how could the creature gratuitously love its Creator, from whom it receives everything it possesses?

Therefore, if we have to give our Creator due love in return, this happens only because we are rearranged according to the Holy Spirit's property. For this, in fact, [the Holy Spirit] is given to humanity, for this he is inspired [to humanity], so that humanity—in the measure in which it is capable—be rearranged to the Spirit. After all, this Gift is sent. This sending is given at the same time and in the same way both from the Father and from the Son, since the Holy Spirit obtains from both [of them] everything that he possesses. Then, if the [Holy Spirit] receives existence, power, and will from both of them, it is right for us to claim that these [persons] are those who send him or give him, since from them he received the power and the will to come and dwell in us.

17. Rom 5:5.

XV

I would like to go back to a question I remember dealing with else-where. Why, according to a certain terminology, is power attributed to the ungenerated, wisdom to the begotten, and love to the Holy Spirit?

We all know what power, wisdom, love, or charity are, as we verify it everyday by experience. Indeed, from clear knowledge of these reali-ties, we can go back to the notion of those which transcend the limit of human abilities. The three abovementioned qualities, in fact, express a certain figure and image of the supreme Trinity and are presented to us as a sort of mirror in which the Spirit can distinguish God's invisible dimension through the creatures.[18] Then, between those things that are present [in the idea of] trinity [in the sensible world] and those [in the divine] Trinity there is a correlation with the number three, with similarities, with properties, and with individual terms. We can see that there may be a manifold power even where there is no wisdom. I will omit all the elements and all the eventual non-sensible objects. However, in living beings and in animals we find the ability of hear-ing, seeing, moving about, eating, drinking, and of all faculties as such. However, no wisdom exists nor can exist in these beings on the natural level. As it has been said before, then, it is clear that there cannot be a manifold power where there is no room for wisdom. To be able to have wisdom, in fact, is, no doubt, a power. Consequently, it is not wisdom that gives to power the power of existing, but it is power itself that com-municates [power] to wisdom.

Similarly, we know that Lucifer, who used to rise up at dawn,[19] pos-sesses a great power, a great wisdom, but absolutely no good will. After all, willing the good is that which is distinctive of goodness: after all, what is goodness, if it is not good will? Lucifer, tenacious in his perver-sion, testifies that there may be a manifold power and a multiform wis-dom where even any trace of goodness is absent. Conversely, there will be no goodness, if wisdom or power are completely absent. The power of willing good is in fact a power. After all, it is a characteristic of wis-dom to discern between good and evil; and without such a discernment the will would ignore that which should be chosen. Thus, if you want

18. Rom 1:20.
19. Isa 14:12.

to possess goodness it is necessary for you to know and to be capable of choosing good. Power is [the one] giving power. Wisdom is [the one] giving knowledge. Without [these two] goodness does not reach being. True goodness, then, receives its being both from wisdom and from power. Therefore, in this trinity of values, it is only power that is not derived from any of the others, while wisdom proceeds only from power and goodness is derived both from power and from wisdom. Certainly, you realize that in this earthly trinity we find a representation of the properties of the supreme and eternal Trinity. In [the divine] Trinity, the person of the unbegotten does not proceed from anyone else, the person of the begotten proceeds only from the unbegotten one, and the person of the Holy Spirit originates both from the unbegotten and the begotten. Thus, since the specificity of the unbegotten is expressed in power, it is right to attribute [power] to him in a special fashion. Then, since the specificity of the begotten is expressed in wisdom, it is logical to ascribe [wisdom] to him. Finally, since the Holy Spirit's specific character consists of goodness, it is not without reason that goodness is ascribed to him in a totally particular way. From this natural trinity, we can develop a reflection that shows—through an example—how that which we read on account of the divine properties can be interpreted.

XVI

Yet, it is very easy to understand why the Father is called "unbegotten" and the Son "begotten," and this does not require a laborious explanation.

It is only the Father who is not derived from anyone else and thus he absolutely cannot be called "begotten," because if he had been generated he would have received that which he is from another. It is right, then, that the name "unbegotten" be ascribed to him who did not originate from anyone else. After all, if he had not generated the Son, there would be no reasons for calling him "Father." Yet, he had this Son from eternity, as it is clear from our previous considerations. Thus, the Son, whom [the Father] had from eternity, has been eternally begotten, and with reason we must say that he has eternally received being.[20] Therefore, he is called "begotten"; and not even just begotten, but also

20. See Hilary of Poitiers, *De Trinitate* 15, 25.

"only-begotten," since in the Trinity there is only one Son. Actually, neither the Father nor the Son have with the Holy Spirit the [same] relationship that the Father has with his Son. In the human nature, when a person is generated by some other [person], the first is called "son," the second one is called "father." Then, it is right not to define the Holy Spirit as "begotten," in order not to mistake for a son him who is not a son. And [the Holy Spirit] is not even called "unbegotten," so not to think that he, who does not exist by his own activity, originates from himself.

Indeed, in some instances we have used the word "begotten" in a narrow meaning, in others instances in a broader sense. After all, in the common language we do not employ the same relationship terms to [indicate] all those who generate or are generated. When a man begets another man, the appropriate language calls the first "generator" and the second "progeny." [We call] one "father" and the other "son," [we call] one "generator" and one "generated." We say: the tree generates the branch; but neither is the tree called "generator," nor the branch his "progeny." The branch generates the flower, but neither the first is ever indicated as "father," nor the second as "son." The worm is born out of the fruit: and yet, we neither refer to one as "generator" nor to the other as "generated" from it. Thus, according to the different meanings of [the term], we either affirm or deny the worm's generation.

In a broad sense, generation is nothing but the production of an existing being by the work of another existing being, according to nature's activity. Conversely, if a production does not happen according to nature's activity it cannot be customarily defined as generation. Eve was not produced from Adam by a natural activity, so she cannot be said to have been begotten by him. Furthermore, certain natural productions allow the use of that relationship terminology mentioned above, while others—as we have already said—absolutely do not.

In summary, since the Holy Spirit's production—according to that which we have said—is of such a nature that he cannot be called son, he cannot rightly be defined as begotten. Yet, since his procession happens in a way suitable to a natural production, he must not be defined as unbegotten either. As we have already said, then, if we do not want him, who is not a son, to be mistaken for a son, it is right not to call [the Holy Spirit] "begotten." Similarly, we can explain in the light of reason [why] he is not called "unbegotten" either: in fact, in this way we would deny [the Holy Spirit] to have a natural origin.

XVII

With regards to the human nature, the production of a consubstantial being from oneself is not different from begetting progeny or from generating a son.

Conversely, in the divine nature the situation is much different. Indeed, the Father produces out of himself both the Son and the Holy Spirit, and both of them are consubstantial to him. However, we cannot call both of them his sons since their productions are different. After all, if both of them had the same production, neither of the two [productions] would have been prime to the other, according to the natural order. Yet, it follows from our previous considerations that one [production] is prime to the other.

We know that in the propagation of human persons we have various modes, according to the different degrees of relationship, as we have previously observed. The way of a son's procession from his father is of one kind, that of a grandson from his grandfather is of another kind, and a great-grandson's [procession] from his great-grandfather is even different. This fact can be seen both in these instances and in other ones. Among all modes of processions, we know that the son's procession from the father is primary and it is prime before all others. In fact, if a son does not come first, none of the others will ever be able to exist.

We know that the words' transposition from the human to the divine dimension is realized by the criterion of similarity, according to the apostle's words: *God's invisible realities are perceived by the intellect through the created objects.*[21] Now, according to the mentioned criterion of similarity, what do we intend when we say that God begets God? [Certainly that,] God the Father begets God the Son. What should we understand? [Certainly that,] he who produces another proceeding from him, produces this being according to the prime procession mode. Our faith tells us and the witness of our reasons confirms to us that the Father begets and that, as a consequence, the Son is born of the Father. On the basis of faith, the Son's procession is a generation, while

21. Rom 1:20.

the Holy Spirit's procession is not a generation. What does it mean that God begets a divine person, however? It means that he produces from himself someone similar and consubstantial, according to the prime procession mode. And what does it mean [to say] that the Son is born of the Father? It means that one proceeds from the other, according to the prime procession mode. As it seems, proceeding by generation corresponds exactly to using the prime procession mode in the procession. Proceeding without generation seems to correspond to not using the prime procession mode in the procession. [Even so], generation, birth, and procession are to be understood, in every aspect, with regard to measure and dignity in such a great excellence, and to the proper character of the super-eminent nature. Which is this mode of production? Certainly it is that one of which we have talked before. Without a doubt, producing another [being] from himself is equivalent—for him who produces—to wanting him, by an absolutely legitimate reason, since he is omnipotence itself. And because of this primary reason, wanting him corresponds to generating him. In fact, even though both modes of procession are based on will, they differ in the [will's] different motivations. For this reason, the prime motivation is the one that constitutes the prime procession mode.

Do you want to listen to a summative exposition on these topics that we have already discussed at length? The desire of the "unbegotten" to have from himself [a person] similar to him and equal to him in dignity seems to me to coincide with the Son's generation. The will of both the "unbegotten" and the "begotten" to have [a person] as the object of love for both of them, seems to be identified with the Holy Spirit's production. You can observe a communion of glory in the first case, [and] a communion of love in the second instance.

We have talked about a "similar" person. Let the diligent reader consider attentively whether perchance we are not referring this to that image of the Father, which only the Son carries in himself. [In fact, there is there] a certain similarity of properties.

XVIII

As we have underlined previously, the limits of the human language often force us to link words with different meanings every time. This is the reason why sometimes we limit and sometimes we widen the meaning of "generation"—as we have already said. That which we have said regarding generation is also valid for procession. In fact, when we talk about "proceeding," we generally do not give a uniform meaning to this word. In a broad perspective, to be generated seems to mean that an existing [being] is produced by another existing [being] according to natural activity. In light of this meaning, in the Trinity we only call the Father "unbegotten." We cannot say this concerning the Holy Spirit.

The production of one existing [being] by another existing [being] is certainly different according to the different nature. Before all other [modes of production], the most important one (on the level of nature's dignity) seems to be that production mode which takes place by natural appetite—absent in the inanimate beings. [This natural appetite] allows us to call him who generates both parent and father, and him who is generated both progeny and son.

By this consideration, we can claim that a son's generation from his father seems to correspond to the natural production of a living [being] from a living [being], consistent with [this being's] substance. In spite of this, not every production of a living [being] by another living [being], according to natural activity, can be included in this definition. For example, [let us think of] a worm born out of a man. Who could affirm that [this worm] is this man's son and that the man is its father?

We must not ignore that if man had not sinned and had kept his nature's integrity, he would be pushed to generate out of rational will rather than out of animal impulse. Thus, in the propagation of the species, the human generating activity would not be instinctive but rather voluntary, according to [God's] image.[22] Then, if man had kept in his integrity his own original purity, he would be closer, in this aspect, to similarity with God.

But let us go back to the topic that gave origin to these remarks. To God the Father, generating the Son seems to be equivalent to producing—naturally and deliberately—from his own person, a person distinguished by a peculiar conformity with his characteristic property. In the Trinity, all [persons] share possession of fullness of divinity. Yet, whilst the Holy Spirit's specific property is that of possessing [divinity]

22. Gen 1:27.

without giving it to any other person, the Father and the Son have the common property of possessing [divinity] and communicating it.

Rightly we must call Son him in whom the Father has most deeply impressed and fully expressed the image of his property and the reproduction of his likeness. Because of such expression of similarity, only the Son is called image of the Father. For this reason only the Son is called *reflection of his substance.*[23] On the other hand, since the Father has not impressed, so to speak, the reproduction of his image in the Holy Spirit, when he produced him, the Holy Spirit cannot be called his son, although he has naturally proceeded from him. After all, we generally do not call one [being] progeny and another one parent, in all natural processions of an existing [being] from another existing [being].

XIX

Yet, just as the Father and the Son have the common [characteristic of] giving out fullness of divinity, similarly the Son and the Holy Spirit share [the fact that] they do not possess fullness of divinity by their own activity. Thus, if it is right to define the Son as the image of the Father, because of his resemblance with the Father due to their [common] property, why should we not call the Holy Spirit the image of the Son, considering his resemblance conferred to him by his common property with the Son? To produce from their own person another person in their image and according to their likeness seems to be common both to the Son and to the Father. He who proceeds from the other appears in both cases as the producer's image. Then, if it is right to call Son of the unbegotten "he whom the unbegotten produced from himself according to his likeness," why should the Holy Spirit not be called "son of the begotten," since the begotten produces him from himself according to his own likeness?

Yet, we do not usually say that an object is in the image of [another] object because both of them do not share something similar, but rather because they both have something similar. Then, how could we affirm that one is the image of the other by that which is absent in both? Neither of the two, in fact, has *being* or *possessing* from himself. If this were not the case, a stone would rightly be called image of man,

23. Heb 1:3; Col 1:15.

and man would reasonably be called image of the stone, since neither of these two have or can have anything from themselves. Everybody understands how stupid this is!

Yet, you could still object to these arguments: just as it is common to both Father and Son to communicate the fullness of divinity, it is common to the Son and the Holy Spirit to have received this same fullness. Then, why should we not attribute the same level of relationship to both of these [two groups] when considering the resemblance that draws them together?

Yet, one should observe that the Holy Spirit receives both from the Father and from the Son. [If we look at the aspect of] receiving, the [Holy Spirit] cannot be called image of the Father (who does not receive anything from anybody). From this perspective, between the Father and the Spirit there is more dissimilarity than similarity. Therefore, it is not that which makes the second [person] different from the first one that authorises us to call him his image or his son. Yet, if he is not son of one [of them], the Holy Spirit cannot be defined as son of the other either, since the same relationship he has with one [person] he also has, no doubt, with the other. Indeed, he proceeds in the very same way both from the unbegotten one and from the only-begotten, and that which he receives from one he also receives from the other. Finally, the very fact that we say that the Holy Spirit has received all fullness, demonstrates that he does not possess it from himself. Yet, as we have just explained, we have no right to define someone as image of another on the basis of that which he does not possess. If he who proceeds is not generated in the producer's image and likeness—by our common way of speaking—we do not speak of either a father who generates or a son who is generated. Regarding Adam, we read that [God] generated him in his likeness.[24] It is only to this type of generation that we generally apply the principle relationship terms of which we have spoken.

In sum, from the considerations that I have formulated, we deduce that the Holy Spirit is not the image of the only-begotten, and that he must not be considered his son.

---

24. Gen 5:3.

XX

Perhaps, some will think that the Son has been called image of the Father because he is perfectly similar and equal to him in power, wisdom, and goodness. However, if this were the reason why the Son is called image of his Father, why should we not consider the Holy Spirit—for the same reason—the image of both the Father and the Son? Actually, when we say: "Such as the Father is, such is the Son," we immediately add: "and such is the Holy Ghost."[25] Where we start saying: "the Father is Almighty, the Son is Almighty," immediately we finish: "the Holy Ghost Almighty." We say: "the Father is God, the Son is God" and there we add: "the Holy Ghost is God." Thus, since by such a similarity or equality, the Son is presented as the image of the Father, why—from analogous considerations—should we not have a similar understanding regarding the Holy Spirit?

Yet, we must underline and consider with greatest care that which we say concerning divine realities in less appropriate terms, due to our limited abilities, and that which we affirm in a more resolute way. Not by chance many things in the Holy Scripture are deliberately said in a less vigorous way, so that our weakness may understand it more easily. After all, these less appropriate affirmations are usually corrected by a more precise formulation. This is why when we start saying: "the Father [is] eternal, the Son [is] eternal, the Holy Ghost [is] eternal," right after—as if we want to clarify truth—we add: "And yet they are not three eternals, but one eternal." Similarly, after we say: "The Father is Almighty, the Son Almighty, and the Holy Ghost Almighty," immediately after, almost as a correction, we add: "And yet they are not three Almighties, but one Almighty." Likewise, after we say: "The Father is God, the Son is God, and the Holy Ghost is God," we swiftly go on: "And yet they are not three Gods, but one God."

Why do we even need to say "such" and "such," where simple unity and supreme simplicity reigns? The expression "Equal to himself" is not justified at all. When there is true unity, we can solidly speak of identity, not just of equality. The Father is power, the Son is power, the Holy Spirit is power, and yet Father, Son, and Holy Spirit are one and the same power. That which we preach on divine power is identical to

25. This and all the following quotes are taken from the *Quicumque* symbol, the so-called Athanasian Creed, with which Richard shows extreme familiarity.

that which concerns divine wisdom and identical in every respect to that which concerns the divine substance. God's power and wisdom are not distinct from his substance.

In human nature we rightly affirm that the son's substance is the image of his father, as the father's and the son's substances are different. Conversely, in divine nature the substance is one and the same in the Father, the Son, and the Holy Spirit. Thus, what sort of comparison is possible where authentic unity dominates? In fact, in the supremely simple unity there can be room neither for similarity nor for dissimilarity. The image of the Father is to be sought where there is reciprocal conformity (which is not to be separated by some sort of difference) and difference (in the context of extreme harmony).

Therefore, he who wants to understand more deeply must go back to the consideration of properties. Yet, as we have repeatedly said, all share the fullness of divinity. Indeed, it is proper for the Father not to have received [this fullness] but to communicate it. It is proper to the Son both to have received it and to transmit it. Thus, there is conformity in giving and difference in receiving. The clear argument that we have previously expounded demonstrates how in this reciprocal conformity the Son carries in himself the Father's image.

XXI

It is necessary to ponder deeply, if we want to understand with greater clarity the reason why the Son of God—[himself] God—is defined as *figure of his substance*.[26] The expression "figure of a substance" can be understood—if I am not mistaken—in two ways. Indeed, if we look at the human dimension—so to observe as in a mirror[27]—man's figure (which is the form of his substance) and the figure of the image representing him are two different things. Yet, in both cases we have a figure, and in both cases it is acceptable to speak about man's figure. Similarly, regarding two substances: on one hand, there can be a figure that is form, and, on the other, there can be a figure that is representation.

Yet the Father and Son's substance is one and the same. Consequently, from this point of view, we cannot say that the Son is the

26. Heb 1:3.
27. 1 Cor 13:12.

figure of the Father's substance. Then, if we cannot speak of representative figure in this sense, will we be able to say that he is figure as form? Yet, if the Son were the Father's form, he would certainly bestow his beauty upon him.[28] Therefore, the Son would not be the one receiving beauty from the Father, but rather the Father from the Son. However, such a thing is not reasonable and it is not admitted by the catholic faith.

Thanks to the testimony of Truth, we have learned that *God is Spirit.*[29] Then, let us ask our spiritual nature about these topics, which are the objects of our investigation. Your soul is a spiritual nature, and your soul is either beautiful or ugly as a consequence of its will. Good will makes it beautiful, evil will makes it ugly. Its goodness grants beauty to it; its evil makes it ugly. From this we can understand what a figure of a spiritual substance is. Certainly, if the Lord allows, the same form of perfection may give form to both your soul and mine. Thus, if we seek conformity or configuration between Father and Son in the similarity of will, we will realize—without a doubt and with no possibility of rebuttal—that in the same way in which the Father wants to have a person proceeding from him and to whom he may communicate the delights of the love he enjoys, also the Son—in a totally similar fashion—wants to have (and [actually] has) [this person] according to his own will. In summary, just as we have previously observed with reference the image, the configuration [between persons] also has to be explained on the basis of the consideration of their properties. As we have already said, we find amongst these a reciprocal conformity, which contains some differences, and a diversity that coexists with the greatest conformity.

XXII

Yet, you could perhaps counter these arguments with the following objections. Where there is no plurality there cannot be conformity either. Well, in the true divinity, even though we really find a plurality

---

28. It is a pity that Richard's play on words, obvious in the Latin, cannot be maintained in translation. In fact, the rhetorical force of Richard's argument is revealed in the fact that if the Son gives form (*informaret*) to the Father, he necessarily makes him beautiful (*formosum*).

29. John 4:24.

of persons, there is no plurality of substances. Thus, why do we define the Son as "figure of the Father's substance" rather than as "[figure of] the Father's person?" Actually, as we have observed, we cannot call him figure of the Father's substance, as if he were his form. Indeed, since the substance of both of them is one and the same, we cannot define him as figure of the Father's substance, just as if he were the Father's representative image.

Now, we must underline that when the apostle presents the Son as the figure of the Father's substance,[30] it is as though he defines him as the figure of the unbegotten substance. If we say, though, "figure of the unbegotten substance" we are saying: "figure of the unbegotten person." You certainly refer to the same person, whether you say "Father," or whether you talk about the "unbegotten substance," or [whether you speak of] the "unbegotten person." There is no doubt: the person of the Father is nothing else but the unbegotten substance. The person of the Son is nothing else but the begotten substance.

Yet, there are many today who do not dare to speak in these terms. Even more dangerously, they rather dare to disapprove [of these affirmations] and try to contradict them in every way, against the holy Fathers' authority and in spite of the many claims of the ancient tradition. These [heretics] admit neither that substance generates substance, nor that wisdom generates wisdom. They stubbornly deny that which is claimed by all the saints, without being able to exhibit any authoritative proof of their assertions. Let them indicate an authority, if they can! Not even many, but just one [authority]! [Let them mention an authority] claiming that the substance does not generate the substance! Conversely, they are the very ones quoting many authorities which uphold that which we affirm and they come forward to fight carrying with them the very sword with which they will be beheaded, just as Goliath did.[31]

"Yet, that which the Fathers teach"—they say—"is to be interpreted in this other way. Indeed, the Fathers do claim that the substance generates the substance, but our exposition disproves it by demonstrating to us that substance does not generate substance." A faithful and very worthy exposition! [This exposition of theirs] declares that that which

30. Heb 1:3.
31. 1 Sam 17:51.

the Fathers manifestly affirm together is false and it presents as true that which none of the saints claims.

But they say: "If the Son's substance is begotten and the Father's one is unbegotten, in what way can they both possess a single and same substance?" There is no doubt that the Son's substance is begotten, [whilst] the Father's substance is unbegotten. It is just as certain that an unbegotten substance is not begotten and that a begotten substance is not unbegotten. Yet, this does not imply that there are two distinct substances, but two distinct persons.

Evidently, in the divine and in the human nature things are different. In the human nature, when someone's substance is begotten and someone else's is unbegotten, it follows that the substance of the first is totally different from that of the second. Contrarily, in the divine nature, we do not doubt that one's substance is unbegotten and the other's substance is begotten. Yet, this does not imply that that there is a difference of substances between the two, but only difference of persons.

You may say: "I do not grasp this. I do not understand." Yet, you may believe through faith that which you are not able to comprehend by intelligence. In the opposite instance, these words would refer to you and to those like you: *If you do not believe you will not understand.*[32] Why do you not believe that which the universal church confesses everyday concerning Christ? "He is God, of the substance of the Father, begotten before the worlds."[33] But perhaps you do not want to believe it because you are not able to demonstrate it by evidence or to understand it at a rational level.

Do you perhaps understand by intelligence or can you prove by an example that the unity of substance is compatible to the persons' plurality, and that the person's plurality is in agreement with the substance's unity? Does that, which you intensely deny, surpass human intelligence more than that, which you faithfully admit with us? If then you know of an explanation for the thesis you support, why do you not make it known? Why do you deny it to your brethren? But if the solution escapes you in both instances, why do you believe the holy Fathers on one hand, and do not listen to them on the other? If it is right to give them

32. Isa 7:9b.
33. Athanasian Creed.

credit, the Father's person is nothing but the unbegotten substance, whilst the Son's person is nothing but the begotten substance.

In order to summarize our thought on the problem discussed, the begotten substance carries in himself the figure of the unbegotten substance. [This means] that the [begotten substance] produces from himself—and in the same way!—the same person that the [unbegotten substance] produces. [This also means] that [the begotten substance] is both the cause and the origin, the author and the cause, of the same gift. Certainly, the same gift of complete fullness bursts forth entirely from both of them, i.e., both from the begotten and the unbegotten substance.

XXIII

When we make an effort to investigate and demonstrate the transcendent, invisible realities, we tend to use a ladder of similarities. [This] allows those who have not yet received the wings of contemplation to be elevated. Thus, in this nature, which we know to be created in the image of God,[34] we love to try and discover something similar to the divine, whereby we are able to be elevated to the understanding of the divine realities.

Let us imagine two men: one of them has reached—by his own thinking—the knowledge of a topic and the skill of an activity and has taught to another man everything he has been able to learn about this and has instructed him in everything as it was appropriate. Well, is it not evident, perhaps, that the same knowledge, the same truth, without a doubt is found in the minds of both of these men? If this were not the case, it would mean that the first man did not teach the second the science that he had discovered. Thus, one of them has communicated knowledge and the other one has received it. As you can see, it is clear that the former person's knowledge has been received by the latter, although the first man's knowledge was completely, so to say, non-received. Yet, the knowledge of one is not different to the knowledge of the other. If all truth is entire and identical in both of them, certainly both of them will essentially have the one, same knowledge. It is clear, however, that received knowledge is not non-received knowledge, and

34. Gen 1:27.

that non-received knowledge cannot be said to have been received, even though—whether received or non-received—it is essentially one.

From this consideration, we are able to deduce, I believe, that which is to be thought concerning divine realities. Then, let us examine, from this perspective, whether it is possible to prove that which some still do not believe regarding the unbegotten and the begotten substances, in the light of that which they believe with us. They agree with us in believing that the Father has from himself everything that he possesses. They agree with us in believing that the Son has received from the Father everything that he possesses from eternity. It is evident that the Son has received fullness of wisdom from the Father. [They] recognise with us that the Father's and the Son's wisdom are not distinct, but that we are dealing with absolutely one and the same wisdom for both the Father and the Son. Nonetheless, it is clear that the Son's wisdom is received, whilst the Fathers wisdom is non-received. It is manifest that a non-received wisdom is not a received wisdom and that a received wisdom is not a non-received one, even though there is no doubt that both the received and the non-received wisdom constitute one, single wisdom. Who could be so gross or foolish to deny in the divine wisdom that which he can see in the human wisdom?

But let us go deeper in our consideration. We all know that the Son possesses being from the Father, by generation from the Father. Thus, if he has his being by generation, in the same way he also has wisdom; in fact, for him to be and to know are not two distinct realities. Consequently, the fountain of essence is to him also fountain of wisdom. Also, since he has received his being by generation, it is clear that he has been generated. It is manifest that the Son's wisdom—or better, the Wisdom [which is] the Son—has been generated from the Father.[35] Saying that the Father has given wisdom to the Son or that the Son has received it, is the same as saying that the Father has generated him, who is Wisdom. Actually, the Father both gives to the Son by generating, and generates him by giving. Then, it is right to say that the Son is generated wisdom and that the Father is non-generated wisdom. Yet, one of them knows absolutely nothing that the other does not equally

35. The construction of the sentence in the Latin could offer two solutions. Following the example of both Salet and Spinelli, as benefits the greater sense of the paragraph, one should prefer to read: "*Sapientia [quae est] Filius sit genita ex Patre*," rather than "*Filius sit sapientia genita ex Patre.*"

know. Therefore, both of them possess one and the same wisdom, even though the non-generated wisdom is not the generated one and the generated wisdom is not the non-generated one.

But if the Son is generated wisdom he is also generated substance, since his wisdom and his substance are not two different realities. Thus, that which has been affirmed about generated and non-generated wisdom is to be attributed, by the same reasoning, to generated and non-generated substance also.

The fear of some to declare that substance generates substance and wisdom generates wisdom, or that the Father is unbegotten substance and the Son is begotten substance is without foundation. In fact, we cannot conclude from this that the begotten and the unbegotten one are two different substances. Actually, as we have already said, from the fact that the Father is the unbegotten substance and the Son is the begotten one, it follows that they are not two distinct substances but rather that they are two different persons.

XXIV

In any case, in order to make clearer that which we have said (i.e., the duality of persons does not imply the duality of substances) we will pause over the example we have previously used. We have demonstrated that one and the same knowledge can be found in two individuals, when a man teaches in full to another the knowledge of an art that he has learned. Then, if the term "instruction" is interpreted in both a passive and an active sense—thus meaning both the instruction of him who instructs and [the instruction] of him who is instructed—clearly, understood in this twofold meaning, one's instruction will be different from that of the other one. Just like "knowledge" is derived from "*knowing*," likewise, "instruction" comes from "*instructing*." In both cases we are talking about the same knowledge, but not of the same instruction: in fact, one teaches and the other is taught; the first man instructs and the second one is instructed. In one we find the knowledge that teaches, in the other, the knowledge that learns. Finally, one's instruction is different from that of the other. In this sense, then, your instruction could be different from mine even though we shared one and the same knowledge, both in learning and teaching. And if in the two of us our substance coincided with our knowledge, in both of us there could be a single substance just as a single knowledge. If, in the two of us, the person were to be identified with the instruction, certainly, the person—as well as the instruction—would relate one to the first, and the other one to the second.

If my knowledge was derived from yours, this would indicate that one would be generated from the other. Then, if knowledge is generated from knowledge in the human nature, why should we not affirm—with much more solid a foundation—that in the divine nature wisdom generates wisdom, since it has been demonstrated that in God wisdom coincides in every aspect with the substance? Just like in the human nature the instructing knowledge and the instructed knowledge constitute one and the same knowledge (although two different instructions are present), so in the divine nature the generating wisdom and the generated wisdom are one and the same wisdom. Consequently, they are one, single, and identical substance, even though they are two distinct persons. Therefore, in the human nature, the fact that one [person's] knowledge is received and [the knowledge] of another is non-received—and that there is sharp distinction between the received and the non-received [knowledge]—does not imply that the two [persons] have two different 'knowledges,' but only [that they have] two different instructions. Similarly, in the divine nature, the fact that one [person's] substance is generated and [the substance] of the other [person] is non-generated—and that there is sharp distinction between the generated and the non-generated [substances]—does not imply in any way that there are two different substances in God, but only two distinct persons.

XXV

We have said that the Father is the unbegotten substance. We have said that the Son is the begotten substance. With regards to the Holy Spirit we must say that he is neither the begotten nor the unbegotten substance. Previous considerations demonstrate how this is to be understood. In any case, even though the Father alone is called "unbegotten substance," the Son alone [is called] "begotten substance," and the Holy Spirit alone [is called] "neither begotten nor unbegotten substance," nonetheless, the Father, the Son, and the Holy Spirit have one, single substance and one, single wisdom. In fact, as we have repeatedly observed, divine substance and divine wisdom are not two different substances.

In fact, we may better understand that which we are saying now by developing our previous example a little further. Let us imagine three individuals: one of them has discovered a knowledge and has taught it; a second one has learned it directly from the discoverer and has written it down; the third one has read it and understood it. The first possesses this [knowledge] because of himself, the second one possesses it only from the first one, the third, both from the first and from the second. Actually, it was because the first one had discovered it and the second one had written it down that the third was able to know it.

Then, if knowledge of the same truth is complete and entire in all [three of them], one's knowledge is not different from that of another one, as concerns essential truth. In other words, if he who learned by listening had learned by reading, or if he who learned by reading had learned by listening, the acquired knowledge would not be different in either of them.

So, if it is true that in thee persons only one, single knowledge can be found, why should we not believe even more that in the three persons of the divine Trinity there is only one, identical wisdom?

And yet, the wisdom received by one [person] is not the wisdom that is unreceived by anyone else, and the wisdom received by two [persons] is neither the wisdom unreceived by anyone else, nor that which is received only by one.[36] Without a doubt, in all of them, there is one and the same wisdom and consequently, one and the same substance. Yet, the Father's substance, just like his wisdom, is not derived from anyone else. The Son's substance is derived only from the Father, and the Holy Spirit's substance is derived from both the Father and the Son. That which has been said about wisdom can also be said entirely of substance, since in God wisdom and substance are not two realities distinct from each other.

The knowledge of the learned man is called "discipline" because it is fully learned, so that "discipline" is understood as "full comprehen-

---

36. I.e., the knowledge of the Son (received only from one) is yet different from the knowledge of the Father (which is non-received). Similarly, the knowledge of the Holy Spirit is different both from that of the Father (non-received) and from that of the Son (received from one).

sion" as well.[37] [If this is the case]—and if we speak of discipline referring to the mode of learning—according to this meaning, the discipline of him who learns by meditating, that of him who learns by listening, and that of him who learns by reading are different.

Therefore, by this interpretation, as you see, in the human nature we can have a trinity of disciplines [even] where we have one and the same knowledge. Why is it so surprising, then, if in the divine nature, where substance and wisdom coincide—why is it so surprising, I repeat, if there are three persons where we have only one, single substance? Here we have confirmed with a clear and manifest example, that which the catholic faith professes on the unity and Trinity of God.

Let us pause for another consideration. Let us suppose that I, you, and a third [person] have the same knowledge, equal in every aspect. Indeed, would my knowledge and that of the third [person] be any greater than your knowledge alone? Or would my knowledge and yours be [greater] than that of the third person, taken by itself? Would his knowledge and yours be [greater] than mine by itself? Finally, would my knowledge, yours, and his together, be greater than my knowledge, yours, and his considered individually? Who would affirm this, if not one who does not realize at all that which he is saying?

In the same way, certainly, two persons of the Trinity—any two of them—or even all three of them, considered together, neither constitute a greater reality than the sole person of the unbegotten, nor that of the only-begotten, nor of the sole person of the Holy Spirit.

To complete this work of ours, we want to reaffirm and impress in the [the reader's] memory that which has been demonstrated with great clarity throughout our previous considerations. That is: by the consideration of omnipotence one easily concludes that God is and cannot but be only one. By [the consideration of] fullness of goodness, God is proven to be triune in persons. Lastly, by [the consideration of] fullness of wisdom one grasps with no hesitation the agreement that exists between the substance's unity and the persons' plurality.

37. See Isidore of Seville, *Etymologiae*, I.1.1.

Bibliography

Abelard, Peter. "Introductio ad Theologiam." In *Petri Abaelardi Opera Omnia*, 979–1114. Patrologia Latina 178. Edited by J. P. Migne. Paris: Garnier Fratres, 1885.

———. "Theologia Christiana." In *Petri Abaelardi Opera Omnia*, 1123–30. Patrologia Latina 178. Edited by J. P. Migne. Paris: Garnier Fratres, 1885.

Adorno, Piero. *L'Arte Italiana*. 3 vols. Florence: D'Anna, 1993.

Alighieri, Dante. *La Divina Commedia: Inferno*. Edited by Carlo Steiner. Turin: Paravia, 1955.

———. *La Divina Commedia: Paradiso*. Edited by Natalino Spegno. Florence: La Nuova Italia, 1957.

———. *La Divina Commedia: Purgatorio*. Edited by Natalino Spegno. Florence: La Nuova Italia, 1956.

Anselm of Canterbury. "Monologion." In *Anselm of Canterbury: The Major Works*, edited by B. Davies and G. R. Evans, 5–81. Oxford: Oxford University Press, 1998.

———. "On the Incarnation of the Word." In *Anselm of Canterbury: The Major Works*, edited by B. Davies and G. R. Evans, 233–59. Oxford: Oxford University Press, 1998.

———. "On the Procession of the Holy Spirit." In *Anselm of Canterbury: The Major Works*, edited by B. Davies and G. R. Evans, 390–434. Oxford: Oxford University Press, 1998.

———. "Proslogion." In *Anselm of Canterbury: The Major Works*, edited by B. Davies and G. R. Evans, 82–104. Oxford: Oxford University Press, 1998.

———. "Reply to Gaunilo." In *Anselm of Canterbury: The Major Works*, edited by B. Davies and G. R. Evans, 111–22. Oxford: Oxford University Press, 1998.

———. "Why God Became Man." In *Anselm of Canterbury: The Major Works*, edited by B. Davies and G. R. Evans, 260–356. Oxford: Oxford University Press, 1998.

Aristotle. *Politics*. Translated by Benjamin Jowett. Oxford: Clarendon, 1905.

Arnobius the Elder. "Arnobii Afri Disputationum Adversus Gentes Libri Septem." In *Sixti Papae, Dionysii Papae, Dionysii Alexandrini, S. Felicis, S. Eutychiani, Caii, Commodiani, Antonii, S. Victorini, Magnetis, Arnobii Afri, Opera Omnia*. Patrologia Latina 5. Edited by J.P. Migne, 713–1288C. Paris: Sirou, 1844.

Athanasius of Alexandria. *On the Incarnation of the Word of God*. London: Bles, 1944.

Augustine of Hippo. *Discorsi: Sul Nuovo Testamento*. Edited by L. Carrozzi. 2 vols. Nuova Biblioteca Agostiniana 30/1. Rome: Città Nuova Editrice, 1990.

———. *Discorsi: sul Vecchio Testamento*. Translated by P. Bellini, F. Cruciani, and V. Tarulli. Nuova Biblioteca Agostiniana 29. Rome: Città Nuova Editrice, 1979.

———. *La Vera Religione*. Translated by A. Pieretti. 2 vols. Nuova Biblioteca Agostiniana 6/1. Rome: Città Nuova Editrice, 1995.

———. *Lectures or Tractates on the Gospel according to St. John*. Translated by John Gibb. 2 vols. Works of Aurelius Augustine 10. Edinburgh: T. & T. Clark, 1873.

———. *On Christian Doctrine*. Translated by J. F. Shaw. Works of Aurelius Augustine 9. Edinburgh: T. & T. Clark, 1873.

———. "On the Grace of Christ, and on Original Sin." In *Saint Augustine: Anti-Pelagian Writings*, 213–55. The Nicene and Post-Nicene Fathers 5. Edited by P. Schaff. Grand Rapids: Eerdmans, 1997.

———. *On the Trinity*. Translated by Arthur W. Haddan. Works of Aurelius Augustine 7. Edinburgh: T. & T. Clark, 1873.

———. *The City of God against the Pagans*. Edited by G. P. Goold. 7 vols. London: Heinemann, 1988.

Baron, Roger. *Hugues & Richard de Saint-Victor*. Témoins de la Foi. Paris: Bloud & Gay, 1962.

Barth, Karl. *Anselm: Fides Quaerens Intellectum. Anselm's Proof of the Existence of God in the Context of his Theological Scheme*. Translated by I. W. Robertson. London: SCM, 1930.

Basil of Caesarea. "Letter XXXVIII On *Ousia* and *Hypostasis*." In *Letters*, translated by Roy J. DeFerrari, 4:197–227. Loeb Classical Library. London: Heinemann, 1972.

———. "On the Holy Spirit." In *The Treatise De Spiritu Sancto, The Nine Homilies of the Hexaemeron, and the Letters*, edited by Philip Schaff and Henry Wace, 1–50. The Nicene and Post-Nicene Fathers 8. Grand Rapids: Eerdmans, 1968.

Benson, Robert L., et al. *Renaissance and Renewal in the Twelfth Century*. Oxford: Oxford University Press, 1983.

Bligh, John. "Richard of St Victor's *De Trinitate*: Augustinian or Abelardian?" *HJ* IV (1960) 118–39.

Boethius, Severinus. *Liber de Persona et Duabus Naturis*. Patrologia Latina 64. Edited by J. P. Migne. Paris: Garnier Fratres, 1891.

Brisson, Luc. *How Philosophers Saved Myth: Allegorical Interpretation and Classical Mythology*. Translated by C. Tihanyi. Chicago: University of Chicago Press, 2004.

Cacciapuoti, Pierluigi. *"Deus Existentia Amoris": Teologia della Carità e Teologia della Trinità negli Scritti di Riccardo di San Vittore († 1173)*. Bibliotheca Victorina 9. Paris: Brepols, 1998.

Celenza, Christopher S. *The Lost Italian Renaissance: Humanism, Historians, and Latin's Legacy*. Baltimore: John Hopkins University Press, 2004.

Châtillon, Jean. *Le Mouvement Canonial au Moyen Age: Réforme de l'Eglise, Spiritualité et Culture*. Edited by P. Sicard. Bibliotheca Victorina 3. Paris: Brepols, 1992.

———. *Trois Opuscules Spirituels de Richard de Saint-Victor: Textes Inédits Accompagnés d'Études Critiques et de Notes*. Paris: Études Augustiniennes, 1986.

Clement of Alexandria. "The Stromata, or Miscellanies." In *Fathers of the Second Century: Hermas, Tatian, Athenagoras, Theophilus, and Clement of Alexandria*, 299–568. The Ante-Nicene Fathers 2. Edited by Alexander Roberts and James Donaldson. Peabody: Hendrickson, 1995.

Coffey, David. *Deus Trinitas: The Doctrine of the Triune God*. Oxford: Oxford University Press, 1999.

Collins, Paul M. *Trinitarian Theology: West and East. Karl Barth, The Cappadocian Fathers and John Zizioulas*. Oxford: Oxford University Press, 2001.

Den Bok, Nico. *Communicating the Most High: A Systematic Study of Person and Trinity in the Theology of Richard of St. Victor († 1173).* Bibliotheca Victorina 7. Paris: Brepols, 1996.

Dumeige, Gervais. *Richard de Saint-Victor et l'Idée Chrétienne de l'Amour.* Bibliothèque de Philosophie Contemporaine. Paris: Presses Universitaires de France, 1952.

Eadmer of Canterbury. "De Excellentia Virginis Mariae." In *Eadmer Cantuariensis Opera Omnia,* 557–80. Patrologia Latina 159. Edited by J. P. Migne. Paris: Migne, 1853.

Ethier, Albert M. *Le "De Trinitate" de Richard de Saint-Victor.* Paris: Librairie Philosophique J. Vrin, 1939.

Fairweather, Eugene R. *A Scholastic Miscellany: Anselm to Ockham.* Library of Christian Classics 10. Philadelphia: Westminster, 1961.

Fedele, Pietro. *Grande Dizionario Enciclopedico.* 20 vols. Turin: Unione Tipografico-Editrice Torinese, 1992.

Ficino, Marsilio. *Platonic Theology.* Translated by M. J. B. Allen. 6 vols. Cambridge: Harvard University Press, 2006.

Gilbert Porreta. *Commentaria in Boethium.* Patrologia Latina 64. Edited by J. P. Migne. Paris: Garnier Fratres, 1891.

Gilson, Étienne. *La Philosophie au Moyen Age: Des Origines Patristiques a la fin du XIVe siècle.* 2nd ed. Bibliothèque Historique. Paris: Payot, 1952.

Gregory the Great. *Omilie sui Vangeli.* Edited by G. Cremascoli. Turin: UTET, 1968.

Gregory Nazianzen. "Oration XII: To His Father." In *Select Orations of Saint Gregory Nazianzen, Sometime Archbishop of Constantinople,* edited by Philip Schaff and Henry Wace, 245–47. The Nicene and Post-Nicene Fathers, 2nd series. Grand Rapids: Eerdmans, 1973.

———. "Oration XXXI; Fifth Theological Oration: On the Holy Spirit." In *Select Orations of Saint Gregory Nazianzen, Sometime Archbishop of Constantinople.* The Nicene and Post-Nicene Fathers. 2nd Series. Edited by Philip Schaff and Henry Wace, 318–28. Grand Rapids: Eerdmans, 1973.

———. "Oration XL; On Holy Baptism." In *Select Orations of Saint Gregory Nazianzen, Sometime Archbishop of Constantinople,* edited by Philip Schaff and Henry Wace, 360–77. The Nicene and Post-Nicene Fathers, 2nd series. Grand Rapids: Eerdmans, 1973.

———. "Third Theological Oration: On the Son." In *Select Orations of Saint Gregory Nazianzen, Sometime Archbishop of Constantinople,* edited by Philip Schaff and Henry Wace, 301–9. The Nicene and Post-Nicene Fathers, 2nd series. Grand Rapids: Eerdmans, 1973.

Gregory of Nyssa. "Oratio Catechetica Magna." In *S.P.N. Gregorii Episcopi Nysseni Opera quae Reperiri Potuerunt Omnia,* 10–106. Patrologia Graeca 45. Edited by J. P. Migne. Paris: Migne, 1863.

———. "Quod non Sint Tres Dii: ad Ablabium." In *S.P.N. Gregorii Episcopi Nysseni Opera quae Reperiri Potuerunt Omnia,* 115–36. Patrologia Graeca 45. Edited by J. P. Migne. Paris: Migne, 1863.

Guimet, Fernand. "Caritas Ordinata et Amor Discretus dans la Théologie Trinitaire de Richard de Saint-Victor." *RMAL* 4 (1948) 225–36.

Gunton, Colin E. *The One, The Three, and the Many: God, Creation, and the Culture of Modernity.* Cambridge: Cambridge University Press, 1993.

———. *The Promise of Trinitarian Theology.* Edinburgh: T. & T. Clark, 1991.

Haskins, Charles H. *The Renaissance of the Twelfth Century.* Cambridge: Harvard University Press, 1927.

Hilary of Poitiers. *On the Trinty.* Translated by E. P. Meijering. Philosophia Patrum 4. Leiden: Brill, 1982.

Hugh of Saint Victor. "De Sacramentis Christianae Fidei." In *Hugonis de Sancto Victore Opera Omnia,* 183–618. Patrologia Latina 176. Edited by J. P. Migne. Paris: Garnier Fratres, 1880.

Irenaeus of Lyon. "Against Heresies." In *The Apostolic Fathers with Justin Martyr and Irenaeus,* 309–566. The Ante-Nicene Fathers 3. Edited by Alexander Roberts and James Donaldson. Peabody: Hendrickson, 1995.

Isidore of Seville. *Isidori Hispalensis Episcopi Etymologiarum sive Originum Libri XX.* 2 vols. Oxford Classical Texts/Scriptorum Classicorum Bibliotheca Oxoniensis. Edited by W.M. Lindsay. Oxford: Clarendon, 1911.

Jacquin, A.M. "Les 'Rationes Necessariae' de Saint Anselme." *EHLDMA* 2 (1930).

Jerome. "Epistola XV: Ad Damasum Papam," In *Sancti Eusebii Hieronymi, Stridonensis Presbyteri, Opera Omnia,* 355–58. Patrologia Latina 22. Edited by J. P. Migne. Paris: Garnier Fratres, 1815.

———. "Letters." In *The Principal Works of St. Jerome,* edited by Philip Schaff and Henry Wace, 1–295. The Nicene and Post-Nicene Fathers 6. Grand Rapids: Eerdmans, 1954.

John Scot Eriugena. *De Divisione Naturae.* Patrologia Latina 122. Edited by J. P. Migne. Paris: Migne, 1865.

———. *Versio Operum Sancti Dionysii Areopagitae.* Patrologia Latina 122. Edited by J. P. Migne. Paris: Migne, 1865.

Kelly, Anthony. *The Trinity of Love: A Theology of the Christian God.* New Theology Series 4. Wellington: Glazier, 1989.

Knell, Matthew. *The Immanent Person of the Holy Spirit from Anselm to Lombard: Divine Communion in the Spirit.* Studies in Christian History and Thought. Milton Keynes: Paternoster, 2007.

Longère, Jean. *L'Abbaye Parisienne de Saint-Victor au Moyen Age: Communications Présentées au XIIIe Colloque d'Humanisme Médiéval de Paris (1986-1988) et réunies par Jean Longère.* Edited by J. Longère. Bibliotheca Victorina 1. Paris: Brepols, 1991.

Maximus the Confessor. "Liber Ambiguorum." In *S.P.N. Maximi Confessoris Opera Omnia,* 1031–418. Patrologia Graeca 91. Edited by J. P. Migne. Paris: J. P. Migne, 1863.

McInerny, Ralph. *Boethius and Aquinas.* Washington, DC: The Catholic University of America Press, 1990.

Melone, Maria Domenica. *Lo Spirito Santo nel De Trinitate di Riccardo di S. Vittore.* Rome: Antonianum, 2001.

Merlo, Giovanni M. and Sergio Moravia. "Persona." In *GDE* 15:768–69.

Meyendorff, John. *Saint Gregory Palamas and Orthodox Spirituality.* Translated by Adele Fiske. New York: St. Vladimir's Seminary Press, 1974.

Migne, Jean-Paul. *Johannis Scoti Opera quae Supersunt Omnia.* Patrologia Graeca 122. Edited by J. P. Migne. Paris: J. P. Migne, 1865.

———. *S.P.N. Gregorii Archiepiscopi Tessalonicae Palamas Opera quae Reperiri Potuerunt Omnia.* Patrologia Graeca 150. Edited by J. P. Migne. Paris: J. P. Migne, 1865.

Moltmann, Jürgen. *The Trinity and the Kingdom: The Doctrine of God.* Minneapolis: Fortress, 1993.

Nauert, Charles G. *Humanism and the Culture of Renaissance Europe.* Cambridge: Cambridge University Press, 2006.

Ngien, Dennis. *Apologetic for Filioque in Medieval Theology.* Milton Keynes: Paternoster, 2005.

Nietzsche, Friedrich. *The Gay Science: With a Prelude in Rhymes and an Appendix of Songs.* Translated by W. Kaufmann. New York: Random House, 1991.

Noble, Thomas A. "The Deity of the Holy Spirit According to Gregory of Nazianzus." PhD diss., University of Edinburgh, 1989.

O'Collins, Gerald. *The Tripersonal God: Understanding and Interpreting the Trinity.* London: Geoffrey Chapman, 1999.

Ottaviano, Carmelo. "Riccardo di San Vittore: La Vita, le Opere, il Pensiero." *MRANL* 4.5 (1933) 411–543.

Paré, Gérard M., et al. *La Renaissance du xiie Siècle, les Écoles et l'Enseignement.* Paris: Librairie Philosophique J. Vrin, 1933.

Peter Lombard. "Sententiarum Libri Quatuor." In *Petri Lombardi Magistri Sententiarum, Parisiensis Episcopi Opera Omnia,* 519–962. Patrologia Latina 192. Edited by J. P. Migne. Paris: Garnier Fratres, 1880.

Petrarca, Francesco. *Il Canzoniere.* Edited by Giancarlo Contini. Turin: Einaudi, 1964.

Phaedrus. *Fables.* Translated by Alice Brenot. Paris: Les Belles Lettres, 1924.

Plato. *Meno.* Translated by B. Jowett. Rockville: Serenity, 2010.

———. *Phaedo.* Translated by D. Gallop. Oxford World's Classics. Oxford: Oxford University Press, 1999.

———. *Phaedrus.* Translated by R. Waterfield. Oxford World's Classics. Oxford: Oxford University Press, 2002.

———. *Republic.* Translated by R. Waterfield. Oxford World's Classics. Oxford: Oxford University Press, 1998.

———. *Timeo.* Translated by F. Fronterotta. Biblioteca Universale Rizzoli. Milan: Rizzoli, 2003.

Plotinus. *The Enneads.* Translated by S. MacKenna. Burdett: Larson Publications, 1993.

Quintilianus, M. Fabius. *Istituzioni Oratorie.* Turin: Einaudi, 2001.

Rahner, Karl. *The Trinity.* Mysterium Salutis. Translated by Joseph Donceel. New York: Seabury, 1974.

Reale, Giovanni, and Dario Antiseri. *Il Pensiero Occidentale dalle Origini ad Oggi.* 3 vols. 18th ed. Brescia: La Scuola, 1995.

Reid, Duncan. *Energies of the Spirit: Trinitarian Models in Eastern Orthodox and Western Theology.* American Academy of Religion, Academy Series 96. Atlanta: Scholars, 1997.

Ribaillier, Jean. *Richard de Saint-Victror, De Trinitate: Texte Critique avec Introduction, Notes et Tables.* Textes Philosophiques du Moyen Âge 6. Paris: Librairie Philosophique J. Vrin, 1958.

Richard of Saint Victor. *Benjamin Minor.* Translated by S. V. Yankowski. Ansbach: Wiedfeld und Mehl, 1960.

———. *De Trinitate.* Patrologia Latina 196. Edited by J. P. Migne. Paris: Garnier Fratres, 1880.

———. *Liber Exceptionum: Texte Critique avec Introduction, Notes et Tables.* Edited by Jean Châtillon. Textes Philosophiques du Moyen Âge 5. Paris: Librairie Philosophique J. Vrin, 1958.

———. "Of the Four Degrees of Passionate Charity." In *Selected Writings on Contemplation,* translated by Clare Kirchberger, 213–33. Classics of the Contemplative Life. London: Faber and Faber, 1957.

———. *Selected Writings on Contemplation.* Translated by Clare Kirchberger. Classics of the Contemplative Life. London: Faber and Faber, 1957.

———. *Sermons et Opuscules Spirituels Inédits.* Translated by Joseph Barthélemy. 2 vols. Bibliothèque de Spiritualité Médiévale. Metz: Desclée de Brouwer, 1951.

———. *The Twelve Patriarchs, the Mystical Ark, Book Three of the Trinity.* Edited by Grover A. Zinn. The Classics of Western Spirituality. New York: Paulist, 1979.

Salet, Gaston. *Richard de Saint-Victor: La Trinité.* Sources Chrétiennes 63. Paris: Les Éditions du Cerf, 1959.

Spinelli, Mario. *Riccardo di San Vittore: La Trinità.* Fonti Cristiane per il Terzo Millennio 4. Rome: Città Nuova Editrice, 1990.

Tertullian. "A Treatise on the Soul." In *The Writings of Tertullian,* 181–241. The Ante-Nicene Fathers 3. Edited by Alexander Roberts and James Donaldson. Peabody: Hendrickson, 1995.

———. "On the Flesh of Christ." In *The Writings of Tertullian,* 521–43. The Ante-Nicene Fathers 3. Edited by Alexander Roberts and James Donaldson. Peabody: Hendrickson, 1995.

———. "The Prescription Against Heretics." In *The Writings of Tertullian,* 243–67. The Ante-Nicene Fathers 3. Edited by Alexander Roberts and James Donaldson. Peabody: Hendrickson, 1995.

Thomas Aquinas. *Quaestiones Disputatae de Veritate.* Edited by R. Spiazzi. 10th ed. Opere di San Tommaso. Milan: Marietti, 2005.

Torrance, Alan J. *Persons in Communion: An Essay on Trinitarian Description and Human Participation.* Edinburgh: T. & T. Clark, 1996.

Torrance, Thomas F. *The Trinitarian Faith: The Evangelical Theology of the Ancient Catholic Church.* Edinburgh: T. & T. Clark, 1988.

Trinkaus, Charles. *The Scope of Renaissance Humanism.* Ann Arbor: University of Michigan Press, 1983.

Vacant, Alfred, et al. *Dictionnaire de Théologie Catholique: Contenant l'Exposé des Doctrines de la Théologie Catholique, Leurs Preuves et Leur Histoire.* 15 vols. Paris: Letouzey et Ané, 1926–1950.

Vignaux, Paul. *La Pensée au Moyen Âge.* Paris: Armand Colin, 1938.

Von Arnim, Hans F. A., and Maximilianus Adler. *Stoicorum Veterum Fragmenta.* 4 vols. Leipzig: Teubner, 1903–1924.

Wolff, Paul. *Die Viktoriner Mystische Schriften.* Leipzig: Hegner, 1936.

Zini, Zino. "Anselm of Canterbury, Saint." In *GDE* 1:893–94.

Zizioulas, John. *Being as Communion: Studies in Personhood and the Church.* New York: St. Vladimir's Seminary Press, 1985.

Author Index

Author Index

Scripture Index

Printed in Great Britain
by Amazon